THE ESOTERIC TRADITION IN RUSSIAN ROMANTIC LITERATURE

Lauren G. Leighton

THE ESOTERIC TRADITION IN RUSSIAN ROMANTIC LITERATURE

Decembrism and Freemasonry

The Pennsylvania State University Press
University Park, Pennsylvania

Library of Congress Cataloging-in-Publication Data

Leighton, Lauren G.
　　The esoteric tradition in Russian romantic literature : Decembrism and Freemasonry / Lauren G. Leighton.
　　　　p.　　cm.
　　Includes bibliographical references and index.
　　ISBN: 0-271-02651-0
　　1. Russian literature—19th century—History and criticism.　2. Occultism in literature.　3. Decembrists.　4. Freemasonry and literature.　5. Romanticism—Russia.　I. Title.
　　PG3015.5.O33L45　1994
　　891.709′003—dc20　　　　　　　　　　　　　　　　　　　　　　　93-13983
　　　　　　　　　　　　　　　　　　　　　　　　　　　　　　　　　　　　CIP

Copyright © 1994 The Pennsylvania State University
All rights reserved
Printed in the United States of America

Published by The Pennsylvania State University Press,
University Park, PA 16802-1003

It is the policy of the Pennsylvania State University Press to use acid-free paper for the first printing of all clothbound books. Publications on uncoated stock satisfy the minimum requirements of American National Standard for Information Sciences—Permanence of Paper for Printed Library Materials, ANSI Z39.48–1984.

Contents

Acknowledgments	vii
Introduction: The Esoteric Tradition and Thaumaturgy	1
1 The Esoteric Tradition in Russia	11
2 The Esoteric Tradition in Russian Romantic Poetry	35
3 Ryleyev's *Voynarovsky:* Decembrist Prescience	67
4 Decembrist Repentance: "The Frigate Hope"	91
5 Decembrist Fate: Pushkin and Bestuzhev	111
6 Numbers and Numerology: Pushkin's "Queen of Spades"	131
7 Thaumaturgy in "The Queen of Spades"	153
8 Freemasonry in "The Queen of Spades"	175
9 Literature and Thaumaturgy: Sources and Tradition	195
Reference Materials	205
Index	217

Acknowledgments

I would like to thank several colleagues in Russian literature who have offered criticism of drafts of this book or the published articles that were later included in it. I especially appreciate their patience with my analyses of thaumaturgical texts. These colleagues are the late M. P. Alekseyev, Stephen Baehr, Lewis Bagby, James Bailey, Diana Lewis Burgin, Kenneth Craven, Anthony G. Cross, Sergey Fomichev, the late M. I. Gillelson, George J. Gutsche, Raisa Iezuitova, Valentin Korovin, Yury Mann, John Mersereau, Jr., Natalya Mikhaylova, Igor Nemirovsky, Aleksandr Ospovat, Irina Paperno, Oleg Proskurin, Nathan Rosen, Vsevolod Sakharov, I. Z. Serman, J. Thomas Shaw, Victor Terras, Vadim Vatsuro, and Harry Weber. I am equally grateful to the scholars of esoteric studies who have led me through the labyrinths of their difficult field and helped me to understand thaumaturgical practices, particularly William F. Ryan of the Warburg Institute in London and Antoine Faivre of the Sorbonne and Bordeaux. I am greatly indebted to Freemasons in North America, England, Australia, and Europe, who opened their archives to me with generous scholarly interest. Here I wish to thank the memory of a Russian Freemason in Paris whom, to my regret, I never met in person, Sergei Pavlovich Theakston. I thank the International Research and Exchanges Board, the American Council of Learned Societies, and the Academy of Sciences of the USSR for the opportunity to conduct research in the library and archives of the Institute of Russian Literature (Pushkin House) in Leningrad in 1977 and 1989–90, and the Lenin State Library and Central State Archives of Art and Literature in Moscow in 1989–90; the Campus Research Board of the University of Illinois at Chicago for support of research at the Warburg Institute in London; and the Institute for the Humanities of the University of Illinois at Chicago, whose director, Gene Ruoff, allowed me to hold down the computer corner of the basement of Stevenson Hall. I acknowledge with appreciation permission to incorporate materials that appeared previously as articles in *Slavic and East European Journal, Russian Literature, Canadian Slavonic Papers, Yale Handbook of Russian Literature, Russkaia literatura, Novoe literaturnoe obozrenie*, and *New Perspectives on Nineteenth-Century Russian Prose* (Slavica, 1982).

Introduction:
The Esoteric Tradition
and Thaumaturgy

It is but one step from religion to superstitious magic.
— Curt Seligmann, *The History of Magic*

The relationship between literature and the esoteric is universal. The link between the love of mystery and the urge to manipulate language was probably forged in the uttering of the first word. Certainly the authors of sacred texts must have believed that gnosis is best revealed through art. Holy writ is replete with intricate relationships between *logos* and *esoterica*.

Logos is the word, the sign, and the signal. It also means more than it seems to sign—it can be arcane, deceptive, conspiratorial. A striking number of writers have been drawn to secret societies: Goethe, Lessing, Burns, and Pushkin were Freemasons. Kipling and John Le Carré were spies who turned love of intrigue into literary mysteries. Poets have long been attracted to plots against the existing order. In all cultures social, political, and religious constraints have driven creative minds to seek release by indirect literary means. In intellectual history the literary love of mystery cannot be disentangled from the snarl of the esoteric tradition—the preoccupation of thinking persons with myth and legend, the ineffable, and the mystical. The relationship goes both ways. The Great Magi of the esoteric tradition, intrigants like Casanova, charlatans like

Count Saint-Germain, theosophers like Swedenborg, mystics like Madame Blavatsky, the Cabalists, the Illuminati, the Rosicrucians, and the Freemasons were prolific writers.

Modern scholars call the history of preoccupation with the arcane the esoteric tradition. "Esoteric" does not necessarily mean "secret"; it can mean "strange." It often signifies gnosis—knowledge of the inexpressible. It is a tradition of mentation not disciplined by obedience to the principle of cause and effect. A word, one acceptation of which can help define the relationship between literature and esotericism, is *thaumaturgy*—the performance of wonders. This word, though itself strange, helps clarify our understanding of the esoteric tradition. In pre-Cartesian science and theology thaumaturgy included such arcana as magic, the occult, demonology and angelology, witchcraft, incantation, and divination. It also included such "crafts" as alchemy, astrology, calendarology, numerology, bibliomancy, cartomancy, and scores of other mantic skills, especially the Cabala and its numerological-orthographic manifestations called cabalism or cabalistics. In their relationship to literature, thaumaturgical skills are tools used for either the interpretation or the creation of texts—either to search for ineffable meaning in an existing text or to embed hidden meaning in a new text. The transmission and reception of meaning through encoded or otherwise camouflaged texts was often based on the need to find covert means to express deep concerns under the watchful eye of a censor. Thaumaturgy in literature is not always lofty. It is often playful, secretive, parodic, and ironic—it is language as used by Rabelais, Cervantes, Sterne, not Dante, Milton, or Spenser.

In this study of the application of thaumaturgy to the creation of literary texts I attempt to discover the role of the esoteric tradition in Russian romantic literature. I discuss extensively the political conspiracy that greatly influenced the romantic movement in Russia and the culmination of that conspiracy in the revolt of 14 December 1825 by which a group of Russia's "finest young men" attempted to overthrow the tsarist autocracy. Their aesthetics—the trend known as literary Decembrism—is a context of this study. Two literary Decembrists who provide some of the most unusual thaumaturgical puzzles are the poet Kondraty Ryleyev and the writer Aleksandr Bestuzhev, pseudonym Marlinsky. Among their sympathizers were other writers and poets. One Russian poet who transformed esoteric symbolism into rich romantic metaphors was Vasily Zhukovsky, a pioneer of the romantic movement in Russia. Zhukovsky's arcane metaphors were developed by a wide range of poets who made the romantic movement Russia's golden age of poetry. The sympathizer with whom these Decembrists were most intricately involved in both the expression of proscribed thoughts and the making of puzzles was Aleksandr Pushkin. The influence of the esoteric tradition on the literary works of these Russian romantics forms the core of this study.

Prior to the Decembrist revolt politically minded Russians were obliged by censorship and other governmental restraints to discuss controversial political and literary concerns in devious ways. In their literary works they had to suggest—never directly say—perilous meaning, sometimes in semantic hints that later became known as "Aesopic language," sometimes in more or less transparent allegories. In their criticism and journalism they had to be guarded, they had to use one word to designate what they all knew was another. They had to paraphrase forbidden ideas to get them by the censor and hope their contemporaries would be led by hints in the work to the "real" contents. Even in their private correspondence and diaries they had to use a hasty shorthand comprised of slang, puns, and unattributed mentions of proscribed ideas. Curiously, except for some disguised mentions in their correspondence, the Decembrists seem not to have used such methods in the conspiracy itself. We are dealing with a purely literary phenomenon.

After 1825 the surviving Decembrists and their sympathizers had to use these devious techniques to reaffirm their ideas and ideals through even more allusive, often actually encoded texts, because now they had deep feelings of guilt that they could not express openly, but felt compelled to express somehow. Some continued their defiance; others, demoralized by defeat, were contrite. Many Decembrists behaved badly under interrogation, attempted to blame others, confessed more fully than they might more honorably have done. In this regard especially they had to justify their actions to their contemporaries and posterity. Ryleyev and Bestuzhev-Marlinsky had been involved in the most extreme activities of the Decembrist conspiracy, including plots to assassinate the imperial family. Ryleyev was defiant and was hanged. Bestuzhev confessed and survived to suffer the guilt of an unpleasant failure of character.[1] The Decembrists' sympathizers had failings to express too. Some, among them Pushkin, had been privy to the conspiracy but had failed to act and were allowed to go free. All were demoralized by the execution or banishment of their friends, and by Russia's loss of rich talent.

Pushkin and the Decembrists were free-thinking young men who had been

---

1. Aleksandr Aleksandrovich Bestuzhev resumed his literary career in the 1830s under the pseudonym Aleksandr Marlinsky; his works are published today under the name A. A. Bestuzhev-Marlinskii. In this book he will be referred to as Bestuzhev; the name Marlinsky and the name of his style—*marlinism*—will be used where appropriate.

spiritually liberated by the European example of the romantic imagination. They were enamored of Byron and Byronism, drawn to the model of the young man of the age, and eager to express their individual personalities by deed and word. The romantic idea—revolution, freedom, justice, fraternity—made them despise Russian autocracy and dared them to dream of a more humane society. Their awareness of Russia's need for a modern national literature attracted them to the patriotic notion of a heroic past on which such a literature could be based. These men believed that history was made by either a mystical or an intentionalist explanation of history, and that revolution would be the most effective way to gain the power needed to transform Russia from a feudal empire into a modern nation.

Many Russian romantics were also Freemasons. They had experience of secret societies and knowledge of sub-rosa methods of exerting influence. They derived from Freemasonry a respect for the moral attainments of self-knowledge, self-perfection, and self-sacrifice. By 1822 they no longer hoped that the closely watched, conservative Masonic lodges could be a vehicle for either reform or revolution. But they carried away from their initiation into the Order of the Grand Architect of the Universe a knowledge of the power of secrecy. They also acquired thaumaturgical skills useful to a literature of indirect meaning: numerology, cabalistics, calendarology, arcane symbolism. They gained from their Masonic work a familiarity with, if not an erudite reading of, the esoteric tradition in European history, including an appreciation of the relationship between literature and thaumaturgy.

Freemasonry per se did not influence the Decembrist movement as much as romanticism did. Freemasonry was only one of many manifestations of the romantic Weltanschauung born of the Russian Enlightenment. Furthermore, Freemasonry included some of the most reactionary government ministers. But Freemasonry was related to Decembrism in ways similar to its role in such revolutionary phenomena as the Carbonari and the Tugenbund, and the teachings of Freemasonry and the esoteric tradition in which they originated are a prominent aspect of romantic literature in Russia.

To appreciate the arcane phenomena in Russian romantic literary works we must struggle to find a way through what a pioneer of modern esoteric studies Frances A. Yates has called "the clouds of nineteenth-century ridicule from which the scholarship of the twentieth century has slowly begun to rescue" the esoteric tradition (1979, 37). Contempt for the popular writing about and the fraudulent practice of thaumaturgy is well justified, but the seriousness of the study of the esoteric tradition is now well established. Indeed, when Yates pointed out the extensive holdings of esoteric material in the archives of

Florence and Elizabethan England that had never been examined, scholars had to wonder whether the received view of European history as the epitome of reason was not out of kilter, whether the Cartesian division of world culture into empirical and nonempirical knowledge was not misleading. Yates emphasizes throughout her work that the Great Magi of the Renaissance were major Christian theologians. Gerschom Scholem similarly restored the study of Jewish Cabalism and Merkabah mysticism to mainstream scholarship. Curt Seligmann, who articulates the unhappy fact that "it is but one step from religion to superstitious magic," nevertheless stresses the value of the Cabala as an interpretive tool (1948, 347). Alastair Fowler, prominent member of an international group of scholars who have recovered the relationships between numerology and prosody, points to the shoddy history of "autonomous speculative criticism" in esoteric scholarship, but believes that modern study "vindicates descriptive analysis as a heuristic instrument" (1970b, x). Modern esoteric studies is now a field that combines empirical measure with heuristic interpretation.

Evidence that the Russian romantics knew of the esoteric tradition is not as scant as was believed when this study was begun. The paths along which the esoteric tradition entered Russia in the eighteenth century and made their way to the nineteenth-century romantics can be traced. The presence of thaumaturgical phenomena in literary texts and the use of such to convey meaning through carefully constructed systems of allusions can, through text-object analysis, be demonstrated. Textual evidence is empirical: the implications of such evidence are not easily judged, but to the degree that a work of art contains its own verification, the text itself can be analyzed. The presence of thaumaturgical phenomena in a text must yield its own verification and the interpretation of their meaning—the solution to the puzzle—must be explored in context.

In this book I have assumed that literary tradition is a dialogic process and that thaumaturgical skills are acquired, transmitted, and transmuted from one need to another, in various forms of writing, as a dynamic process of broad cultural intertextuality. Effective means for decoding the complex puzzles posed by thaumaturgical phenomena in literary works can be developed by joining formal textual analysis to the empirical-heuristic methodology developed by intellectual historians of the esoteric tradition. Text-context and text-subtext analyses are essential to the analysis of thaumaturgical discourse because, although one pioneer of esoteric studies has advised that "no deliberately symbolic numerical value can be interpreted with any degree of accuracy, unless a hint is given of . . . the intent of the author" (Hopper 1938, 64), it is equally true that the author's intent sometimes cannot be identified without first decoding the text. In other words, a code cannot function without a key; *however,* the key might be in the text itself, and the text might yield enough information for the key to be worked out and tested by trial and error. The key might be lodged in another text, or another text might yield the information needed to discover the key. Once the code is broken and the text deciphered, the author's intent often becomes apparent. Perhaps the relationship is symbiotic: authorial intent—hypothesized or known in advance—facilitates the decoding process, decoding the text helps reveal authorial intent. Whatever the case, interpretation, empirical or heuristic, should be verified wherever possible. Evidence often raises as many questions as it answers, and autonomous speculation must be avoided by clearly distinguishing between *verifiable* links and *suggestive* associations.

The problems of dissociating verifiable interpretation from heuristic exploration, and the latter from enigmatic possibilities, are several. The influence of the Decembrist movement on Russian romantic literature has been exhaustively studied, but the ambiguous connections between literary works and political conspiracy have not been adequately measured. This aspect of Decembrism is difficult to gauge because although the political meaning of many literary texts is usually quite plain, the movement's conspiratorial character—the romantic love of intrigue—encouraged a mingling of matters at once political, historical, literary, and personal. The innermost secrets of the Decembrist conspiracy are now well known, and sometimes it is easier for modern scholars to decipher encoded texts than it was for the Decembrists' contemporaries. The publication of the Decembrists' testimonies before the Investigatory Commission (Pokrovskii et al. 1925–) revealed a wealth of previously unknown information, and historical studies of the Decembrist movement have proved a boon despite an ideologically motivated tendency in the Soviet period to distort the all-too-human Decembrists into noble revolutionary heroes. When the vagaries of the imperial censors are added to the tendency of some historians to overlook the unsavory behavior of the conspirators, the connections between literary works and political realities become even more difficult to identify. Interpreting troubling matters of conscience is also difficult because the individual's psychological need to confess often conflicted with the writer's desire for immortality. Obfuscatory self-justification distorted frank self-accountability, and what was covert became merely devious.

Many codes, once broken, yield readily to empirical analysis that can be substantiated by secondary evidence. Discovering the source of the user's skills provides additional evidence. Biographical information often supplies intentions, and literary allusions contain telling hints. But problems of interpretation are created by the devious character of thaumaturgical practices—the use of wit to camouflage serious hints and signals, for example, or simply the love of play even when sacred matters are close by. The solution to the puzzle often leads through a maze of verifiable links and possible associations that, however apparent the author's intent may be, resist clarification. Some mazes are cul-de-sacs—the evidence does not exist or cannot be found—others lend themselves to contradictory interpretations. Authors sometimes like to deceive, and of course deception is often the very basis of esoterica. Pushkin's prose tale "The Queen of Spades" contains both intentional links and suggestive associations that lead the reader into a game as risky as the game of cards on which the tale is based. This is in fact a point of game-playing and puzzle-making: the reader is led through a maze of literary and biographical hints not toward but away from understanding into ever greater irony.

Problems also arise from the character of the esoteric tradition itself: beware of invoking the spirits of arcane ambiguities, they may appear and raise hell with causal principles. To the same degree that thaumaturgical skills lend themselves to both profound theosophy and the conniving of hoaxers, so also does literary thaumaturgy freely mix foolishness and seriousness. But this, too, is the point: the mix of the sublime and the ridiculous with deception and disguise results in texts that provide intriguing problems—multilevel creations that express curious literary and extraliterary meanings.

Modern scholars of the highly specialized field of esoteric studies have established the lines of the history of esoterica, and many previously misunderstood thaumaturgical works have been convincingly explicated. They have defined terms: they know that mysticism, magic, the arcane, the supernatural, the occult, and theosophy are not identical phenomena, and they do not, like many other scholars, use these words interchangeably (see Faivre 1987). I am deeply indebted to the work of these esotericists, who are essentially intellectual historians, and in this book attempt both to introduce their knowledge to the Slavic field and to conjoin their historiography with the formalist methods that have shaped modern Slavic studies. Because these two approaches are not easily reconciled, I found it necessary to define strictly the limits of this study: my subject is Freemasonry, Decembrism, and the writings of Russian romantic poets and writers whose thaumaturgical practices are closely related and can be traced along a single if also intricately meandering path. My intent is not only to explore these subjects per se, however, but also to explore the relationships between literature and esoterica on the model of one literature in a period characterized by a political conspiracy in which thaumaturgical phenomena played an exceptionally prominent literary and extraliterary role.

Examination of the relationship between literature and thaumaturgy begins with an overview of the Decembrist movement and of Decembrist literature, known because of its orientation to political ideals as civicism or civic romanticism. Although the political movement needs to be considered because of its importance as context, my intent here is not to rehearse the history of Decembrism, but, first, to highlight those events of the conspiracy that became the secret subjects of literary and extraliterary communication and, second, to demonstrate that literary texts, not history, are the raison d'être of this study. The esoteric tradition and the vehicles of its introduction into Russian culture in the late eighteenth and early nineteenth centuries are outlined in Chapter 1, with attention to Freemasonry as the chief source of knowledge of thaumaturgy.

In Chapter 2, I explore and attempt to show, on the basis of one Masonic symbol that attracted the Russian romantics and helped them express a wide variety of concerns peculiar to their national cultural experience, how thaumaturgical practices were introduced into Russian literature, and how these practices developed along the different paths of romanticism in Russia. The symbol is the "Star of Hope." It was introduced into Russia from an arcane European Masonic system by the eighteenth-century "enlighteners" of the Novikov group known as the Moscow Mystic Masons or Rosicrucians and developed into a richly romantic poetic metaphor first by the early Russian romantic Vasily Zhukovsky and thereafter in different ways by poets throughout the course of the romantic movement. This chapter is meant to provide a context for the subsequent tracing of this and other thaumaturgical phenomena along a winding path through the works of the Decembrists Ryleyev and Bestuzhev and their best-known contemporary, Russia's national poet Aleksandr Pushkin.

Examination of thaumaturgy in the literary works of leading Decembrists begins in Chapter 3, a study of the radical Decembrist and fanatic idealist Kondraty Ryleyev and his allegorical prediction of the failure of the Decembrist revolt in his historical verse tale *Voynarovsky*. Ryleyev's tale is a prescient foretelling of his own and Bestuzhev's fates; Ryleyev's desire for immortality and martyrdom was realized by Bestuzhev in ways resembling the role of the "accomplice" in a Masonic rite called love of death. The Masonic Star of Hope becomes in the poetry of Ryleyev a tragic symbol of fate and hopeless rebellion. After the rebellion, the star becomes, in the works of Bestuzhev and Pushkin, the symbol of the painful loss of hope. In Chapter 4, I analyze the romantic prose tale "The Frigate Hope," in which Bestuzhev, writing as Marlinsky, reenacts and confesses his role in the Decembrist conspiracy and tries to banish from his conscience his remorse over the execution of Ryleyev. Here the erstwhile symbol of hope stands allegorically for tragic fate and loss of faith. In Chapter 4 I attempt to decode a text shaped by hints and allusions governed by the thaumaturgical skills of numerology and calendarology. In Chapter 5, I continue my analysis of Bestuzhev's tale as a "message to Pushkin."

Bestuzhev's obsessive signals to Pushkin prompted the latter to respond in similarly covert ways in "The Queen of Spades," his tale of the supernatural, magic, and "the secret of the three cards." In Chapter 6, I analyze the numerology of "The Queen of Spades" and conclude that Pushkin used a system based on the cabalistic numbers three, seven, and one to organize the structure and style of the tale. Numbers are more than a subject or a feature of "The Queen of Spades"—they virtually create it and govern it in every aspect. In Chapter 7, I attempt to show how Pushkin used numerology and cartomancy to organize the tale's pattern of ironic hints, allusions, and coincidences and to identify the sources of the poet's knowledge of cartomantic and other arcane skills. In "The Queen of Spades" Pushkin plays a game of allusions and leads his reader through a maze that has inspired the many interpretations that constitute the legacy of this tale. I have tried to chart the literary and biographical connections that go into the making of this puzzle. In Chapter 8, I discuss the elements of Cabala and Freemasonry that can be found in "The Queen of Spades" and analyze the tale as a parody of the Masonic legend of Hyram-Abif. Indications that Pushkin used some of the same thaumaturgical skills demonstrated by Bestuzhev in "The Frigate Hope" are examined, together with the struggle of both men to ease their consciences. I find evidence that Bestuzhev used allegory, numerology, and calendarology to structure "The Frigate Hope" and that Pushkin used numerology, cartomancy, and the stylistic-semantic system of the Cabala known as gematria to structure "The Queen of Spades."

Because the esoteric tradition is ambiguous and thaumaturgical phenomena are contradictory, understanding requires that findings be verified and false or irrelevant leads be eliminated. Such is my aim in the concluding chapter. The creation of an encoded text is an arcane practice, and the ultimate meaning of such a text is, as I have said, ineffable. The esoteric tradition entered Russia by many routes, but the subsequent development of the esoteric tradition in Russia is still terra plerumquate incognita. I hope, however, that if one route is traced using a carefully defined methodology, the way can be shown to a new view of Russian literature and culture of the romantic period. In the concluding chapter I intend, therefore, to answer lingering questions by providing a summary of the meaning of the esoteric tradition in Russia and to suggest new paths to be followed toward a final understanding of this unusual—and arcane—culture.

1

The Esoteric Tradition in Russia

Divine . . . writing consists of its secret meaning, understanding of which is incorporated in the cabalistic-numerical science.
—I. P. Elagin

The conspiracy known as the Decembrist movement and its culmination in the revolt of 14 December 1825 that gave it its name radically changed the direction of Russian culture. Hope of liberation died, and a vigorous romantic movement ground to a halt. On the fatal day thirty members of a secret organization known as the Northern Society took advantage of a confusing interregnum following the sudden death of Alexander I and led some three thousand soldiers of three regiments onto Senate Square in Petersburg in an effort to prevent the swearing of the oath of loyalty to the new tsar, Nicholas I. The revolt never gained momentum because when the rebels reached the Square late in the morning they learned that Nicholas had had the oath administered before dawn. It did not help, either, that the "dictator" they had chosen to lead them proved to be too fainthearted to show up or that they deceived the soldiers by telling them they were preventing Nicholas from usurping his older brother Constantine, who had in fact refused the throne. Nicholas acted decisively on that cold winter day by deploying loyal troops against the rebel forces across the Square. After declaring reluctance to become emperor "at the price of my subjects' blood," he ordered his cannons to disperse the rebels.

Fifteen days later, on 29 December, members of a second secret organization, the Southern Society, succeeded in inciting soldiers of the Chernigov regiment to seize the town of Vasilkov in Ukraine. On 3 January 1826 the rebels were intercepted near the town of Belaya Tserkov by a detachment of government troops and defeated in a bloody confrontation. Russia's first modern revolution had come to an end. (For studies of the Decembrist movement, see Nechkina 1955 and 1978, Mazour 1937, and Raeff 1966.)

The Decembrist Affair

Five hundred and seventy-nine men were investigated and brought to trial after the failure of the Decembrist revolt. They were incarcerated, most of them, in the bastions of Peter-and-Paul Fortress in Petersburg, and a special Investigatory Commission was appointed. The method of interrogation was to isolate each prisoner, give him pencil, paper, and a list of questions, and then to collate the separate answers, extract evidence, and present a new set of more incriminating questions. Few withstood this psychological pressure: many broke down and confessed; others cooperated out of a belief that defeat signified guilt. The most damning crimes were two: republicanism and plans to assassinate the tsar and expel or even exterminate the Romanov family. At the end, 289 men were found guilty. Five Decembrists were hanged on 13 July 1826. Among these were Colonel Pavel Pestel, leader of the Southern Society, chief advocate of a republican form of government and of assassination as the only way to end the autocracy, and the poet Kondraty Ryleyev, "chief instigator" of the revolt on Senate Square, secret supporter within the Northern Society of Pestel's plans, and advocate of assassination as an instrument of justice. One hundred and twenty-one Decembrists were sent to Siberia; others suffered punishments ranging from running the gauntlet to service in penal regiments to transfer to the pacification campaign underway in the Caucasus.

All Russians had ample cause in the early nineteenth century to oppose the autocracy. Napoleon's invasion of Russia in 1812 aroused great patriotism in Russians of all classes. The trauma of the invasion had led to the rise of modern nationalism. The subsequent European campaigns of 1813–14 exposed large numbers of Russians, including soldier-peasants, to the more democratic life of Europe. The Decembrists reached their majority during the relatively liberal years of the early reign of Alexander I, but Alexander's turn to the Alliance of Europe and increasing reliance on reactionary, religious-mystical advisers disappointed hopes for reform. A constitution, the abolition of serfdom, a more humane military system, agricultural and economic reform, reform of the courts, tolerance for the non-Russian nationalities within the Empire—by 1820 it was clear that these promises would not be kept. Revolution was in the air—the Greek Revolution was underway, rebellions had occurred in Spain, Portugal, and Italy. Thinking Russians dreamed of a republican Russia modeled on the French revolution or a constitutional monarchy based on the American example.

The movement is said to have originated in 1814 in Paris when young officers formed "discussion groups" to ponder the relatively freer societies and marvelous new ideas they were encountering. Some of these men reportedly came into contact with secret political societies. This might not be true, but they certainly learned a great deal about such conspiratorial phenomena as the German Tugenbund. In 1816 thirty army officers formed or soon joined a Union of Salvation to discuss, formulate, and consider ways of implementing reforms. Two years later the group organized a Union of Welfare and adopted a radical program calling for the abolition of serfdom and absolutism. By 1820 the membership had grown to two hundred. As it grew stronger and angrier, the new organization discarded its plans for a constitutional monarchy and began to look forward to a revolutionary republic.

In 1820, frustrated by the timidity of many members, the radical leaders of the Union of Welfare adopted a program calculated to drive moderates away and prepare a new, more decisive secret society. Instead, they got two. The program of the Northern Society called for a constitutional monarchy and planned a federative government to be introduced by an elected Constituent Assembly. The Southern Society preferred a republic, planned to introduce it through a supreme revolutionary government appointed to represent the will of the Russian people, and envisaged a new social order. The two societies agreed on the need to abolish autocracy and serfdom. Their leaders knew they could accomplish their mutual and differing reforms only through force. Members shifted back and forth between the two societies, but in Petersburg Ryleyev, with Aleksandr Bestuzhev's help, formed a conspiracy within a conspiracy to turn the Northerners to the Southerners' program. The two men apparently did not believe in republicanism, but they hoped that an alliance with Pestel would put them in a position to gain control after power was seized (Lebedev 1954; Zakharov 1954). In the spring of 1825 the two societies agreed on a plan to seize Alexander I during his annual inspection of the Army of the

South in May 1826 and take control of the army and the government. Details of the takeover and the choice of the form of government were left for later discussions. Unhappily, the plan—or rather, lack of plan—was preempted when Alexander died suddenly in November 1825. Aware that the tsar had discovered the existence of their conspiracy, and having good reason to believe that one of the tsar's brothers, either Constantine or Nicholas, would take severe measures against them, they had little choice but to put together their hasty plans of revolt in the north and rebellion in the south.

As Machiavelli knew, conspiracies are not efficient. They almost always fail, and the usual result of such failure is not the inauguration of a new order, but reaffirmation of the old. This was, in fact, the result of the revolt of 14 December 1825: Nicholas I inherited and strengthened the autocracy. According to recent studies, secrecy causes rampant problems of organization and communication, not least by provoking mutual distrust. Conspiracies attract eccentric personalities who seek to glorify an ego that has proved inadequate in normal human discourse. Paranoia and other psychological disorders among the members of a conspiracy thereby take a toll on organizational effectiveness (Tefft 1980). One problem of "secrecy" among the Decembrists was that they were prone to confide their plans to others. Another problem was that, truth be told, planning sessions usually turned into champagne-and-oyster banquets. The results of the Decembrists' efforts are therefore mixed, and this shows up in their attempts to subvert other organizations to their programs. They influenced literary societies, and Ryleyev and Bestuzhev almost gained control of two prominent journals. The chief result of these efforts, however, was to divide both the Northern and Southern societies into right and left wings (Bazanov 1964, 85–102). The Decembrists had less luck with the Masonic lodges, because these were too closely watched by the tsar's gendarmes. The majority of Decembrists were initiated into the lodges of the Grand Lodge of Astraea, Orient of Petersburg (which existed from 1815 to 1822). The early Decembrist unions and the literary societies they influenced often shared the same membership as the Masonic lodges. Decembrist activities bear the stamp of Masonic ideals of social progress, philanthropy, intellectual perfectibility, and resort to sub-rosa means to achieve moral goals. But by 1822 most had lost hope in Freemasonry as a vehicle of change.

Failures of communication became more serious. The Southern Society was more effectively unified only because of the influence of the Napoleon-like Pestel, whose penchant for secrecy kept the membership ignorant of his more extreme intentions. The Northern Society was divided by Ryleyev's conspiracy within a conspiracy. The leaders of the two societies had been foolish to settle on a plan of action without reconciling their most basic political differences. Imagine their dilemma. The Northerners were forced to act in part because they knew the Southerners might revolt and damn them all. The Southerners had to revolt for the same reason, and when they did, they did not even know their cause had already been lost in the north. Not the least reason for Nicholas's victory was that the plan for revolt on Senate Square was so poorly communicated to the membership that many overslept on the crucial morning.

Problems of communication were caused by class resentments. As a rule, the aristocrats formed a moderate right wing, whereas the less-privileged members of the lower nobility, especially those of the Southern Society, tended to be republicans.[1] The case of Pavel Pestel is illustrative. Despite the Napoleonic brilliance with which he overwhelmed all who met him, the aristocratic Davydovs and Volkonskys who worshiped him did not consider him comme il faut. Kondraty Ryleyev's standing is revealing too. Ryleyev, who came from a minor landowner family, was a born democrat and worshiper of the people. Known as the Brutus of the Decembrist movement, he despised the elite guards officers of both societies and worked against the aristocrats of the Northern Society. Aleksandr Bestuzhev seems to be an exception to Ryleyev's prejudice, but class complications are present here too. Bestuzhev's family was distinguished, and he used his social standing to enter an elite dragoon regiment and obtain duty at the Winter Palace. But his father, General A. F. Bestuzhev, had married a merchant's daughter, for which "offense" high society snubbed the entire family. Aleksandr's brothers Nikolay and Mikhail, minor writers and naval officers, scorned privilege, shared Ryleyev's contempt for aristocrats, and were angered by the corruption they had witnessed in the Admiralty and by Alexander's use of warships for pleasure cruises.

The United Slavs—a third society and an ally of the Southern Society—were also motivated by social resentments. The United Slavs provided Pestel with several potential assassins. They were more radical than the Southerners in other ways as well. One of the crucial differences between these plebeians and the liberal noblemen was their insistence on a disciplined revolutionary

---

1. Legend and history have it that the Decembrists were elite guards officers and poets inspired by the high ideals of the enlightenment and romanticism. However, according to W. Bruce Lincoln (1978), the aristocrats were a minority; most members of both societies belonged to the petty gentry or were sons of merchants or Orthodox priests; and only five are remembered as significant poets and writers. Lincoln divides the Decembrists into four categories. Closer to the centers of power, the Northerners tended to be more cautious. The Southerners were more radical because they were generally less privileged. The members of a third organization, the Society of United Slavs, differed from their allies in the Southern Society in that they were officers and noncommissioned officers of the line. The fourth category comprises nonmembers who joined the revolt at the last moment.

organization whose members surrendered their wills to a Ruling Directorate. As for the two assassins recruited by Ryleyev and Bestuzhev—A. I. Yakubovich and P. G. Kakhovskoy—their hatred of aristocrats became a loudly proclaimed intention to avenge wrongs against themselves by killing Alexander I. The romantic ideal of the assassin's dagger became an integral aspect of the literary expression of Decembrism known as civicism and an image central to the relationship between literature and thaumaturgy. In the late 1820s the Russian romantic movement was torn by a schism between literary aristocrats led by Pushkin and literary plebeians whose badly written literary works he despised. Before 1825 literary Decembrism was defined in large part by Ryleyev's advocacy of democracy and his formulation of an ideology based on civic patriotism. His dislike of the literary aristocrats led to significant differences between him and Bestuzhev on one side and the aristocratic Pushkin on the other, differences that all three men expressed in their works.

Literary Decembrism

Political Decembrism is inseparable from literary Decembrism, and that fact is central to an understanding of why arcane practices became so important to Decembrist writers and their contemporaries, so deeply troubled by the December uprising and its consequences. Nevertheless, it is not the political movement, but the literary one that produced the texts whose secret subjects are matters of political conspiracy. Russian literary Decembrism is variously labeled: Decembrist romanticism, civicism, civic Decembrism, and Decembrist romantic civicism. The terms indicate the difficulty of defining a self-contradictory sociopolitical-literary phenomenon. Most narrowly defined, literary Decembrism comprises only those actual members of the conspiracy who wrote and whose works express the ideals they were attempting to realize through political action. This definition implicates Ryleyev, Aleksandr Bestuzhev, V. K. Küchelbecker, A. I. Odoyevsky, Nikolay and Mikhail Bestuzhev, and the poet V. F. Rayevsky. Decembrism is usually broadened to include those sympathizers who were generally aware of the conspiracy and cultivated similar sociopolitical or civic themes in their works. Drawn in here are Pushkin, the dramatist A. S. Griboyedov, the student-poet N. M. Yazykov, P. A. Vyazemsky, and others who were cleared of complicity despite their open sympathy. Also drawn in by this definition are the journalists and publishers N. I. Grech and

F. V. Bulgarin, who were close to the conspirators but later became supporters of the government.

The problem of defining literary Decembrism is further complicated by many years of Soviet scholarship devoted to systematic inclusion of any writer who cultivated civic themes or was in any way associated with the Decembrists. (See, for example, Bazanov 1953, 1961, and 1964.) Literary Decembrism became so broadly defined that the Russian romantic movement is sometimes divided into Decembrism and whatever is left over. A more reasonable general definition would state that literary Decembrism is a demand for original, passionate, lofty, and free creativity, including the fullest expression of the ideals of patriotism and love of liberty. The slogan used for this literature is "national in form and civic in content." Literary Decembrism calls for "national-historical distinctiveness in poetry" and equates this with the concept of *narodnost'*—national originality, autocthony, *Volkstümlichkeit*. It is devoted to the national past and thus to the cultivation of folklore, legends, chronicles, and all other available sources of historical themes. The literary Decembrists believed that literature has political value. Theirs is a literature of protest and revolution, of sympathy for the Russian people. It is democratic in both political and social terms. It may be called plebeian in that it was one of the first attempts to reach a mass audience—a popular literature in the sense that it desired to educate newly literate readers and a low-class literature in the sense that it was willing to forego the sophistication of high literature.

The word *civicism* (*grazhdanstvennost'*) originated in the enlightenment ideal of civic Rome, perceptions of the poet as a patriotic citizen and son of the fatherland, and Decembrist dreams of a republic. For Russians in the eighteenth century civicism meant the duty of the court poet to praise state and autocrat. For the Decembrists civicism implied a literature of opposition to established authority and a yearning for individual freedom and dignity. Decembrist literature is a desire for equality and justice, a call for national originality, an expression of hatred for serfdom. Civicism is the poet's duty to enlighten the masses, promote democracy, and glorify the democratic past, especially as represented by the medieval republic of Novgorod. The civic ideal was most clearly expressed by Ryleyev in the line, "I am a Citizen, not a Poet." Decembrist civicism was a trend of the romantic movement, and thus succeeded the civic poetry of the eighteenth-century neoclassicists and preceded the civic writers and radical critics of the realist period.

Romantic Decembrism grew out of the trauma of 1812, was shattered by the failure of the revolt, and existed thereafter in anonymously published works of the surviving conspirators and in covert reaffirmation of Decembrist ideals in the works of sympathizers. The trend reached its peak in the years 1823–25 with the publication of three annual issues of the literary almanac *Polar Star,* edited by Bestuzhev and Ryleyev. Their literary-political platform was enunciated in "Glance," a review written by Bestuzhev as a preface to each issue. The editors emphasized civic works and managed to get strong statements past the censors, but their first concern was to publish the best, most profitable works of the time. Among the editors' chief interests were the modernization of the Russian literary language and its liberation from the pernicious influences of the French language and neoclassical dictates. They championed the "spirit of the time" in literature—emphasis on content over form in poetry—and used the word *narodnost'* for the first time in print. Their bible of history was N. M. Karamzin's *History of the Russian State,* but they rejected, without daring to say so publicly, Karamzin's conservative ideology. They also cautiously opposed the prestigious older poets of the Karamzinian "sentimental-elegiac" school (the first generation of Russian romantics) and openly opposed the philosophical poets who called themselves Lovers of Wisdom (*liubomudry*). Ryleyev disliked their Schellingian faith in poetry as philosophy and the preference of the "Pushkin Pleiad" for poetry as form. The Decembrist writers glorified the post-1812 yearning for democracy and freedom. They were Byronic, and to them Byron was a revolutionary.

The Decembrists preferred conventionally romantic genres—literary ballad, elegy, sonnet, modern ode, verse tale, prose tale, drama. The only genre that can be called distinctively Decembrist is the short historical poem known as the *duma* (meditation), cultivated most successfully by Ryleyev. The *duma* is a lyric poem of varying lengths that came to the Russians from the Polish romantics, who in their turn had developed this short form under the influence of a Ukrainian folk epic of that name. Ryleyev's *dumy* celebrate and are each named after a hero of the national past interpreted as a leader of the people who expressed the spirit of the time at a crucial historical moment. Each is accompanied by a prose account of the hero, his historical epoch, and his contribution. The *duma* as Ryleyev wrote it is a lofty genre imbued with patriotic fervor and love of freedom. He chose for his subjects the ancient hero Svyatoslav, who died rather than set off another fratricidal struggle for power in Kievan Rus; Boyan, the singer of Igor's campaign; Dmitry Donskoy, who defeated the Tatars; Prince Kurbsky, who defied Ivan the Terrible; and Natalya Dolgorukaya, who died a victim of Catherine's envy.

Decembrist literature is remarkable for its high idealism and the poet's sense of lofty mission. The civic poet is at once an admirer of the past and a would-be liberator of the present. This comes out with particular force in Ryleyev's historical verse tales *Voynarovsky* (1823–24) and *Nalivayko* (1824–25), which glorify Ukrainian, not Russian, history. Arguably, Ryleyev is the only Russian romantic who fully meets the definition of literary Decembrism. Küchelbecker's political poetry constitutes a small portion of his total oeuvre, for example, and A. I. Odoyevsky's political poetry was irrelevant to the Decembrist movement because it was not published until many years later. Ryleyev's poetry is predominantly civic, and he was the most active campaigner against noncivic trends. His disagreements with Pushkin are precisely on the point of civic versus formal aesthetics. In his definition of the essence of poetry as the "spirit of the time" he meant that poetry ought to advance sociopolitical causes.

Nor were other Decembrists as committed to Decembrism as Ryleyev. Bestuzhev shared his convictions, but hardly with such force. Bestuzhev created magnificent heroes of the past, as in the patriotic tale "The Raiders" (1831), the historical tale à la Walter Scott "Tournament at Reval" (1825), and the Novgorod legend "Roman and Olga" (1823). The hero of "Tournament at Reval" is a merchant who outwits and outfights his aristocratic rivals. In "Roman and Olga" the young Roman, also a merchant's son, is aided by robbers to save democratic Novgorod from autocratic Moscow and win the hand of the beautiful Olga. His historical heroes are also villains, as is the case with the main character of "The Traitor" (1825), who betrays Russia out of envy of his popular brother, his lust for power, and a misdirected longing for the admiration of his people. The early Bestuzhev's tales of Livonian history, "Castle Wenden," "Castle Neihausen," and "Castle Eisen" (1821, 1824, 1825), and the tale from Russian history "Gedeon" (1820) are Gothic tales of terrible vengeance. When he resumed his career as Marlinsky in the 1830s, Bestuzhev created heroes who are often beset by doubt, whatever their commitment to lofty ideals. "The Frigate Hope" (1832), a tale of a naval captain who deserts his ship for an illicit love affair and dies knowing he has failed both duty and love, is a psychologically painful confession of the author's feelings of guilt. Even the hero of "Ammalat-Bey" (1831–32), one of his most positive heroes, is a man beset by terrible conflicts of loyalty, which lead to death and dishonor.

A popular genre of the civic trend is the revolutionary song. Ryleyev and Bestuzhev coauthored a series of "Agitational Songs" (1823–25), which were well known to their fellow conspirators and others in manuscript form. One of these songs, "Tell me, say, how tsars are murdered in Russia," mocks the assassination of Paul I and other victims of eighteenth-century palace revolts.

"Our tsar is a Russian German" satirizes the Romanov family and ridicules Alexander I in a strong jeering rhyme: "Ay-da tsar, ay-da tsar, Orthodoxy's Star!" "Akh, it makes me sick" is an attack on the banality and brutality of the serf system in the language of serfs. The song complains of "Russian lords" who "rob us shamelessly" and "strip our skins." Russian landowners are "thieves, fleecers, they suck our blood like leeches." These are the songs the Decembrists loved to sing at their champagne-and-oyster banquets. There is no evidence that they appealed to their intended audience, the Russian people.

The revolutionary song was cultivated beyond the confines of Decembrism strictly defined. Early in the century the hussar-poet Denis Davydov wrote several ringing satires and songs against Petersburg society and the army command; in the 1830s he wrote a bitter invective titled "Hungry Cur" (1832). Other authors of revolutionary songs and verses are P. A. Katenin and Yazykov. Some of the most extreme views were expressed by Pushkin, notably in "Liberty. An Ode" (1817); "Noël, Hurrah" (1818); and "The Dagger" (1821). When Pushkin casts his eye over Russia in "Liberty," he sees "everywhere scourges, everywhere irons, the destructive shame of laws, the impotent tears of slavery, everywhere unjust power." In "The Dagger" Pushkin celebrates the assassins of history, Brutus, Marat, Charlotte Corday, and Karl Sand.

After 1825 literary Decembrism sounds notes of despair. Understandably, the conspirators themselves expressed the deepest regret and disillusionment. A. I. Odoyevsky wrote his first Decembrist laments while incarcerated in the Peter-and-Paul Fortress in Petersburg and some of his most defiant post-December verse while in Siberian exile. Küchelbecker wrote sad poetry of loss and exile. Some of the best poetry of lonely exile belongs to Bestuzhev, who expressed regret in verses while exiled to Yakutsk. Among the best of these is "Dream" (1829). Better known is Pushkin's post-December expression of his fate as a fellow-traveler of the Decembrists, "Arion" (1827). Loss of hope frequently resulted in bitter contemplations of an inhuman Russia and denunciations of Russian backwardness. Typical is D. V. Venevitinov's poem "Homeland" (1826), in which he renounces all hope of change.

Hope was not fully lost, however, and the ideals of Decembrism did not die. The first tale published by the new authorial persona Marlinsky, "The Test" (1830), is a humorous story of two frivolous hussars that contain behind its wit several covert reaffirmations of Decembrist ideals. In 1827, in his "Message to Siberia," Pushkin reaffirmed his allegiance to his fallen friends and sent them words of hope. One year later the exiled Odoyevsky replied by expressing continued defiance and his comrades' faith that their example would indeed live on. It did, in fact, live on. After 1825 thinking Russians were alienated from the state and from society. Russian writers were prevented by censorship from expressing their true views, but it is not easy to find in the history of Russian literature an advocate of the autocracy; the integrity of most was firmly based on contempt for it. The Decembrists were admired not only by the radicals of the revolutionary movement that led to 1917, but by almost all whose dignity was expressed in the word intelligentsia. The tradition of democracy in Russia did not die in 1825 (or, as we now understand, in 1917), and Russian literature is of course world renowned for its spirit of protest. The Decembrists themselves could not protest, but those who survived continued to express their views, thoughts, and feelings. However, they could do so only covertly, and this is why they turned to the skills of arcane, sub-rosa, secret communication provided them by the esoteric tradition.

Russia and the Esoteric Tradition

Whereas Decembrism has been thoroughly studied and Freemasonry in Russia partly studied, the esoteric tradition has received scant attention. As a result, the rich scholarship on esoteric, arcane, or thaumaturgical phenomena in the works of such European writers as Dante, Rabelais, Spenser, Milton, Sterne, and Goethe has not been matched in the study of Russian literature. Many problems of irregular texts and covert expression of proscribed meaning have been studied, however, and this is especially true of literary Decembrism.[2] Esotericism coexists in history with reason; sometimes it dominates a culture, sometimes it recedes into obscurantism. (For an excellent overview of the history of the tradition, see Faivre 1987 and 1992.) The origins of the modern European tradition have been traced largely to the Middle Ages and the

---

2. Major literary works like A. S. Griboyedov's play *Woe from Wit* (1822–23) have been thoroughly analyzed for their Decembrist allusions, and such outright Decembrist allegories as Pushkin's poem "Arion" have been convincingly interpreted (Mikkelson 1980; Vickery 1976). The encoded "Decembrist chapter" of Pushkin's *Eugene Onegin* (1823–33) has been analyzed (Tomashevskii 1934; Nabokov 1964, 3:311–75; Morozov 1910). The Decembrist meaning of *The Bronze Horseman* (1833) has been decoded (Lednicki 1955) and the Decembrist connections of "The Queen of Spades" (1833) have been established thanks to brilliant sleuthing on Pushkin and the Decembrists (Eydelman 1979). Pushkin's relationship to the conspiracy has been exhaustively researched (Meilakh 1958a, 1958b; Vatsuro and Meilakh 1966). Allusive language and disguised themes in Decembrist works have been attended to; commentaries to collected works offer shrewd explications of key phrases; and specialists in Decembrist literature have pointed to both allegorical and encoded literary texts (Bazanov 1953, 1961).

Renaissance, and to the sources to which the men of these eras ascribed authority. The most important ancient origin is Hebrew gnosis of the Old Testament—the "ineffable writ" ascribed to Moses and Merkabah mysticism—and the Jewish Cabala (Scholem 1960, 1961, 1971b, and 1987). Closely related to this source is the Christian Cabala deciphered by the Great Magi of the Renaissance from the New Testament, primarily the Book of Revelation (Blau 1944). The second origin is Platonism and Hellenic gnosis, primarily Pythagorean geometric numerology and astrology.[3] The third is Hermetic gnosis, an ambiguous tradition supposedly passed down from the ancient Egyptian gnostic Hermes the Thrice-Fold Great (see Hermes Trismegistus 1964). The Christian Cabalist tradition began in the late fifteenth century in the Medici Circle of the Renaissance Neoplatonic thinkers Marsilio Ficino and Pico della Mirandola. They found their authority in the Platonic and Neoplatonic Greek manuscripts brought to Florence after the fall of Byzantium and in the *Corpus Hermeticum* of Hermes, who, they believed, was the precursor of Plato himself. Ficino and Pico adapted the Cabala invented by Ramon Lull at the end of the thirteenth and beginning of the fourteenth centuries and a fifteenth-century variant known as the Spanish or Lurean Cabala after its author Isaac Lurie. Their contribution was to introduce into it an amalgamation of Renaissance and pre-Renaissance Hermeticism and Hermetic magic. The Renaissance Cabalist tradition flourished in Italy after the Expulsion of 1492 in the movement known as Lullism (Yates 1979, 29–30, 32–34). Lullism is an esoteric philosophy based on the search for truth in all areas of knowledge and a belief that the secrets of mundane and celestial levels of existence can be deciphered by manipulating the letters of the alphabet. The Cabala (the word means "tradition") can be exegetic (an existing text is deciphered and interpreted) or "practical" (a specially encoded text is written). That is to say, arcane knowledge can be discovered or invoked (French 1972, 47–49; Hillgarth 1971; Blau 1944).

The esoteric tradition founded in the Medici Circle was additionally enriched with Hermetic and Christian Cabalism by the Franciscan friar Francesco Giorgi, whose architectural symbolism of the Temple of Solomon, *De harmonia mundi* (1525), later became a major authority of the Freemasons. The tradition reached one great expression in the writings of Giordano Bruno (Yates 1964).

---

3. According to Heinrich Schneider, an authority on the esoteric tradition (1947, 102–3), the Cabala attracted the Renaissance Neoplatonists because it was itself Platonic and anti-Aristotelian. Their view of the Cabala was not shaped so much by Plato directly, as by Plotinus.

Modern historians of the esoteric have now traced a significant origin of modern science to the alchemistic, numerological, and magic researches of Paracelsus (Webster 1982). Under the influence of Lullism the esoteric tradition moved north to connect with French humanism and eventually with the German Reformation in Johann Reuchlin's *De verbo mirifico* (1494) and *De arte cabalistica* (1517) (Yates 1979, 2–4, 17–18, 24–25). In France Henry Cornelius Agrippa published his "handbook of the Renaissance occult sciences," *De occulta philosophia,* in 1531 and republished his diatribe *De vanite scientarium* in 1533. Agrippa's works are "a compendium of the glories of French Humanism": grammar, rhetoric, poetry, the art of memory, dialectics, music, architecture, astronomy and astrology, arithmetic, geometry and numerology, physics, metaphysics and ethics, medicine and jurisprudence, magic, cabalistics, chemistry and alchemy, angelology, and cosmology (Yates 1979, 37–46; also Nauert 1965). In Elizabethan England Agrippa's erudition was reexpressed in the Lullism, Cabalism, and Hermeticism of the Great Magus John Dee, chiefly in *Monas hieroglyphica* (1564).

With the triumph of Cartesian and post-Cartesian empiricism, esotericism was consigned to the realm of quackery. This attitude remained dominant in European thought until the mid-twentieth century when modern scholars of esoteric studies began to appreciate that in the humanities Pascal with his faith in faith was as influential as Descartes and that the Great Magi were the theologians and scientists of their time. In the natural sciences astrology prepared the foundations for astronomy, alchemy for chemistry, physics, and biology, numerology for mathematics. The Cabala in all its varieties is one basis of modern poetics, stylistics, and textual analysis (Fowler 1970a). The Great Magi were wrong in their mystical assumption that human beings can manipulate the natural forces of the universe through numerological or astrological means, conjure celestial beings, or divine the mysteries through occult rituals, but they were not wrong in their faith or the respect for intellect that enabled them to recover mountains of lost humanistic knowledge. They were able to do so in no small part through cabalistic decodings, and in this way they contributed greatly to the development of science and the humanities. John Dee was wrong to believe that numbers and letters are actual forces, rather than symbolic signs that can be made to stand for objective phenomena, but his "erroneous" knowledge of astrology and numerology created the maps that led to the New World, and his *General and rare memorials pertayning to the Perfect arte of Nauigation* (1677) provided Elizabeth with the ideology of British imperial destiny (French 1972; Yates 1975, 85).

Among the most important post-Renaissance esoteric works are *The Hermetick Romance, or The Chymical Wedding* and *The Fame and Confession of the Fraternity of the Rosie Cross (Fama fraternitas)* (1614–16) that are ascribed to "Christian Rosenkreutz," a legendary figure imagined by the founders of the first Rosicrucian movement, but were written in Dutch and Latin by Johannes Andreae. Christian Rosenkreutz exerted significant influence on Freemasonry and became the basis of Rosicrucianism (see Allen 1968). The influence of Robert Fludd and Jakob Böhme was powerful in the seventeenth century, particularly in the former's *Utriusque cosmi historia* (1617–21) and the latter's *Mysterium magnum* (1623). Their work on the Cabala and numerology was systematized by Georg von Welling in his *Opus Mago-Cabbalisticum et Theosophicum* (1735).

In the eighteenth century theosophy is represented by Emanuel Swedenborg, who described his work, especially *Coelestia Arcana* (1749–58), *De Coelo et Inferno* (1758), and *Apocalypsis revelata* (1769), as a spiritual system common to both the Apocalypse and the Cabala. The tradition descended to charlatanry in the posing of Count Saint-Germain and Joseph Balsamo, Count Cagliostro, to both or either of whom are ascribed *La Très Sainte Trinosophie* (see Saint-Germain 1949) and the so-called *Roman Rites of the Egyptian Order of Masons* (Yates 1972).[4] It remained on the high level of theosophy in the writings of the mystics Martines de Pasqually (Martinez Pasqualis), author of *Traité de la réintégration des êtres* (1754; see 1899), and Louis-Claude de Saint-Martin, especially *Des erreurs et de la verité* (1775), *L'Homme de désir* (1790), and *De l'esprit des choses*. The European esoteric tradition was shaped in the eighteenth century most prominently, but not entirely, by the rise of the Order of the Grand Architect of the World, known more commonly as Freemasonry. Among the eighteenth-century thinkers who influenced the moral character of the Masonic movement were John Pordage (Johann Pordadsche), author of *Göttliche und wahre Metaphysica oder Wunderbare* (1715), A. I. Kirchweger, author of *Aurea Catena Homeri* (1723), and Christian von Haugwitz, author of *Hirten-brief* (1785). These works are cited among the most influential of many "hermetic"

---

4. It is difficult to distinguish among the deeds and works of Saint-Germain and Cagliostro, especially since Cagliostro often found it convenient to claim that his works were entrusted to him by Saint-Germain. At least one of Cagliostro's biographers credits him with the authorship of *La Très Sainte Trinosophie* (Ribadeau Dumas 1967, 305–6), but most scholars agree that Saint-Germain was the real author and that Cagliostro wrote the *Roman Rites of the Egyptian Order of Masons*. Although many of Cagliostro's works were sequestered by the Inquisition, some scholars claim to have identified titles of works on cabalistics, astrology, alchemy, and invocations of spirits (Chetteoui 1947, 24).

works brought to the Moscow Mystical Freemasons (Vernadskii 1917, 126–27).[5]

To these moral treatises and instructions in the intricacies of alchemy, numerology, and cabalism may be added a source not previously mentioned by historians of Russian Freemasonry, but greatly influential: the texts of rites and teachings of the eighteenth-century Masonic author Théodore Henri, baron de Tschoudy, his rites of the Order of the Flaming Star–Der flammende Stern (1866; see also *Der Signatstern* and Tschoudy 1766, 1779).

Freemasonry in Russia

The history of Freemasonry is shrouded in secrecy and beset by controversy. Serious historians will probably never sort out the relationships among the many directions the Masonic movement has taken through the years.[6] Amateur historians, especially anti-Masonic searchers for sinister conspiracies, have obfuscated the history of Freemasonry. Fortunately, the work of several reputable historians facilitates a search for the road the esoteric tradition took into Russia.[7]

---

5. Craven (1988, 401–2) has recently added to this list the mystic Jan van Ruisbreck, the philosopher Jean Baptist van Helmont, and the quietist Jeanne Maria Guyon. Among Masonic theosophists frequently mentioned by such prominent Russian Freemasons as the writer and national historian N. M. Karamzin are Carl von Eckartshausen, Heinrich Jung-Stilling, Charles Bonnet, and Johannes Caspar Lavater. Karamzin traveled through Europe in the 1790s with the express purpose of meeting these Masonic teachers. His *Letters of a Russian Traveler* shows that Freemasonry was also a chief concern of his meetings or attempts to meet with such literary Freemasons as Wieland, Klopstock, Kleist, Lessing, Uhland, Schiller, and Goethe. An excellent overview of the influence of Eckartshausen and others on Karamzin is provided by Faivre (1969).

6. For one of the most reliable brief histories of Freemasonry in the eighteenth century, including its partings of the ways with Templarism, Rosicrucianism, Illuminism, and other branches of the movement, see Faivre 1973, 145–86.

7. The most authoritative historians of Freemasonry and Rosicrucianism are A. N. Pypin and G. V. Vernadsky, who disentangled and recorded a wealth of factual materials. Among the earliest serious scholars are M. N. Longinov, A. I. Nezelenov, and S. A. Petrovsky. Thanks to correspondence and other documents collected and published by Ya. L. Barskov, historians have been given access to the cabalistic, theosophical, and other esoteric interests of the group of enlightener-philanthropists led by the writer and publicist N. I. Novikov and known for their deep involvement in esoterica as the Moscow Rosicrucians (1915). The most ingenious analyst of Masonic and Rosicrucian rituals is T. O. Sokolovskaya. Three indispensable sources are V. L. Tukalevsky, P. N. Sakulin, and N. K. Piksanov. Among other standard works are an index of Russian Freemasons compiled by Tatiana Bakounine and

Russians made contact with the European esoteric tradition in the eighteenth century.[8] Their knowledge came almost exclusively through Freemasonry and the mystical expression of the movement known as Rosicrucianism. Although "rudimentary" Masonic lodges were opened in Russia in the early eighteenth century during the reign of Peter the Great, it was not until the 1760s that Masonic thought and esoteric ideas exerted serious influence on Russian culture. In 1763 the writer and publicist I. P. Elagin received permission to found lodges in Russia under the authority of the Berlin lodge Zu den drei Weltkügeln. In 1770 Russian Freemasonry gained European status when the Order of Royal York in Berlin, center of rational English Freemasonry in Germany, granted Elagin a formal charter or patent for a Directorial or Grand Provincial Lodge to work in accordance with the Ancient English System. Other lodges were opened under the auspices of various French, German, English, and Swedish orients and orders. The Grand Lodge of England acknowledged the authority of the Directorial or Grand Provincial Lodge in 1771, but the Swedish System, which was more receptive to esotericism, was introduced in 1775 and quickly gained dominance. Russian Freemasonry flourished until 1794 when it was suppressed by Catherine II, whose ban was continued by Paul I. It was revived in the early nineteenth century and flourished until Alexander I closed the lodges in 1822 and Nicholas I banned the Order in 1826.

The main carrier of esoterica into Russia was I. G. Schwartz, professor of German at Moscow (Lomonosov) Imperial University and "emissary" of German Freemasonry (Longinov 1857). The greatly respected Schwartz was replaced by an enigmatic German Freemason, Baron G. J. Schroeder.[9] The most influential recipients of their teachings and documents were Elagin and N. I.

---

a bibliography compiled by Paul Bourychkine. A superb two-volume collection of articles on Russian Freemasonry edited by S. P. Melgunov and M. P. Sidorov has recently been reprinted. Please see the appropriate listings in "Reference Materials" for all the foregoing. The primary sources used by these historians (and by Tolstoy for his novel *War and Peace*) are the Masonic documents preserved in the Rumyantsov Museum in Moscow (Berdnikov 1900), now in the Russian State Library (Lenin), and particularly in Fund 14 of the Manuscript Section ("V. S. Arsen'ev—Sobranie Masonskikh Rukopisei [XVIII–XIX v.v.]). A less well known source is the Masonic collection of the Institute of Russian Literature (Pushkin House) in Petersburg (Razdel II, opis' 2, nos. 51–140).

8. For an excellent study of a major Masonic trend in eighteenth-century Russian culture, see Baehr 1991.

9. So far as the influence of Schwartz and Schroeder is concerned, Vernadsky substantiates Pypin's belief that both worked closely with Elagin, Novikov, and Lopukhin (1917, 65, 68–69, 72). Vernadsky (1917, 65–79, 80–83) and Pypin (1916, 337–68, 368–80) agree that Schwartz brought his authority from the Berlin lodge Zu den drei Weltkügeln, and introduced materials from French Rosicrucianism, shaped by Pasqually and Saint-Martin. Schwartz's credentials are sound. Schroeder, however, is a con-

Novikov. Novikov and the group of men around him became known as the Moscow Rosicrucians or Mystic Masons (Longinov 1867).[10] I. V. Lopukhin exerted great moral influence on Russian culture through three religious-mystical treatises, "The Spiritual Knight, or The Seeker of Supreme Wisdom" (1791), "On the Church Within Thee" (1798), and "A Morally Edifying Catechism of the True Free Masons" (1790; see also 1913). Also influential was I. P. Turgenev, a pioneer of Russian pedagogy, director of Moscow Imperial University and founder of the Moscow Pension of the Nobility, where many well-known early romantic poets were educated in accordance with his Masonic ideals.[11] The best of these poets was V. A. Zhukovsky, whose translations of German and English romantic and preromantic poetry were a chief vehicle of the Russian romantic movement.

Historians agree that the most influential source of esoteric knowledge and mysticism was Louis Claude de Saint-Martin. G. V. Vernadsky stresses the importance of *Des erreurs et de la verité* (1917, 162–63, 165), and A. N. Pypin states that Saint-Martin was so influential as to justify the name Martinists for the Novikov group (1916, 141–42, 210–17). Vernadsky lists Fludd's *Utriusque cosmi*, Welling's *Opus Mago-Cabbalisticum et Theosophicum,* and "a huge number of works" by Böhme among the "Divine Wisdom [*Bogomudrye*] works" that attracted the Moscow Rosicrucians (1917, 126–27). To this list he adds Anton Kirchweger, Christian Haugwitz, and John Pordage. Among the other prominent sources of esoteric knowledge most often mentioned by historians are Christian Rosenkreutz (Andreae), Hermes Trismegistus, and Emanuel Swedenborg. Swedenborg's influence is indicated by the word-for-word explications of the Old Testament à la Swedenborg in the Barskov collection. As for

---

troversial figure whose claim to Schwartz's authority is not fully convincing. According to Pypin, Schroeder was accepted as a legitimate representative of Zu den drei Weltkügeln, but might have been a poser (1916, 224–25). But Vernadsky actually says that despite a sharp break in Novikov's friendship with Schroeder, Novikov once considered the baron to be "his chief in everything" (1917, 123, 79). Whatever the case, there is no doubt that Schroeder's influence was substantial. His Masonic name "Sacerdotos" figures prominently in the documents published by Barskov (cf. 1915, 227).

10. Historians have always had difficulty separating Freemasonry from Rosicrucianism, or for that matter from Templarism and other orders and systems. Many orders claimed precedence and considered the others apostate. To complicate matters, the members of the Moscow group called themselves both Freemasons and Rosicrucians; subsequently, scholars of Russian Freemasonry followed suit and added to the term Mystic in an effort to clarify their definition. What is important as a general rule is that nonrational Freemasonry and Rosicrucianism often were identical: the same esoteric sources were sought, the same practices developed.

11. In addition to Novikov, Lopukhin, and Turgenev, the Moscow Mystic Masons include N. N. Trubetskoy, A. M. Kutuzov, P. A. Tatishchev, S. I. Gamaleya, and A. F. Labzin. All are listed in major Masonic encyclopedias.

the sources of thaumaturgical skills, these seem to be Saint-Martin, Swedenborg, Welling, and especially Tschoudy. The thaumaturgical works of these four men subsume the skills taught by Böhme and Fludd, who in their turn learned from such predecessors as Giorgi, Reuchlin, Agrippa, Dee, and Andreae.

Unhappily, the links between European and Russian esotericism were broken when Novikov was arrested and his library burned by order of Catherine I. In 1970 the Russian bibliographer Evgeny Beshenkovsky, now in the United States, found a list of Novikov's books comprising some 3,500 titles (Martynov 1976). Among these books was a Masonic Library divided hierarchically in chambers. The chambers contained a virtual treasury of the works of the Great Magi from the medieval theosophist Roger Bacon through the eighteenth century (Craven 1988). Beshenkovsky's discovery leaves no doubt that the Moscow Rosicrucians' reputation for erudition is deserved.

So many prominent Russians of the second half of the eighteenth century and the early nineteenth century were Freemasons that it would be easier to list those that were not, rather than those that were (Bakounine 1967; Leighton 1982). Although Freemasonry is usually considered a singular phenomenon, it is actually a diverse and wide-ranging complex of many different orients; orders; directorates; societies; national, provincial, and grand lodges; rites; and systems. At different times and different places Freemasonry can be politically revolutionary or reactionary, actively involved in public affairs or in retreat from the world, rational or mystic. Some orders and lodges have fallen into obscurantism, charlatanry, and religious intolerance. Freemasonry has thrived in different forms in Catholic countries such as France, Italy, and Poland, predominantly Protestant countries like the United States, Orthodox countries like Russia, Islamic countries like Turkey, and recently in Israel. (To this must be added the rapid revival of Freemasonry underway in Russia and other countries of the Commonwealth of Independent States.) Freemasons trace their founding variously to the builders of Solomon's temples, the Knights Templars of the Crusades, and the craftsmen of medieval English and European guilds. But Freemasonry as such was founded in the early eighteenth century. Freemasons have been accused of attempting to supplant religion, but Masonic teachings insist that Freemasonry is devoted to the development of moral virtue, not to the establishment of a church.

Masonic symbolism is based on the principle of "work." Freemasons—that is, architects, craftsmen—are "working" members of the Order of the Grand Architect of the Universe. Masonic work consists of participation in rites or rituals and in "study," that is, in memorizing the texts of the rites and mastering their symbolic meanings. This basic "practical" or "working" Freemasonry is characterized by three grades or degrees of advancement toward "mastery" of or "adeptness" in the craft: Apprentice Mason, Fellow Craft Mason, and Master Mason. Every initiate into the secrets of the craft must "build a temple within," that is, achieve the goals of self-knowledge, self-perfection, and self-sacrifice or self-renunciation. These basic ethical-moral qualities are attained in turn by the mastery of seven virtues, listed variously as (to cite the most common) prudence or tolerance, obedience, morality or religiosity, love of one's brothers, courage, disinterestedness or unselfishness, and love of death. Love of one's brothers leads to love of family, friends, country, all of mankind. Love of death, the highest possible attainment, means the overcoming of fear of death, that is, perfect faith in the existence of God and "a better world."

In some orients (usually a city) work is divided differently, as it is, for example, in the American Free and Accepted Scottish Rites, which has thirty-three degrees. Masonic "authority" or "obedience" is usually centered in a grand orient or grand lodge, to which "regular" lodges are subordinate. Some "orders" or "systems" are confined to the three working degrees; others add a number of higher "theoretical" degrees, for example, Templarism, Rosicrucianism (Rosie Cross), Golden Cross, Scottish Rites; still others subscribe only to the higher degrees. Those orders which include the Rosicrucian and Templar degrees should not be confused with Rosicrucianism or Templarism per se, which are sometimes considered offshoots (or forerunners) of Freemasonry, sometimes entirely different phenomena. Whatever the common origins of a general movement called Freemasonry may (or may not) have been, by the end of the eighteenth century Freemasonry proper was often at odds with Rosicrucianism, Knights Templar, Knights of Malta, Illuminati, and other orders and systems.

Every Freemason swears to preserve the secrets of the craft. Freemasons communicate with one another through "the signs, the signals, and the words."[12] Scholars usually divide Freemasonry into "mystic" and "rational" trends or "strict" and "lax" rites. It is often said as a generalization that German Freemasonry tended to mysticism, English Freemasonry to rationalism. The word "strict" signifies purity of the rites and the necessity to observe both the letter and the substance of the texts. Obedience, sometimes surrender of one's will, is obligatory. "Lax" rites emphasize substance over form, a more liberal

---

12. However strictly secrecy was observed in the past or is observed in some lodges and orders today, the texts of the rites are readily available in published form, as are most Masonic writings. Masonic libraries and archives are accessible, and Masonic scholars share their research with others.

observance of the rules, and initiation into the secrets of the order by and of one's own free will. The rite of Strict Observance was founded in 1754 by Johann Gottlieb von Hund, and the even stricter Swedish System was founded by Count von Eckleff in 1759.[13] A third, more complex rite of strict observance is the Zinnendorf System, founded by J. W. Zinnendorf (Ellenberg). The different, most mystic Rosicrucian system of thirty-three degrees was centered in Frankfurt and in Bordeaux, Lyons, and other orients in the south of France, most notably in L'ordre des Élus Coéns (Le Forestier n.d.). Lax systems are usually called Free and Accepted Rites. The most prominent of these is the Ancient English System, simplified to the symbolism of the three practical degrees. The Ancient English System exerted significant influence on German and other European Freemasons through the Order of Royal York.[14]

The popularity of the Swedish System in eighteenth-century Russia was equaled by the Rosicrucian system of thirty-three degrees. The Zinnendorf System also played a significant role in Russia, as did Templarism. In the early nineteenth century, however, when Freemasonry was revived during the reign of Alexander I, the Free and Accepted Rites prevailed. Tolerance and reform were the new order of the day in European Freemasonry. German Freemasonry was transformed by such modern Freemasons as Lessing, Fichte, Ignatius Fessler, and Friedrich Schroeder, who were disillusioned by mysticism and drawn to the unpretentious Ancient English System. When Fessler was appointed professor of philosophy at the Petersburg Spiritual Academy in 1810, he influenced the Russian Freemasons in the direction of Free and Accepted Rites.

The goals of the new Russian Freemasons were modernization of the rituals, religious tolerance, organization and development, and, usually, straightforward cultivation of the Masonic ideals of self-knowledge, self-perfection, and self-renunciation. Their concerns were recruitment (initiation), opening new lodges, inculcating Masonic ideals, protecting the integrity of the rites, and philanthropy. The reopening of the lodges was encouraged by Alexander in 1803 and officially approved in 1809. By 1815 two Masonic organizations were

---

13. Indicative of the contradictory character of Masonic history is that the Swedish System is called lax despite its strictness.

14. The St. John's Rites, which define the craft degrees, originate in the legend that St. John introduced Freemasonry to Scotland. They are also called Primitive to denote their alleged ancient origin, Solomonic to reflect their origin in the temples of Solomon, and Scottish (Écossais). There are many different forms of these rites, but the Scottish Rites are not like the American so-called Scottish Rite. Not all systems are based on architectural symbolism. For example, the symbolic systems of Templarism and Rosicrucianism are based on the age of chivalry and the Crusades.

at work: a revived Grand Directorial Lodge and a newly founded Grand Lodge of Astraea, both in the Orient of Petersburg. Whereas the Grand Directorial Lodge clung to the Swedish System, the Grand Lodge of Astraea was authorized to work in accordance with the Ancient English System. By the time the lodges were closed in 1822, Astraea was clearly dominant, with twenty-five lodges under its authority, including several that retained the Swedish System (see Pypin 1916, 398–457).

There was no lack of political motivation among the new initiates. Pestel and Ryleyev are examples of this, and one of the most active nineteenth-century Freemasons was A. Kh. Benckendorf, the reactionary secret policeman who headed the dread Third Section under Nicholas I. Pushkin's lodge of Ovid in Kishinev was one of several hothouses of political intrigue whose members—V. F. Rayevsky and M. F. Orlov among others—worked closely with the Greek revolutionary Alexander Ypsilanti and welcomed Pestel to their debates (Chereiskii 1975, 163–64, 339–40). But the membership lists of the Grand Lodge of Astraea show that honorary and active positions were occupied by police and court officials whose task was to discover and discourage political activism (Leighton 1982). Even despite this close surveillance, Alexander I was finally persuaded by his religious-mystic advisers that Freemasonry constituted the same revolutionary peril that it had in France, Italy, and the North American colonies. Those Freemasons who became Decembrists turned to their own societies because they realized reform could not be effected through the closely watched lodges, and many were disillusioned by the absence of social conscience in Russian Freemasonry itself. If the lodges had not been closed, it is likely that those Decembrists who had not already left by 1822 would have left sooner or later; and whatever their commitment to Masonic ideals, they had no respect for the social and political significance of the Masonic movement. Only one Decembrist leader—Pestel—wanted to introduce ritual into Decembrist proceedings; Ryleyev, however, expressed contempt for the idea that rituals could be used to strengthen political discipline (Nechkina 1951, 159).

Given this condition, it does not seem likely that the new Freemasons could have become as adept in the craft as their predecessors. The majority were rational Freemasons and were not attracted to Rosicrucianism. Continuity had been disrupted by Catherine's suppression of the craft. But mastery of the three skills of alchemy, the Cabala, and numerology was the first requirement of Apprentice Masons in Russia as elsewhere, and the members of the Grand Lodge of Astraea shared with their predecessors the Masonic emphasis on such virtues as philanthropy, brotherhood, and love of wisdom. Their interest was primarily intellectual—they saw the utility of thaumaturgical skills, and they appreciated the symbolism of the craft. They were not erudite readers of the Great Magi, but evidence suggests that they were more than passingly familiar with the esoteric tradition.[15]

Theosophy, mysticism, Cabalism, nonempirical science, and thaumaturgy flourished in the Russian Enlightenment in the form of Rosicrucian mysticism and Masonic theosophy; the Novikov Freemasons were clearly erudite in these branches of arcane knowledge. How adept the later romantics were, however, is not clear. All that can be said for certain is that in the romantic period Masonic symbolism and the arcane skills of thaumaturgy were welcome in arenas of social and political action like the Decembrist affair, as well as in the larger arena of public journalism inhibited by ubiquitous censorship and private discussion made perilous by surveillance. The connections between thaumaturgy and literature have to be seen in this context, and additionally in relation to the attitude of the more rational, more skeptical Freemasons of the romantic period.

This attitude can be likened to a more extensively studied phenomenon, the early nineteenth-century European attitude toward conspiracy. According to J. M. Roberts, an authority on the mystique of secret societies, conspiratorial explanations of political events were acceptable in the early nineteenth century and were "held by men who were socially and intellectually respectable and who prided themselves, often, on their practical grasp of political affairs." The

---

15. Some of the most interesting evidence exists in the Moscow Masonic archives and in the character of the documents contained there. These documents generally date from the two periods when the craft flourished. The eighteenth-century documents are either esoteric or rational—texts of the rites, organization work, opening of new lodges, social and political interests. Many of the esoteric documents in the Arsen'ev Fund are copies, paraphrases, and adaptations to Russian needs of the European sources already specified. Many bear the names of or are known to have belonged to leading Moscow Masons. Similarly, the Masonic holdings of the Institute of Russian Literature in Petersburg are divided by about half between thaumaturgical documents and such rational documents as texts of rites, financial accounts, correspondence, and speeches. Some belonged to the Grand Directorial Lodge, most to the Grand Lodge of Astraea. The esoteric documents in Petersburg are written in French, German, and Russian, or were translated from French and German. They seem to have originated with the Moscow Rosicrucians, for they bear the same titles, and some were written or translated by I. V. Lopukhin and other Moscow Rosicrucians (Razdel II, opis' 2, nos. 60–62, 76–80, 85–86, 88). A document titled "A Masonic Collection" (no. 65), contains Lopukhin's theosophical treatise "On the Church Within Thee." Many bear the Grand Lodge of Astraea's indicators or are copied on its distinctive paper. They deal with such subjects as alchemy, the wisdom of Solomon and Hermes Trismegistus, the Chemical Garden, and the Philosopher's Stone. Some are German Rosicrucian works (nos. 64, 66, 80, 86). Some are translations of the chief works brought to the Moscow Rosicrucians from Germany and France: Kirchweger's *Aurea Catena Homeri* (no. 63), Haugwitz's *Hirten-brief* (no. 77), and Pordage's *Göttliche und wahre Metaphysica* (no. 53).

early nineteenth century was a time of radical change, and in seeking explanation of these changes "many people accepted the explanation that secret societies were behind them because it was coherent with widespread views about the origins and springs of historical change" (1972, 2, 9–10). This was also the attitude toward esoterica. Esoteric, sometimes even mystical, interpretations of events were acceptable to intellectually skeptical men who prided themselves on their empirical views. Simultaneously, however, their post-Cartesian minds knew better. Pushkin, for example, was superstitious and able to laugh at himself for it. The new Freemasons rejected mysticism yet were interested in esotericism. The majority of Freemasons did not subscribe to a mystical-conspiratorial view of history, but they did not reject the possibility of such explanations and to the degree that they accepted the romantic emphasis on free will, they accepted intentionalist explanations of public events. They had no doubt, for example, that the Napoleonic wars were a consequence of the conspiratorial machinations of European statesmen, and they joined other Europeans in searching for the secret masters of the Alliance of Europe. With the exception of eccentrics and unstable personalities, of which there were of course many in the Decembrist movement, they seem not to have believed literally in thaumaturgy, but they intellectually appreciated the symbolism of alchemy, numerology, Cabalism, and the other magic skills they were required to learn in the Masonic lodges. And those among them who were writers perceived the literary potential of thaumaturgy, just as they perceived the efficacy of secrecy and conspiratorial methods.

2

The Esoteric Tradition in Russian Romantic Poetry

> It visited on us a promise;
>   Illumined our life but a moment
> And left us but a legend
>   That once in our life it was.
>   —V. A. Zhukovsky,
>   "Lalla Rookh"

How did the esoteric tradition make its way into Russian culture? The chief vehicle was Freemasonry, brought to Russia in the 1760s and 1770s and received by the Enlightenment philanthropists known as the Moscow Mystic Masons or Rosicrucians. This is a certainty; the sources of their knowledge have been largely identified. But precisely what the interests of these pioneers of esotericism were, is not known. What knowledge they assimilated, what skills they mastered, how they adapted the European esoteric tradition to Russian needs—these things are only slightly known. The evidence shows that knowledge of esoterica was passed on to the Freemasons of the early nineteenth century and influenced the Russian romantic movement. The most apparent influence was on Decembrist literature in the form of an attraction to the efficacy of esoteric symbolism as means of expression and of thaumaturgical practices as literary devices. But we know even less about the esoteric interests of the romantics, and we do not yet fully know the paths along which the esoteric tradition was passed from one generation to the next.

A basic principle of esotericism is to hide knowledge from all but the most carefully chosen and prepared adepts. This resort to "other meaning," arcane language, and encoded texts hinders disclosure. But many texts can be analyzed—the "code" can be "broken"—and it is possible to begin research by identifying one significant source of esoteric knowledge and marking out the path along which it developed. It can be shown how one esoteric symbolic system was introduced into Russian culture, assimilated into the Russian Enlightenment, and transformed during the romantic period into an elaborate poetic metaphor cultivated in different ways by a significant number of poets. If this path can be traced clearly enough through the development of romantic poetry, it can then be followed through the tangle of other paths, through subsequent developments of the relationships between the esoteric tradition and Russian literature in the romantic period.

The European source chosen for this preliminary exploration is a little known but important Masonic symbolic system authored in the eighteenth century by Théodore Henri, baron de Tschoudy (Tschudy), an elaborate set of texts of rituals with exhaustive explications that became the basis of Masonic lodges known as The Flaming Star (*L'Etoile flamboyante, Der flammende Stern, Zum flammenden Stern*).[1] The system and its symbolism, published again in the nineteenth century together with a twin set of explications under the title Sign-Star or Signal-Star (*Der Signatstern*), were introduced into Russia by Grand Masters N. I. Novikov and I. V. Lopukhin. They were developed primarily by Lopukhin and in other ways by I. P. Turgenev. The ideals represented by this esoteric system were passed on to Turgenev's sons Andrey and Aleksandr and to their friend and fellow student at the Moscow Pension of the Nobility V. A. Zhukovsky. According to one recent authoritative source, Zhukovsky rejected Freemasonry along with the Enlightenment (Sakharov 1988, 41–42). Zhukovsky never became a Freemason for the simple reason that Freemasonry was banned before he reached maturity and revived after his views were already formed. He shared his mentor N. M. Karamzin's skepticism about Freemasonry, and in the Arzamas Brotherhood he enjoyed the society's

---

1. Tschoudy wrote originally in French and translated his work into German. Despite his influence on the Moscow Mystic Masons and the extensive use of his symbolism by Russian romantic poets, he is not mentioned by Pypin or other historians of Russian Freemasonry, and is mentioned only in passing by Vernadsky. Literary scholars have not noted the significance of the Star of Hope metaphor in Russian romantic poetry.

parodies of the pseudo-Masonic proceedings of the Society of the Russian Word. It is not likely that Zhukovsky or other men of his generation practiced alchemy, and they were not as carried away by the esoteric tradition as Lopukhin and other Moscow Rosicrucians.

Nevertheless, there is no doubt that Zhukovsky, the most influential pioneer of romanticism in Russia, believed in the ideals of Freemasonry, for he developed these ideals into a polysemantic poetic metaphor that can be traced throughout his oeuvre. The metaphor—"the Star of Hope"—can be traced further through Russian romantic poetry from the early nineteenth century to the 1820s, when Russian romanticism reached its peak, and to the aftermath of the Decembrist revolt in the 1830s. The image, or symbol, or metaphor, of the Star of Hope implicates thaumaturgical practices—cabalistic, numerological, calendarological, cartomantic—which were transformed into literary devices. This exploration can begin with an examination of the role of the Star of Hope in the poetry of Zhukovsky.

A Poet of Hope and Faith

"Poet of the imagination of the heart," representative of German "dreamy" romanticism in Russian literature, leader of the early Russian romantic movement known as the sentimental-elegiac school—these are the roles assigned to V. A. Zhukovsky (1783–1852) in the history of Russian romantic poetry. Zhukovsky was the nominal successor in Russian literature to the great sentimental writer N. M. Karamzin. He was the "singer" of disillusionment, melancholy, religious mysticism, and escape from reality (Veselovskii 1918; Gukovskii 1965, 46–148). But Zhukovsky was far more than a sentimental-religious poet; he was a bold and versatile innovator. He created striking epithets, images, and metaphors. His verse devices are innovative, his lexicon unprecedented. He introduced into Russian poetry new rhymes, metric patterns, and phraseology (Eikhenbaum 1969, 348–90; Semenko 1980; Iezuitova 1989). Zhukovsky was also one of Russia's best translators of poetry, and it is no exaggeration to say that he almost single-handedly introduced romanticism into Russia with his translations of the poetry of the German and English romantics and preromantics.

He was the illegitimate son of a Russian landowner named Bunin and a

Turkish captive. Although his father found a husband for his mother, Zhukovsky was raised by his real father's widow and then by his older half-sister. He was educated at the Pension of the Nobility founded by I. P. Turgenev and directed by Turgenev's Masonic brother A. A. Prokopovich-Antonsky. While still in their teens at the Pension, Zhukovsky and the Turgenev brothers founded a Literary Friendship Society devoted to the study of European romantic poetry and aesthetics. Zhukovsky began his career as editor of the prestigious journal *Herald of Europe*, founded by his mentor Karamzin. His reputation as a "sentimental-elegiac" poet stems from his and his early romantic generation's continued devotion to Karamzin's language reforms and to a preference for the romantic elegy over the neoclassical ode. The beginning of Russian romanticism is sometimes dated from the appearance of his first translation of Thomas Gray's "Elegy Written in a Country Churchyard" in 1802. In the 1810s his translations and imitations of German and English romantic ballads brought him a reputation as the "Russian balladeer." In 1821 his translation of Byron's romantic verse tale *The Prisoner of Chillon*, appearing shortly before Pushkin's first Byronic verse tale *The Captive of the Caucasus*, brought Byronism into Russia by storm.

Two tragedies marked Zhukovsky's life and shaped his Weltanschauung. In 1803 his friend Andrey Turgenev, the inspiration of the Literary Friendship Society, died. Neither Zhukovsky, nor the other members of the Society ever forgot this remarkable young man. In addition, Zhukovsky was deeply in love with his half-sister's daughter Maria Protasova. Their plans for marriage were put to an end after many years of hopeless attempts to persuade Maria's mother. Masha—Zhukovsky's muse, the Maria Protasova loved for her beautiful soul by all who knew her—married another man, and several years later died in childbirth.

Zhukovsky wrote little original poetry after the early 1820s, but his work as a translator continued, culminating in publication of his still canonical translation of *The Odyssey* in the early 1840s. In the early 1820s he became the official tutor of the children of the future Nicholas I, and thereby a formative influence on Alexander II. In both character and outlook Zhukovsky was very much like William Wordsworth, but although he too planned to retreat from the world, he remained active in social and literary circles throughout his life. His influence at court enabled him to protect Pushkin on several occasions the great poet incurred official wrath, he did much to help the exiled Decembrists, he was a mentor to Gogol. His identification with the autocracy was not approved by the Decembrists and other romantic writers of the 1820s. His was the lot of those who choose to attempt to realize their moral goals by working within the power establishment. For this he had to pay the usual terrible price. Perhaps the most humiliating task he had to perform was to help Nicholas I prevent the reaction to the death of Pushkin from becoming a public demonstration and, simultaneously, protect the poet's memory from the sordid affair of the duel with Dantes. By 1825 his sentimental-elegiac style and German "dreaminess," to say nothing of his more conservative views, marked him as out of date with the forceful developments of the romantic movement he originated. Despite this loss of popularity, he remained an active member of the romantic grouping known as the Pushkin Pleiad or the Literary Aristocrats. He lived his final years abroad in the 1840s, by which time he had become an outspoken foe of the "new men," the plebeian representatives of the crassly commercial "iron age."

Zhukovsky's education at the Pension of the Nobility under the tutelage of I. P. Turgenev must be appreciated. After many difficulties following the arrest of Novikov and the suppression of Freemasonry by Catherine II, Turgenev was called to Moscow by Paul I and appointed director of Moscow Imperial University in 1797. Contemporaries and historians agree that the university flourished under his leadership (Tarasov 1915, 2:5–18). He loved his sons; he did not long survive the loss of the brilliant Andrey. He became the father that Zhukovsky never really had; Zhukovsky joined his brothers and the other students of the Pension of the Nobility in referring to their teacher as "the old man." Turgenev was a devout Freemason and developed his Enlightenment theories of pedagogy on the model of two Masonic virtues: love of one's brothers, understood as friendship, and selfless moral purity. Education in Turgenev's view was a process of moral development leading to self-perfection. Whereas the more impressionable I. V. Lopukhin was drawn to the mysticism of Saint-Martin and the thaumaturgy of Baron de Tschoudy, Turgenev was indebted to the pedagogical theories of John Mason, particularly his treatise *Self-Knowledge* (1745), which he translated in 1783. Mason's pedagogical theories became a fully developed program in the basic text used at the Pension of the Nobility, Prokopovich-Antonsky's *Children's Readings for the Heart and the Mind* (1785–89). The Literary Friendship Society continued I. P. Turgenev's moral values and was one of the first expressions of the Russian romantic cult of friendship, a social phenomenon that became a strong trend of the Russian romantic movement (Sakharov 1988, 31–47; Iezuitova 1989, 45–46).

The Star of Hope as Romantic Metaphor

A remarkable characteristic of the metaphor of a Star of Hope in Zhukovsky's poetry is that although it appears only once in his extensive lyric oeuvre, it is implicated in virtually every area of his aesthetics and Weltanschauung. The metaphor seems clearly to be his own: its variants often appear in his verse translations of such poets as Millevoye, Schiller, Hebel, Wetzel, Matthisson, and Byron, but is not present in the originals of these poets, nor does its rich symbolism resemble theirs. It and its variants function consistently as "signal-words" that evoke particular feelings through alliterative and semantic association. It is developed throughout the poet's lyric oeuvre in intimate association with correspondent verbal elements into a unified symbolic system expressed in several well-defined lexical-semantic categories. Zhukovsky's metaphoricization of the symbol of hope in the form of a star is on first consideration conventionally romantic, but in the diversity of its expressions it becomes a rich metaphor behind which hides arcane meaning.

The metaphor itself appears in 1811, in a romance titled "The Blossom," an imitation of a poem by Charles Millevoye titled "La Fleur" (Zhukovskii 1980, 1:79):

> Smotri . . . ocharovan'ia net;
> Zvezda nadezhdy ugasaet . . .
> Uvy! kto skazhet: zhizn' ili tsvet
> Bystree v mire ischezaet?
>
> Behold . . . there is no enchantment;
> The star of hope is fading . . .
> Alas! Who shall say: life or flower,
> Which shall more swiftly perish?

The melancholy mood for which Zhukovsky is known can be felt strongly in these lines. Life is fleeting, there is no enchantment, the star of hope is dying. Which will vanish more quickly, life or the fragile blossom? The same motif of disillusionment is expressed by a variant of the Star of Hope in an epistle titled "To Turgenev, in Reply to His Letter" (1813; 1980, 1:182–86). In this poem Zhukovsky shares the sorrow of his friend Aleksandr Turgenev over the death of Aleksandr's brother Andrey and their father. We do not know "where our path will lead us, or when it shall end." We do not know what hides in the darkness of fate. All we have is friendship, "So let friendship be our star of solace; And naught for else give care." Despair and hopelessness sound forth in this poem: "all is darkness there," "life offers us nothing," "there is no path to happiness for the good."

It is not melancholy per se, but how melancholy is created and how it functions in Zhukovsky's aesthetic system, that is important. In these and other poems noted for their sadness, the poet's disillusionment is tempered or ultimately denied. The most important word in the poet's lexicon is not melancholy, but hope (Fridlender 1987, 10). Sooner or later Zhukovsky overcomes his disillusionment and affirms faith in more consoling values. This is usually accomplished through faith in hope. The most consoling hope is friendship. In his free translation of Schiller's poem "Die Ideale"—the poem "Reveries" (1812; 1980, 1:84–87)—the poet seeks hope in love, happiness, glory, and knowledge in vain. Only one "beacon of hope . . . shines o'er the path" of the poet's life. That beacon of Hope is Friendship, "the sole sharer of my joys and sorrows." Friendship eases worldly burdens, it is "A loving light in spiritual darkness":

> Ty, Druzhba, serdtsa istselitel',
> Moi dobryi genii s iunykh let.
>
> Thou, Friendship, art the healer of my heart,
> My kind genius from my years of youth.

In Zhukovsky's aesthetics the star symbolizes hope, which in its turn denotes a defined series of spiritual values, including friendship, Providence, poetic inspiration, memory or remembrance, and a whole complex of concepts expressed within these lexical-semantic categories. Friendship (*druzhba*) is the highest of these values. This priority, which is central to Zhukovsky's poetic vision, reflects the romantic cult of friendship and is itself one of the best expressions of the trend. The cult, which was expressed in the founding of many societies in the early nineteenth century, developed under the influence of a feeling of isolation from the mass of Russian people shared by all Russian intelligentsia of the late eighteenth–early nineteenth centuries, and from fear of the power of the arbitrary autocratic state. Freemasonry and the Decembrist societies were one result of this widespread sense of alienation, and so was the Literary Friendship Society. Zhukovsky was also an active member of the Arzamas Brotherhood, a friendship society founded in the mid-1810s to provide the Karamzinian sentimental-elegiac poets with mutual support and, not incidentally, to parody the ultraconservative, anti-Karamzinian Society of Lovers of the Russian Word (Gillel'son 1974). Zhukovsky was one of the first poets to cultivate the "friendly epistle" of camaraderie and good humor, which are the best result of the cult of friendship.

Quite often, hope of friendship comes to Zhukovsky through the prism of memory or remembrance (*vospominanie*), as in the poem "Remember, remember, my beloved friend" (1813; 1980, 1:80). "What's past let oblivion have!" We—"our circle of friends"—are under the care of Providence. As a rule, remembrance (implying oblivion as well) arouses feelings of nostalgia, melancholy, disillusionment, as in one of many poems titled "Song" (1818; 1980, 1:109):

> Minuvshikh dnei ocharovan'e,
> Zachem opiat' voskreslo ty?
> Kto razbudil vospominan'e
> I zamolchavshie mechty?
>
> Bygone days' enchantment,
> Why hast thou returned?
> Who has wakened remembrance
> And my long silent reveries?

The same sad motif characterizes the poem "Remembrance" (1816; 1980, 1:96–97). The poet's "days of enchantment" have passed, all they have left behind is "a sad remembrance": "Ah! far better to forget them forever!" Nevertheless, even in poems expressing deep grief, such as "Lines on the Death of Her Majesty the Queen of Würtemberg" (1819; 1980, 1:56–62), in which life itself is treated as sorrow, sadness, suffering, the poet reaffirms the consolatory power of hope:

> Svyatyi simvol nadezhd i uteshen'ia!
> My vse stoim u tainstvennykh vrat;
>
> Sacred symbol of hope and comfort!
> We all stand at the gates of mystery;

Behind these gates we hear voices; we listen, they speak:

> "Muzhaites'; dushoiu ne skorbite!
> S nadezhdoiu i veroi pristupite!"

"Take heart; Grieve not your soul!
With hope and faith do enter you here!"

Closely associated with the signal-word *remembrance* are the words *past* (*proshloe*) and *bygone* (*minuvshee*) (Mann 1976, 26–27). Even in his youth Zhukovsky was oriented to the past. The Star of Hope evokes thoughts of youthful dreams, former friends, past enchantments. The poet habitually addresses the past with a question or "interrogative intonations" (Semenko 1980, 11). Memories are almost always evoked with a query: "Who has awakened remembrance?" In another poem titled "Song" (1818; 1980, 1:109) past, future, and hope are conjoined in a quick procession of questions:

> O milyi gost', sviatoe *prezhde*,
> Zachem v moiu tesnish'sia grud'?
> Mogu l' skazat': *zhivi* nadezhde?
> Skazhu l' tomu, chto bylo: *bud*'?
>
> O dear guest, sacred *was*.
> Why dost thou crowd my breast?
> May I say *live*, to hope?
> Say to what once was: *be*?

The poem "The Inexpressible" (1819; 1980, 1:287–88) is filled with terrifying questions through which Zhukovsky expresses his romantic-ironic belief that neither poet, nor poetry, nor even language itself can express "the sacred secrets" of nature: "What is our mundane language in compare with wondrous nature?" "Does not life in vain with death commune?" "Who dares recreate creation in words?" "Does the inexpressible e'er yield to expression?" The poem "To a Fleeting yet Familiar Genius" (1819; 1980, 1:114–15), a free paraphrase of Schiller's poem "Lied," is structured almost in entirety on interrogative constructions. Is it not thee, the fleeting yet familiar genius, who brought sensual dreams to the poet in his youth, "And in days of old did whisper of a celestial guest—of dear hope?"

Hope is often metaphorized in images of light, ray, lamp, beacon, as in the poem "Reveries":

> O! gde ty, luch, putevoditel'
> Veselykh iunosheskikh dnei?
> Gde ty, nadezhda, obol'stitel'
> Neopytnoi dushi moei?

> O! where art thou, ray, beacon
> Of my happy youthful days?
> Where art thou, hope, enticer
> Of my unpracticed soul?

The image of a beacon (*putevoditel'*) is in its turn integral to a motif of a journey; the signal-words *road, path, way* thereby enter prominently into the symbolic system based on the Star of Hope. The star ("beacon / Of my happy youthful days") that lights the path in the translation of Schiller's "Die Ideale" is indicative here. So are the sunrise, bright clouds, and shining skies that lie ahead of the danger, terror, and shadows of night in Zhukovsky's translation of Schiller's poem "Song of the Mountains" under the title "Mountain Road" (1818; 1980, 1:108): "High above a dread abyss a road runs, / Rushing between life and death." In a translation of Schiller's poem "Der Pilgrim"—"The Traveler" (1809; 1980, 1:74–75)—the image of a road is replaced by a metaphor of a frail craft or bark in a stormy sea, a popular Russian romantic motif. The poet has set out on his path, his road, "With faith as my guide": "And in hope, in confidence, / The path seemed short." Suddenly a river stands before him. It flows to the east, and "Along the bank stands a bark":

> Ia v nadezhde, ia v smiaten'e;
> Predaiu sebia volnam;
> Schast'e vizhu v otdalen'e;
> Vse, chto milo,—mnitsia—tam!

> And I in hope, in agitation;
> I entrust myself to the waves;
> I see happiness in the distance;
> All that is dear—it seems—is there!

A conventional play with the words *hope* (*nadezhda*) and *faith* (*vera*) functions in this poem. Zhukovsky's biographer A. N. Veselovsky has noted that in Zhukovsky's Weltanschauung hope is subordinated to Providence (1918, 197). To this it may be added that in Zhukovsky's symbolic system hope strengthens faith, which leads to Providence. This relationship is vital to an understanding of the metaphor: hope is not an end, it is a means. By affirming truth, hope facilitates faith. By strengthening faith, it ensures salvation. By lighting the way, it shows that Providence exists. This becomes clear in the "The Sailor" (1812; 1980, 1:81–82):

> Vikhrem bedstviia gonimyi,
> Bez kormila i vesla,
> V okean neiskhodimyi
> Buria cheln moi zanesla.
>
> . . . .
>
> V tuchakh zvezdochka svetilas';
> "Ne skryvaisia!"—ia vzyval;
> Nepreklonnaia sokrylas;
> Iakor' byl—i tot propal.
>
> By storms of misery pursued,
> Without tiller and oar,
> Into a boundless ocean
> The storm carried my bark.
>
> . . . .
>
> In the clouds a star shone forth;
> "Do not hide!" I beseeched;
> But, unrelenting, it vanished;
> An anchor I had—it was lost.

All around are the sea, waves, abysses, menacing cliffs—"There is no hope of salvation!" But there is hope of salvation:

> O bezumets! Providen'e
> Bylo tainyi kormshchik tvoi.
>
> O mad fool! Providence
> Was thy secret steersman.

The very structure of this poem is shaped by a careful arrangement of signal-words in defined lexical-semantic groupings. A powerful storm is contrasted with a fragile bark (*chelnok*). Where the component or correspondent words of the latter metaphor are *oar, anchor, tiller,* and *steersman,* the night is metaphorized by such evocative images as *darkness, dark, gloom,* and *clouds,* and the stormy sea by *waves, billows,* and *cliffs.* At the end of the poem—the end of the storm, danger, journey—the darkness is dispersed with the words *star, light, ray, lighthouse,* and *beacon.* Hope has led to Providence and thus to salvation.

Hope, Memory, Providence, Inspiration

In Zhukovsky's order of values—his moral priorities—the Star of Hope is a Christian symbol, but it can also be Roman and ancient Greek. It is Hesperus, Venus, Astraea, Orion. It can be a star of morning or evening, a polar star and a northern star. Most often it is a star of the east. In a translation of Johann Hebel's poem "Der Morgenstern" under the same title (1818; 1980, 1:110–12), the sun chases a "beauty-star" across the morning sky. "Were I that eastern star . . . I'd fear not the sun." Zhukovsky's eastern star is in this poem a "star-friend." It fears the sun, runs from it, "fades away." But nevertheless, it is there in the sky; it cannot be seen, but it exists. It cannot be known, but it can be felt.

Memory is again important. In the poem "Elysium" (1812; 1980, 1:83–84), a translation of F. von Matthisson's poem of the same name, Psyche bows her head to the waters of the Lethe and in the moment of oblivion (*zabvenie*) sees her face "in the ripples." He sees hope in her, and expectation, "Thus shines in that spring / The golden torch of Hesperus." In another poem titled "Song" (1815; 1980, 1:94), a translation of F. G. Wetzel's "Nach Osten," a soul again shines in the eastern sky:

> K vostoku, vse k vostoku
> Stremlenie zemli—
> K vostoku, vse k vostoku
> Letit moia dusha.
>
> To the east, ever to the east
> Strives all on earth—
> To the east, ever to the east
> Soars my soul.

Zhukovsky's religious concept of soul (*dusha*) is prominent in his symbolic system. Just as friendship comes to the poet through the prism of memory, so Zhukovsky becomes aware of his soul through the prism of oblivion. In "Elysium," when Psyche sees the eastern star—herself—in the reflected image of Hesperus's golden torch, she instantly forgets her former life:

> Lish' fial vody zabven'ia
>   Podnesla k ustam ona—
> Dnei minuvshikh priveden'ia
>   Skrylis' legkoi ten'iu sna.

> Scarce had the cup of oblivion
>   Been raised to her lips,
> Than visions of bygone days
>   Vanished in the shade of sleep.

Memory and dream (*mechta, son*) are often synonymous; the soul often becomes Beauty (*Prekrasnaia*). In "To the east" the poet's soul becomes "the Beautiful," understood as "she." It "seems" to the poet that "Far off there to the east . . . Abides the Beautiful." The poet cannot know the Beautiful, but he senses who she is. She comes to him in a blissful dream of a forgotten past, and it seems to him that he has met her before. She is "a beautiful legend of a wondrous past," and it seems to the poet:

> Chto mne ona iavilas'
> Kogda-to v drevni dni,
> Chtob mne ob nei ostalsia
> Odin blazhennyi son.

> That she appeared to me
> Sometime in ancient days,
> So that all that remained of her,
> 't would be ought but blissful dream.

The poet does not actually remember or recall the forgotten past. "She"—the Beautiful that abides far off there to the east—"seems" to him; he senses her. The forgotten past exists not in this life, but "sometime," before this life. The Beautiful "Is a beautiful legend / Of a wondrous past." Her appearance "seems," and when she was gone, he was left with only a "blissful dream" that once she was.

This fleeting sense or sensation is essential to the metaphor of the eastern star that appears in one of Zhukovsky's best poems, "The Appearance of Poetry in the Guise of Lalla Rookh" (1821; 1980, 1:120):

> K vostoku ia stremlius' dushoiu!
> Prelestnaia vpervye tam
> Iavilas' v bleske nad zemleiu
> Obradovannym nebesam.

> To the east I strive in my soul!
> There it is that first this beauty
> Appeared in a light o'er the earth,
> Gladdening the heavens.

In this poem, however, the star symbolizes not only the soul, but poetic inspiration (*vdokhnovenie*). Interesting in this respect is the poem "Reveries," the poet's translation of Schiller's "Die Ideale." In the penultimate stanza hope is "Friendship." Friendship is a healer of the heart, "My kind genius from youthful years." In the final stanza, hope becomes "the guardian of my soul," "my trusty friend," meaning "Unrelenting labor, to whom a sacred power is given." In Zhukovsky's aesthetics, labor—creative work, creativity (*tvorchestvo*)—begins with inspiration, which "appears" to the poet in the form or guise of a visitor, a guest, an apparition, a specter. In "The Mysterious Visitor" (1824; 1980, 1:122–23) inspiration "visits" the poet like "an apparition, a beautiful guest." It "appears" to him, flies down on him, and then, before he can grasp it, flees, vanishes. The poet wonders, is it Hope, or Love, or Thought? The mysterious visitor is in fact Hope, Love, and Thought, but above all it is Poetry. The poet does not "comprehend" inspiration, he senses it. It is a Premonition, the signal of the appearance of creative power. It flees, beckons, entices. "Often in this life is it wont to be" that "some light being flies down up on us," raises its veil, "And beckons us into the distance."

Zhukovsky's aesthetic credo is best expressed in "Lalla Rookh" (1821; 1980, 1:118–19).[2] In this poem a mysterious visitor descends from heaven like a

> Milyi son, dushi plenitel',
>   Gost' prekrasnyi s vyshiny,
> Blagodatnyi posetitel'
>   Podnebesnoi storony.

---

2. The poem was written in honor of Grand Duchess Aleksandra Fedorovna, bride of the future Nicholas I, when she made her appearance at a pageant in the guise of Thomas Moore's eastern beauty.

> Dear dream, captor of my soul,
>   Beautiful guest from on high,
> Heavenly visitor
>   To this earthly realm.

Inspiration appears to the poet in the form of "a blessed herald ... of the heavenly." It shines and beckons "like an angel of heaven." It is "youthful chastity" and "timid diffidence." Poetic inspiration is a "specter" that comes near, but "flees never to return":

> Posetil, kak upovan'e;
>   Zhizn' minutu ozaril;
> I ostavil lish' predan'e
>   Chto kogda-to v zhizni byl.

> It visited on us a promise;
>   Illumined our life but a moment;
> And left us but a legend
>   That once in our life it was.

Above all, inspiration is the poet's "Genius of pristine pure beauty," which "visits us from the heavenly heights":

> A kogda nas pokidaet,
>   V dar liubvi u nas v vidu
> V nashem nebe zazhigaet
>   On proshchal'nuiu zvezdu.

> And when it leaves us,
>   In sign of love for us to see
> In our sky it lights
>   A farewell star.

The same metaphors and similes shape the symbolism of "The Appearance of Poetry in the Guise of Lalla Rookh" (1821; 1980, 1:120). Here the visitor is again feminine—a "charming beauty," "a captress," "a young goddess of song," "divine harmony personified." "She" shines like "a fiery wreath of the east," she captivates with her "beauty."

The most active word in these three poems devoted to inspiration is the verb "to appear" (*iavit'sia*). Inspiration "appears" to the poet, it is an "apparition" (*iavlenie*). In "The Appearance of Poetry in the Guise of Lalla Rookh," Poetry "Appeared in a light o'er the earth, gladdening the heavens." In "Lalla Rookh," Beauty "Appeared to me, a heavenly herald of the good." In "The Mysterious Visitor," "Wherefore thy appearance from heaven on high?" This notion that poetic inspiration can be intuited but not known, sensed but not expressed, is a sublime Russian expression of the torment of romantic irony. It came to Zhukovsky—"appeared" to him—not only through German romantic idealist aesthetics, but as a Masonic teaching: God can be felt in a fleeting moment of inspiration, but He cannot be known except through faith.

In another poem of this cycle on the theme of poetic creativity, "My youthful Muse, as was wont to be . . ." (1822 or 1824; 1980, 1:300), the theme of poetic inspiration is developed on a play with the less active verb "to be" (*byt'*, *byvat'*). In the poet's past, "Life and Poetry were as one." At that time Inspiration cast its "life-creating ray" on all earthly existence, and

> Ia muzu iunuiu, byvalo,
> Vstrechal v podlunnoi storone,
> I Vdokhnovenie letalo
> S nebes, nezvanoe ko mne;

> My youthful Muse, as was wont to be,
> I used to meet in our realm beneath the moon,
> And Inspiration used to fly down
> From heaven, uncalled, to me.

Now, however, Inspiration no longer visits the poet. "The gift of song" has not visited him for many years. "The visions that once were, are in my soul no more." Nevertheless, the poet remembers (recalls) those beautiful times and "All that from my dear, vague, clear / Past days I have preserved":

> Tsvety mechty uedinennoi
> I zhizni luchshie tsvety,—
> Kladu na tvoi altar' sviashchennyi,
> O Genii chistoi krasoty!

> The flowers of lonely revery
> And the finest flowers of life—

> I place on thy sacred altar,
> O Genius of pristine pure beauty!

Zhukovsky's "bright inspiration" is a Genius (*Genii*) and, simultaneously, a Genie. Inspiration is gone, but nevertheless the poet still knows it:

> No ty znakom mne, chistyi Genii!
> I svetit mne tvoia zvezda!
> Poka eshche ee siian'e
> Dusha umeet razlichat':
> Ne umerlo ocharovan'e!
> Byloe sbudetsia opiat'.

> But thou art known to me, pure Genius!
> And still thy star shines for me!
> And still its light
> My soul can discern:
> Enchantment has not perished!
> What was, shall be again.

Especially in this poem, in its very structure, the poet destroys the view of him as a poet of unassuaged melancholy and disillusionment. The poem is structured on a principle of rise and fall that J. Thomas Shaw has called in relation to Pushkin's best-known love poem "To Anna Kern" enchantment—disenchantment—reenchantment (1981). Zhukovsky's Muse, "as was wont to be," used to appear to him (rise), she no longer appears "before me" (fall), but he remembers her (rise): "Enchantment has not perished! What was, shall be again." The poet affirms, in the successful realization of this poem's symbolism, and in no other poem so forcefully, that "what was wont to be" (*byvalo*) and "what was" (*byloe*) will not only "be again" (*sbudetsia*), but still is wont to be (*byvaet*). Even though the poet adds that he cannot expect "the desired return" of Inspiration, the quality of the poem itself is proof that once again Inspiration has flown down from heaven, uncalled, to him (Kaspryk 1990).

The Star of Hope has not expired, it still shines in the sky, in the form of a farewell star, an eastern star, a star-friend, "the sacred symbol of hope and consolation." It is "Friendship," "the healer of the heart," "the trusty friend of my soul." It is "Memory," "bygone days' enchantment," "the kind genius of my youthful years." It is "the captress of my soul" and "the guardian of my soul." It is "a lamp on the path of life," a "secret steersman" in a stormy sea—

"Providence." It is inspiration that "appears" to the poet as a "mysterious visitor," "a guest from the heavens above," "a herald of good from heaven on high," an "apparition," a "specter," a "dear dream," and above all the poet's own "Genius of pristine pure beauty."

The Flaming Star

Clearly, the Star of Hope motif is not simply a series of random associations, but a fully developed and unified symbolic system, one that is profoundly romantic. It is comprised of spiritual values or moral virtues organized into lexical-semantic categories that in their turn are composed of a logical series of signal-words. The key to this system is the Star of Hope, the metaphoricization of hope in the form of a star and a whole series of symbols correspondent to or proceeding from this symbol. This can be seen most clearly by a graphic representation of the poet's moral-aesthetic priorities and their organization by lexical categories and semantic associations:

Star of Hope

Friendship	Providence	Inspiration	Memory
friend	soul	creativity/labor	memory/oblivion
fidelity	faith/belief	enchantment	disenchantment
love	imagination	apparition/vision	dream/revery
consolation	salvation	poetry	past
happiness	divinity	beauty/purity	peace/quietude
light/beacon	angel	genius/muse	specter/visitor

The semantic designations and lexical variants of Zhukovsky's symbolic system are polysemic and at the same time oriented to a unified moral-aesthetic vision of the universum. Interestingly, the absence of possible symbolic associations tells almost as much about the system as its defined meanings. In Zhukovsky's Weltanschauung the metaphor does not designate either established neoclassical values such as enlightenment or new romantic concerns such as victory, glory, or freedom. It evokes strong feelings for the past, received through the prism of memory, but signifies neither the future, nor hope for the future. It denotes happiness, but states that life is an unhappy journey through suffering to Providence. As Veselovsky has noted, in Zhukovsky's view "there is ultimately no true happiness on earth, there is only its shadow, lost happiness, the happiness of self-denial" (1918, 230). Although the Star of Hope sometimes lights the path to love—the poet's love for Maria Protasova—love does not occupy a prominent place in the system. Often the poet speaks of hope in connection with fate (in the epistle "To Turgenev," for example: the poet does not know ". . . what in the dark of fate yet hides"; 1980, 1:186); but thoughts about fate are less frequent in his poetry than is typical of romantic poetry, perhaps because a Christian poet who believes in Providence is not drawn to the Hellenic symbolism of fate. The metaphor does not signify hope of political liberation, and certainly not protest or revolt.

The absence of interest in knowledge or enlightenment is especially revealing. Despite the romantic rejection of the Enlightenment, the romantics found in images of light—sun, moon, star, ray, lamp, beacon—effective metaphors for illumination of the way to wisdom and knowledge. This is true of Masonic symbolism in both the Enlightenment and in the romantic period, in which the virtue known as "love of wisdom" is greatly valued. Zhukovsky, however, excludes Enlightenment values, even as he makes friendship his supreme moral value.

The significance of this omission is to be found in the role of friendship in Zhukovsky's education at the Moscow Pension of the Nobility. In Masonic symbolism the Star of Hope signifies the seven virtues that every Freemason must cultivate. The Moscow Mystic Masons seem to have especially appreciated the virtues of faith (in Providence), purity (of moral behavior), love of death (the overcoming of the fear of death through faith in the existence of God), love for one's brothers (and family, friends, country, all of mankind), and love of wisdom (knowledge, enlightenment). These are not separable values—they are part of a single system in which, for example, love for one's brothers is closely associated with love of wisdom in the sense that a Freemason who possesses true knowledge loves his brothers so dearly that he is prepared to sacrifice himself for their salvation. This is why, first in the Novikov group, then in I. P. Turgenev's continuation of the group's Masonic ideals in the Pension of the Nobility, education and friendship were so closely related. Zhukovsky, however, was one of the first Russian poets to reject the Enlightenment; for him, the Star of Hope shows the way not to knowledge but to spiritual perfection. In his poetry, friendship is developed into a richly romantic symbolic system, implicating the poet's other values—creativity through inspiration and imagination, the Christian concept of Providence, the mysterious power of memory, and especially faith in the existence of God and a better—a spiritual—world. It is here in the transformation of a Masonic symbol into a literary-spiritual metaphor that the path of the esoteric tradition from the eighteenth to the nineteenth century can first be traced.

Whereas Turgenev emphasized the Masonic virtue of love for one's brothers, his Masonic brother I. V. Lopukhin was drawn to the virtues love of wisdom and love of death. A true Freemason, Lopukhin believed that it was possible to achieve both "higher knowledge" or "Supreme Wisdom" (*Premudrost'*) and higher faith (love of death) through the development of one's spiritual strengths by study of such "arcane sciences" as alchemy, astrology, numerology, and theosophy. This does not mark a schism between the two men, still less in Russian Freemasonry as a whole. It suggests, instead, two distinct emphases that eventually became differing, but not dissociable, trends of intellectual development.

I. V. Lopukhin is known in the history of Freemasonry as a strict moralist and profound Orthodox believer (Piksanov 1915). He believed that a Freemason had to work "in this world." In an introduction to the *Memoirs of Senator Lopukhin,* Aleksandr Herzen writes that Lopukhin was never afraid to express his opinion to the autocrats he served, from Catherine II to Paul I to Alexander I, and he worked tirelessly to secure justice for peasants and Old Believers (Lopukhin 1859, v–vi). Even when pressured by a powerful minister in the name of Catherine II to overlook certain disreputable matters, he refused on the grounds that his oath of absolute obedience to his empress obligated him to uphold her laws in spite of her royal will. This was a man of high moral character who in an age of obscurantism pioneered the Russian concept of an enlightened, responsible intelligentsia and struggled to show others by his example that moral courage is not an impossible ideal. If his memoirs show any frailty, it is only that he tended to take pride in his humility.

Lopukhin was drawn to mysticism and practiced alchemy. In his memoirs and treatises he preached the teachings of Saint-Martin and the "divine knowledge" of Hermetic and Solomonic sciences (1859, 19–20, 21–23, 38–40). He propagated his Masonic ideals by two chief means: his treatises on moral virtue "The Spiritual Knight, or The Seeker of Supreme Wisdom" (1791), "On the Church Within Thee" (1798), and "A Morally Edifying Catechism of the True Free Masons" (1790); and his work as Grand Master of the Moscow lodge The Shining Star (*K blistaiushchei zvezde*). In Lopukhin's treatises the Star of Hope is a "signal-star" or "beacon-star." These terms originate, as does Lopukhin's symbolic system almost in its entirety, from the Masonic system authored by Baron de Tschoudy. Lopukhin's lodge, opened in 1784 by Grand Master N. I. Novikov, is the only "seven-degree" Russian lodge (Pypin 1916, 515).

The system on which the lodge was based corresponds to the system founded by Tschoudy.

Tschoudy's system—a fully developed Order of the Flaming Star—is unique. It is comprised of the first three working or craft degrees (or grades) and seven "Knightly" degrees (Templarism), for a total of ten "steps" on the "ladder" to ultimate self-perfection. Tschoudy propagated his Order in *L'Etoile flamboyante* in 1766 and *Der flammende Stern* in 1779. His work constitutes an allegorical history of Freemasonry from its legendary origins in the Garden of Eden and the Temple of Solomon through the Middle Ages and Renaissance into the eighteenth century and synthesizes esoteric teachings, including those of Ficino, Pico, Francesco Giorgi, Reuchlin, Christian Rosenkreutz (Andreae), Fludd, Böhme, Swedenborg, Saint-Martin, and especially Baron von Welling, whose numerological-cabalistic system he incorporates. He explicates the "arcane knowledge" of these "adepts" in a series subtitled "Articles of the Nameless Philosopher," whose "secret name," he finally reveals, is Plato (1866, 2:160–69, 1:263–64; see also *Der Signatstern*, 1:287–92).

Tschoudy elucidates the rites, rules, and symbolism of his Order, particularly in a catechism titled "An Explication of the Flaming Star." He explicates the seven Masonic virtues and the three high attainments of a Freemason. He emphasizes the virtues of brotherhood and friendship ("the flaming star") and wisdom or enlightenment ("the rays of light," "the rays of learning"). He terms his flaming star a "star of hope," a "star of faith," a "star of truth," and a "star of learning." In Tschoudy's view, the true work of a Freemason is not participation in formal rites, but active realization of Masonic virtues in life. Above all, a Star of Hope is a Masonic Master, a Freemason who has attained the higher values of self-perfection, self-knowledge, and self-sacrifice. It is the duty of a Master Mason to become a "shining light of friendship," to show his brothers, by the example of his own moral purity, selfless behavior, pure love, and mastery of "Supreme Wisdom," the way to the higher degrees. In this sense, a Master is himself a light, a ray, a beacon, a guide, in short a flaming or shining star, a "sign-star" or "signal-star," the Star of Hope. A Master Mason does not fear death, he loves it. And he loves his brothers so dearly that he is prepared to sacrifice himself for a brother's salvation (1866, 1:51–54, 1:122–24, 2:90–111; see also Papius 1911, 67–68).

Lopukhin placed great emphasis on Tschoudy's belief that a true Freemason is prepared to sacrifice himself for the salvation of his brothers. For him, as for Tschoudy, the "beacon-star" or "signal-star" symbolized all learning, enlightenment, Supreme Wisdom, love of wisdom (*liubomudrie*). Like Tschoudy,

Lopukhin linked love of wisdom with the virtue of brotherhood/friendship. In his treatise "The Spiritual Knight" he teaches that the highest duty of a Master Mason is to become a "shining star," a "shining example" to his brothers. The shining star is a "seeker of wisdom," a teacher, an enlightener. Every shining star is distinguished for his "inner light" and "banishment of the darkness within." A shining star feels such strong love for his brothers that he is prepared "to joyfully perish for the salvation of his brothers" (Lopukhin 1924, 9–10, 12–13).

Lopukhin knew that the notions of self-sacrifice and love of death were so important to Masonic beliefs that the rite of initiation into the craft was itself a rite of love of death. In this rite the initiate "dies" and is "born again" or "resurrected" by the power of the knowledge revealed to him. In his own "Catechism," appended to his treatises and included in his memoirs, Lopukhin asks, "How is this secret [i. e., the secrets of the craft] acquired?" and he replies, "By resurrection." He emphasizes the idea that "every man must, so to speak, be morally reborn." In his view, "this moral rebirth . . . cannot occur, of course, without the action of the power of the All-Powerful. . . . Knowledge of the Creator and creation reveal to man his links with them and the purpose of his own creation. Without this knowledge there can be no fundamental understanding of oneself. And without understanding of oneself there can be no supreme wisdom" (1859, 32, 21–22).

Here are the signal words and symbols that Zhukovsky transformed into his complex lexical-semantic system based on the metaphor of the Star of Hope. According to Zhukovsky's biographer Veselovsky, the most important values Zhukovsky acquired from Turgenev were the ideal of the free personality and the importance of friendship. Lopukhin, however, strengthened Zhukovsky's faith in Providence (1918, 47, 44). Zhukovsky did not accept Lopukhin's emphasis on knowledge or enlightenment; he was not attracted to the Star of Hope as a symbol of love of wisdom.

Nevertheless, Lopukhin exerted a powerful influence on Zhukovsky, who testified in notes and letters that the Masonic leader transformed his life. The two men met in February 1814 at Lopukhin's estate near Moscow. Zhukovsky called that meeting a day of "joy and delightful hope." And he continued: "I did not pray . . . but what I felt in my soul became a vow I made to God to deserve the happiness which hope depicted for me. . . . I was offered a completely new existence: tranquility, spiritual repose, trust in Providence . . . at that moment, with live hope, there awakened in me a most vital sense . . . of it's [religion's] necessity" (Veselovskii 1918, 141, 151–53). Clearly, Lopukhin must have been a charismatic person to have so strongly affected an established poet, already over thirty years old. Zhukovsky did indeed acquire a strong faith in Providence at that meeting with the Moscow Mason—a faith that he repeatedly characterized as hope. It is at just this time, 1814, that Providence enters into his poetry as the ultimate goal of hope, faith, and truth, and into his symbolic system in close association with friendship.

The Star of Hope in Russian Romantic Poetry

For the romantic poets who developed Zhukovsky's symbol of the Star of Hope, the most important value was friendship. Freemasonry was important to some of the poets, and many were privy to the origin of the metaphor in Masonic teachings. But like Zhukovsky, most developed the symbol in concert with the cult of friendship. They also had other ideas about what values the metaphor should represent. To Pushkin, for example, the most attractive value of the older poet's poetry was not friendship, but inspiration. Friendship poetry is important in his oeuvre, including friendly epistles to Zhukovsky. One of the most important expressions of the cult of friendship is his lifelong devotion to his classmates at the Lyceum of Tsarskoye Selo: V. K. Küchelbecker, I. I. Pushchin, and Baron A. A. Delvig, among others. Even though he used some of Zhukovsky's finest verse phraseology, he did not use the metaphor of the Star of Hope per se, but his attraction to the key phrases on the theme of inspiration is nowhere so striking than in his poem "To Anna Kern" (1825; 1937–59, 1:406–7). Like Zhukovsky, Pushkin is in this poem reenchanted. Inspiration comes to him, too, through the prism of memory. The concept of a marvelous, fleeting apparition in "Lalla Rookh" is repeated in Pushkin's poem in a line too perfect not to lift from the poet he called his teacher:

> Ia pomniu chudnoe mgnoven'e,
> Peredo mnoi iavilas' ty,
> Kak mimoletnoe viden'e,
> Kak genii chistoi krasoty.

> I recollect a magic moment,
> When thou didst appear before me,
> Like a fleeting vision,
> Like a genius of pristine pure beauty.

In Pushkin's poem, as in Zhukovsky's, the addressee is a beautiful woman, but the true addressee and subject of both poems is inspiration and the return of enchantment. Pushkin's poem is structured on the same principle of rise and fall, enchantment-disenchantment-reenchantment. He was enchanted in his youth, he became disillusioned, the (re-)appearance of the lovely Anna Kern, and his muse, brought him enchantment anew. Pushkin's worldly muse in no way resembles Zhukovsky's angel, but she also loves to "appear" to her poet: "And thou didst appear again before me . . . Like a genius of pristine pure beauty."

For free-thinking Russian romantic poets attracted to the metaphor of the Star of Hope, the most important value was not inspiration or Providence. For them the metaphor was an ideal symbol of freedom. To the student-poet N. M. Yazykov, known for his poetry of beerhall bawds and free-wheeling student camaraderie, the metaphor was an effective vehicle for the motif of lost youth, again as received through the power of recollection. In his epistle "To A. N. Vulf" (Iazykov 1828; 1964, 256–58):

> Ia pomniu, plamennoi dushoiu
> Ty voskhishchalsia, kak togda
> Vossiiavala nado mnoiu
> Nadezhd vozvyshennykh zvezda;

> I recollect how thy ardent spirit
> Took such delight
> When high above me burst
> The star of my exalted hopes;

In this poem Zhukovsky's metaphor is stripped of its religiosity. In Yazykov's aesthetic priorities it signifies hope of literary glory. But Zhukovsky's phraseology is apparent, especially in a motif of loss of ability to love. Vulf once admired and encouraged Yazykov's ability to love, "But where is it now, that sweet rapture,"

> Moia zvezda, pechal' i radost',
> Moi svetlyi angel chistoty?

> My star, my sorrows and my joys,
> My shining angel of purity?

In the poetry of V. F. Rayevsky (1795–1872), the metaphor of the Star of Hope also signifies freedom, but in the Weltanschauung of this poet, known as "the first Decembrist" because he was imprisoned before the Decembrist movement gained its momentum, freedom is a fully developed philosophical and political theme of liberation, even revolution. Rayevsky was an active member of the Union of Welfare in Kishinev in the late 1810s and an early member of the Southern Society. He fought in the Moscow Campaign of 1812 and in the subsequent campaigns in Europe. Arrested for political activism in 1822, he spent the next five years in prison and then in Siberian exile until the amnesty of 1856. He was a supporter of the leader of the early Decembrist movement, the hero of 1812 General M. F. Orlov. Pushkin was a close friend during his southern banishment, and so was the leader of the Southern Society, Pavel Pestel. Rayevsky and Pushkin were initiated into the Masonic lodge of Ovid, Grand Lodge of Astraea; unlike Pushkin, who was unable to become an adept in the craft before the closing of the lodges in 1822, Rayevsky was an erudite Freemason. Not the least reason for this is that he shared with Zhukovsky the remarkable education offered at the Moscow Pension of the Nobility. Rayevsky's early poetry deals with themes of friendship, nature, political liberation, and a philosophy oriented to the natural sciences. A convinced Rousseauian, he despised urban society and often retreated to nature at his family estate. During his exile he continued to express his political ideals, his love of nature, and his faith in science (Arkhipova and Bazanov 1967).

Even though Rayevsky, too, used Zhukovsky's poetic phraseology, this politically radical poet was in no way like the "passive" older romantic. In his early epistle "My Farewell to My Friends" (1817; 1967, 74–78) the Star of Hope symbolizes freedom shining in the darkness of autocracy:

> Eshche skvoz' mrachnykh tuch
> Blestit nadezhdy luch—
>
> Once again through gloomy clouds
> The ray of hope shines—

Similarly, in the epistle "To My Friends in Kishinev," written shortly after his arrest (1822; 1967, 151–55), Rayevsky expresses his hope for freedom:

> V soiuze s veroi i nadezhdoi,
> S mechtoi poezii zhivoi

> Eshche v besede vechevoi
> Shumit tam golos vash miatezhnyi.
>
> In union with faith and hope,
> With dreams of vital poetry,
> Again assembled in debate
> Your rebellious voices sound.

By joining the words *hope* and *faith* (*nadezhda* and *vera*) with the word *union* (*soiuz*), Rayevsky encodes the Union of Welfare; he uses the word *veche*—the assembly through which the medieval republic of Novgorod ruled itself—to liken the Union to the Russian tradition of democratic freedom. His poem is a call for the Kishinev radicals to revolt: "Take heart! The dread hour is at hand," "'tis time, my friends! 'tis time to raise / The age of midnight glory from the dark [of our time]." Where in Zhukovsky's system of lexical-semantic priorities the eastern star symbolizes the soul, Rayevsky finds in it a perfect allusion to the Greek Revolution. "Farewell, friends . . . for you"

> Gorit dennitsa na vostoke
> I otrazilasia zaria
> V shumiashchem kroviiu potoke.
>
> The morning star burns in the east
> And the dawn is reflected
> In a noisy sweep of blood.

Like Zhukovsky, Rayevsky expressed hope through the symbolism of a journey embodied in the popular motif of a bark in a stormy sea. In the idyll "Autumn" (1810s; 1967, 110–11) he assures his friends that "A hundred-fold fortunate is he," who has not known secret torments, whose bark has sailed calmly, far from the hidden rocks, far from bad weather and stormy agitations. All the more fortunate is he "Whose steersman was the rule of golden freedom" and whose strivings were always toward "nature and peace." Where in Zhukovsky's aesthetics the signal-word "secret steersman" (*kormshchik*) signifies Providence (cf. ". . . Providence / Was thy secret steersman!"), in Rayevsky's poem "steersman" or "helmsman" (*kormchii*) denotes a striving for freedom (*svoboda*). The poet knows that he cannot escape the dangers of the storm, but he knows also that freedom must bring the right to live in peace. Nor does he leave any doubt that the helmsman is Decembrism, for the phrase "rule [*ustav*] of golden freedom" refers to the ruling Decembrist directorate (also *ustav*).

Although Zhukovsky is considered an escapist romantic, and Rayevsky a romantic rebel, both men periodically retreated from active social life into nature. They did so under the influence of the teachings of Rousseau, with whom they agreed that nature is morally superior to civilization (Kanunova and Ianushkevich 1985; Kanunova 1987). To Zhukovsky, such a retreat—or journey—was a search for the contact point between "the inner world of the soul" and "the external world of nature." This is an essential aspect of his symbolic system: light, ray, sun, moon, and star are visual signs that the world is ruled by "a mighty and wise power" (Providence) that communicates "the secret thoughts of the soul" in symbols (Iezuitova 1989, 35). To Rayevsky, however, a retreat is an attempt to revive his spiritual strengths in "nature and peace." He needs to replenish his spirit for the struggle for freedom. This belief is expressed most clearly in "To My Rural Retreat" (1810s; 1967, 108–9): "With each passing day my spirit takes life with the fire of freedom."

Rayevsky also departs from Zhukovsky in that whereas the latter valued in Rousseau the ideal of the free personality, Rayevsky discovered Rousseau the revolutionary. In "To G. S. Batenkov" (1817[?]; 1967, 82–83), an epistolary poem considered the poet's philosophical manifesto, Rayevsky declares, "I've broken with the world," and cites his agreement "with Rousseau and Timon" that the more he avoided the company of men, the more bearable became his heavy chains. For Zhukovsky freedom is personal and individual; for Rayevsky Rousseauism represented a belief in liberation through political action. In his "Epistle to G. S. Batenkov" (ca. 1817–19; 1967, 84–86) he again develops the motif of the sailor in a stormy sea ("A sailor, poised above a bottomless abyss"), this time as a metaphor of active involvement in life. The poet seeks his way "In hope of finding land," but he always sets out again into the open sea of "life's follies."

The theme of fate (*sud'ba*), absent except as a conventional word in Zhukovsky's poetry, is dominant in Rayevsky's aesthetics, especially where he develops the motif of a sailor or bark at sea. In the epistle "To My Friends in Kishinev" the poet likens himself to a sailor deprived of his freedom ("Sailor, thy journey along the shore is ended") and understands fate as a test of his courage:

> Skazhite ot menia O<rlovu>,
> Chto ia sud'bu moiu surovu
> S terpen'em mramornym snosil,
> Nigde sebe ne izmenil.

> Send the word to O(rlov),
> That my severe fate
> I bore with granite endurance,
> And nowhere betrayed my self.

The Decembrist poet remains defiant: send the word to Orlov—Rayevsky will not betray his comrades or their cause.

Not a Freemason, Zhukovsky transformed the symbolism of the Star of Hope into his own romantic aesthetics based on a profound Orthodox faith. Pushkin was a Freemason, but not a very serious one. Rayevsky was adept in the craft. His poetry is an example of both philosophically rational and politically radical Freemasonry. His encoded allusions to "the union of faith and hope" and "the rule of golden freedom" are indicative here, as are his comparisons of the Kishinev spirit with Novgorod and its *veche*. Among the addressees of Rayevsky's epistle "To My Friends in Kishinev" are General Orlov and Pushkin ("the fortunate singer").[3]

The strong mix of spirit of protest and Freemasonry in Kishinev characterizes many of Rayevsky's poems at this time. In the epistle to G. S. Batenkov, one of the most radical Decembrists and a devoted Freemason, Rayevsky writes about Siberia, "Where the sons of liberty reside, / Where the ray of learning burns!" The references are to Batenkov's lodge in Tomsk, Light of the East ("sons of liberty"), and to its most distinguished Master Mason, the fallen government minister M. S. Speransky ("ray of learning"), author of the unrealized reforms of Alexander I. The phrase "sons of liberty" is, of course, an allusion to the American Freemasons, who began the revolution at the Boston Tea Party. The Decembrists hoped that if they were successful they could persuade Orlov or Speransky to head a new government.[4]

In the poetry of A. I. Polezhayev (1804–38), the "last Decembrist," so considered because he, although never a member of the movement, was arrested for propagating Decembrist ideals after 1825, the metaphor of the Star of Hope becomes a powerful expression of cruel personal fate. Whether Polezhayev was a Freemason or had knowledge of the craft is not known, but his use of the metaphor does not contradict its Masonic origins. The son of a servant woman and a Penza landowner, who paid a local merchant to marry the girl,

---

3. Indicative here is a letter Pushkin wrote to Zhukovsky after the failure of 14 December 1825, in which he ascribed the closing of the Masonic lodges in 1822 to the radical activities of his lodge of Ovid in Kishinev (Shaw 1967, 1:302).

4. Ironically, one of Speransky's last official tasks was his appointment as head of the Decembrist Investigatory Commission.

Polezhayev lacked the high social standing that ultimately shielded Pushkin and others from official wrath. Thanks to a generous uncle, he was able to study as a correspondence student at Moscow Imperial University. But he wrote a long political-pornographic poem that enraged Nicholas I, who consigned him to forced military service. Polezhayev's tragedies are two. Had he been allowed to lead a normal life, he might have been admitted into the rich poetic culture of the 1820s (Zhukovsky helped him in his student years) and in this remarkable environment would surely have developed into a major Russian poet. Sadder yet, he was several times imprisoned and many times savagely beaten or forced to run the gauntlet for insubordination. In 1838, Polezhayev, after another brutal whipping, died of cholera in a military hospital. His poetry reflects his lifelong isolation and despair, as well as his profound religious faith. In the former, but not the latter respect, his life and poetry parallel Rayevsky's: arrest, trial, exile, prison, rebellion. To this he adds themes of brutal barracks life, military discipline, and longing for freedom. His poetry is often bitter and rebellious; at other times he expresses humiliation and cries out against cruel fate (Bel'chikov 1957).

Polezhayev must be honored for having written one of the finest, most intricately constructed romantic poems on the theme of bark (*chelnok*) and storm, "Song of a Drowning Sailor" (1828; 1957, 87–90):

> Vetr svistit,
> Grom gremit,
> More stonet—
> Put' dalek ...
> Tonet, tonet
> Moi chelnok!

> The wind whistles.
> The thunder roars,
> The sea groans—
> The way is far ...
> It sinks, it sinks,
> My bark!

Hope is scant in this poem. Instead, the sailor is beset by waves, darkness, misery, and inevitable death. The only hope is absence of hope, and most terrifying of all is loss of friends:

64   The Esoteric Tradition

>   Tusklyi luch
>   Iz-za tuch,
>   Problesk dali
>   V t'me nochei—
>   Zameniali
>   Mne druzei!

>   A dim ray
>   Behind the clouds,
>   A distant light
>   In the dark of night—
>   Has taken place
>   Of friends!

Here again hope is associated with friendship. But there is no hope in this loner's life, because there are no friends. Either he has no friends, or his few friends abandon him when he needs them most. In the poem "Evening Glow" (ca. 1826–28; 1957, 51–53) the poet complains that "I placed my hope / In trusted friends," but they "fled in swarms" from his adversity.

The poet Polezhayev—a common soldier and political rebel—knows that he will sooner or later perish. His poems on the theme of personal fate express hopelessness. The persona of his poetry is a hero deprived by fate of both hope and faith, as in "The Embittered Poet" (1832; 1957, 90–91): "The divine spark of solace, / The hope of my faith has been taken from me!" In Polezhayev's poetry the "ray of hope" is almost always hidden in darkness, as in "To My Genius" (1836; 1957, 183–84), another poem on the motif of bark and storm. The poet's "lonely bark" braves "savage waves"; in the darkness he sees no "Welcoming star in the heavens." Hope is not totally absent in Polezhayev's poetry. The poet shares Zhukovsky's faith in Providence, as in the line "Cherished gift of Providence" in the poem "Song of a Drowning Sailor." But his suffering hero knows that for him, in this life, there is no hope for a better future. In "The Condemned Man" (1837; 1957, 158–61), written on the eve of corporal punishment ("I am condemned! To humiliating punishment"), the poet sees the Star of Hope, but he finds no consolation in it. The "star of early morning" rises as before, the sky is lit by its beauty:

>   No ia! ... Ia nebu i nadezhde
>   Skazhu: "Prostite navsegda!"

> But I! . . . To heaven and to hope
> I say: "Farewell forever!"

Polezhayev was beaten. He was beaten in the barracks, in prison, in the ranks. Not even Rayevsky suffered as terribly as Polezhayev. It is not difficult to understand why this poet could not find solace, neither in friendship, neither in hope of salvation from cruel fate. His suffering and his despair are powerfully expressed in "Evening Glow":

> Ia uvial—i uvial
> Navsegda, navsegda!
> I blazhenstva ne znal
> Nikogda, nikogda!
>
> I withered—and withered
> Always, always!
> And bliss I knew
> Never, never!

The esoteric tradition traveled a long path from Baron de Tschoudy to I. V. Lopukhin and I. P. Turgenev, to V. A. Zhukovsky, and then on through the Russian romantic movement from the first to the last Decembrist. By the time the Masonic symbolism of the flaming star became the romantic Star of Hope metaphor and made its way through Russian poetry to the 1830s, its origins in Freemasonry had begun to fade from conscious knowledge. The path is true if not straight, however, and the most remarkable thing about the symbolism is not loss of clarity in its arcane meandering, but the consistency of its moral and aesthetic development. Even as Zhukovsky transformed the symbolism from a Masonic system into a new romantic aesthetics, he did so without violating the integrity of its original meaning. Even as other romantic poets adapted the metaphor to their own Weltanschauung, they deliberately or unknowingly preserved and even enriched its values. Just as strict observance of the system yielded deep meaning to specifically prepared adepts, its transformation by poets of broader romantic diapason remained faithful to the spirit and often even to the letter of the original. From the seven virtues and three ultimate moral goals of the Order of the Supreme Architect of the Universe to Zhukovsky's valuation of friendship, Providence, inspiration, and memory, and on to freedom and political activism in the poetry of Rayevsky and the cruel personal fate of Polezhayev—the symbolism changed, expanded, developed, but remained morally coherent. This is nowhere truer than in the interpretation and reinterpretation of Masonic symbolism in the poetry of one of the most highly moral Russian romantic poets. In the poetry, and especially in the fate of the Decembrist Kondraty Ryleyev, the Star of Hope achieves dramatic realization of its original moral intentions. It does so in close association with a broad range of other esoteric systems.

3

Ryleyev's *Voynarovsky*: Decembrist Prescience

"Alas! my prediction came true . . ."
—Kondraty Ryleyev, *Voynarovsky*

One does not choose to be a Freemason, one is chosen. However, whether one chooses to be initiated is a matter of free will. Once initiated, Freemasons are also free to choose how seriously they wish to work.[1] Some Freemasons are "serious," others are not. Rayevsky was a serious Freemason; Pushkin was not. The Decembrist leader and poet Kondraty Ryleyev was a serious Freemason, fully adept in the secrets of the craft. He was initiated in 1820 into the German lodge Zum flammenden Stern. He was sufficiently committed to the craft to learn German and work to the highest degree of Master Mason in the

---

1. So, at least, are the principles of Lax Observance to which the majority of the new Freemasons of the Grand Lodge of Astraea subscribed in the early nineteenth century. This does not necessarily apply, however, to those lodges that continued to observe Eckleff's Swedish System or to the eighteenth-century Freemasons who preferred the Swedish System and Hund's rites of Strict Observance. The Moscow Mystic Masons seem not to have abused the Masonic virtue of obedience—as it had been abused throughout the history of Freemasonry and pseudo-Masonic charlatanry—but they were often criticized for intolerance. This is one reason why Russians such as Karamzin left the Order.

same year as his initiation (Semevskii 1908, 145). He was still an active Freemason when the lodges were closed in 1822 (O'Meara 1984, 68–69). Before his initiation the Star of Hope appears in his poetry as a purely romantic symbol, complete with the older Zhukovsky's phraseology and imagery. After his initiation, it meant to him high morality, quest for knowledge, and, especially, brotherhood. After the lodges were closed in 1822, and he shifted his activism to the Decembrist Northern Society in 1823, he transformed the symbol into a referent for freedom and, in keeping with his tragic life, of terrible fate and a complex desire for death and martyrdom. The path to this new meaning of the Star of Hope leads to different implications of the development of the esoteric tradition in Russian romantic poetry.

Decembrist Hope, Decembrist Fate

Ryleyev first used the symbolism of the Star of Hope in a lyric poem titled "Signal-Star" (1816–18; 1971, 294–96). The poem is an adaptation of Zhukovsky's poem "The Sailor" and incorporates some of the signal-words used in Zhukovsky's translations of Schiller's poem "Die Ideale" and Millevoye's poem "La Fleur":

> S pylkoi iunosti strastiami,
> I nadezhdy sladkoi poln,
> Ia napravil za mechtami
> V more burnoe svoi choln.

> With ardent passions of youth,
> And filled with sweet hope,
> I set a course to my dreams
> In my bark on a stormy sea.

The poet suffers in the storm, even begs for the release of death, but is comforted by "the glimmer of a certain light":

> Dolgo, dolgo tak uzhasno
> Svod Nebes skryvala mgla!
> Nakonets zvezda prekrasna,
> Ia uvidel, tam vzoshla!

> Long, long and fearsomely
> Were the Heavens hidden in darkness!
> At last a beautiful star
> Caught my sight as it rose!

And though the Star of Hope hides in the clouds, fades away ("Again I was left without Hope!"), it returns to comfort him and show the way to salvation:

> Vot zvezda-putevoditel'!
> Glas moi vnutrennii skazal—
> Vot tvoi Genii uteshitel'
> Konets bed tvoikh nastal!
>
> Here is the signal-star!
> My inner voice told me—
> Here is thy Genius, thy succor!
> Thy woes are at an end!

Like Rayevsky, Ryleyev searches the shore for a landing, and finds it "On the way marked by the lovely star":

> O zvezda-putevoditel'!
> V pristan', v pristan' poskorei!
>
> O signal-star!
> To land, quickly to land!

The poet's friends wait to embrace him, his love awaits him. Happiness awaits poor travelers, and

> Tam s Nadezhdoi obitaet
> Vera, Druzhba i Liubov'!
>
> There with Hope abides
> Faith, Friendship and Love!

In the years 1823–24 Kondraty Ryleyev wrote a historical verse tale on the romantic theme of the controversial Ukrainian leader Mazepa. It was at just this time that he became involved in the political conspiracy that culminated in the revolt of 14 December 1825 and his execution in July 1826. He prefaced his tale with a verse dedication to his friend, coeditor of the literary almanac *Polar Star* and fellow conspirator in the Decembrist Northern Society Aleksandr Bestuzhev. Often anthologized under the title "To A. A. Bestuzhev," the dedication (1824; 1971, 185–86) is a heartfelt expression of gratitude because Ryleyev believed that he had come to hate and distrust men until Bestuzhev revived his faith in true friendship.[2] The poem is one of the most far-reaching Decembrist interpretations of the Star of Hope:

> I ia v bezumii derzal
> Ne verit' druzhbe beskorystnoi.
> Nezapno ty iavilsia mne:
> Poviazka s glaz moikh upala;
> Ia razuverilsia vpolne,
> I vnov' v nebesnoi vyshine
> Zvezda nadezhdy zasiiala.

> And I in my delusion dared
> Not believe in selfless friendship.
> Then suddenly you appeared before me:
> The blindfold fell from my eyes;
> I was fully undeceived,
> And once again the sky in its heights
> Was brightly lit by the star of hope.

Three years after Ryleyev's death, Aleksandr Bestuzhev wrote a lyric poem titled "Dream" (1829; Bestuzhev-Marlinskii 1958, 2:502–4) in which he expressed the fate of a fallen Decembrist in Siberian exile. The poet is alone, "death is all around me," and:

> Plyvu. Na tikhom serdtse khlad,
> Dremotoi leni tiazhki vezhdy,
> I zvezdy iskrami nadezhdy
> V ugriumom nebe ne goriat.

---

2. The poem is important in the history of Russian romantic poetry because it ends with the line that became a manifesto of Decembrist civic poetry, the belief that political action is more important than poetry: "I am a Citizen, not a Poet!"

I sail. My quiet heart is cold,
The weight of drowsy indolence is heavy
And the stars' sparks of hope
Do not burn in the gloomy sky.

Prior to the failed revolt, Ryleyev could place hope in the union of friends known as the Decembrist affair. After the revolt, an isolated Bestuzhev could neither hope for friendship, nor believe in "the stars' sparks of hope" represented by Ryleyev and their shared hope for freedom.

The Assassin's Dagger

Political conspiracy, dreams of freedom, the assassin's dagger, selfless martyrdom—these notions, the stuff of which a certain Weltanschauung is made, ran through the early 1820s when the romantic movement reached its maturity in Russia. For political idealists like the Decembrists the impetus came from the French revolution as one model, the American as another. For the literary romantics, dreams of freedom were aroused by Lamartine, Chénier, Schiller, especially by the verse tales of Byron, and even more by the liberating effects of the free romantic imagination.

Russians were carried away by a flood of new possibilities in the early 1820s. Urged to the sublime by fresh hope on one side, goaded to rage by the visible corruption of a despotic autocracy on the other, it is understandable that lofty ideals and assassination came to stand together in the minds of young idealists. Brutus became the ideal. Aleksandr Pushkin, in "Liberty. An Ode" (1817) and such other poems as "The Dagger" (1821), felt no incongruity in singing simultaneously of "freedom's proud inspiration" and the bloody death of tyrants. His rhetoric was echoed by Kondraty Ryleyev's expressions of the same motif, as in the historical *duma* "Dmitry the Pretender" (1823; 1971, 149–52): "For the tyrant there is no salvation: the only friend to him is the dagger!" No matter where the tyrant hides, "the assassin's dagger waits."

Several kinds of extremists may be marked out among the Decembrists. Wilhelm Küchelbecker, poet and dramatist, boyhood friend of Pushkin, was a gentle bumbler whose beliefs could never be compromised. On the day of the revolt he armed himself with a pistol and wandered around Senate Square in search of Nicholas I. A. I. Yakubovich swore that he would kill Alexander I for what he considered an imperial act of injustice against himself. The psychotic P. G. Kakhovskoy also swore vengeance against the tsar. In the summer of 1825 Ryleyev and Bestuzhev persuaded Yakubovich and Kakhovskoy to put their services at the call of the Northern Society. Yakubovich's oath turned out to be a deliberately cultivated pose; he did not show up on the day of the revolt. Kakhovskoy approached Nicholas I several times on Senate Square, but could not muster the courage to shoot; finally, he worked himself into a rage and shot the Governor-General of Petersburg instead. Pavel Pestel, the brilliant leader of the Southern Society, was the ambitious Napoleon and devious Cassius who looked to Robespierre as his ideal. His attention was attracted by I. I. Gorbachevsky, a member of the Society of United Slavs, whose strongly expressed plebeian hatred of the autocracy made him an ideal assassin. And finally there was Kondraty Ryleyev, the Brutus of the Decembrist conspiracy whose fanatic idealism gave him the resolve to sacrifice both life and honor in the cause of the liberation of the Russian people. Ryleyev was the ultimate martyr, a man so deeply committed to his ideals that a willingness to sacrifice himself for a just cause became a desire to die for immortality. Franklin Walker is right that "there is a Zoroastrian conflict of good and evil in Ryleyev which contributed to the element of fanaticism in the Russian revolutionary movement" (1969, 446).

Fanatic Idealist

Kondraty Ryleyev (1795–1826) was a literary and political idealist. His character allowed no compromise of beliefs. His testimony before the Investigatory Commission and the testimonies of his friends show that he more than once overwhelmed his reluctant—and more sensible—fellow conspirators. N. M. Lebedev goes too far when he says that the three Bestuzhev brothers, their naval officer friend Konstantin Torson, and the assassins Yakubovich and Kakhovskoy were under Ryleyev's control (1954), but they were all fatally influenced by him, not least by action he took without their knowledge. Ryleyev prompted Aleksandr Bestuzhev to recruit the two assassins. He urged the other Bestuzhev brothers and Torson to organize a revolt at the naval fortress of Kronstadt in the Gulf of Finland, and to stand by with a "reliable frigate" to carry the imperial family abroad. Ryleyev, a man who despised hypocrisy, formed the conspiracy within the conspiracy to subvert the Northern Society's program for a constitutional monarchy to Pestel's plans for a republic. He was willing to support Pestel's proposal to exterminate the imperial family (Zakharov 1954, 97–101). On the night of 13 December 1825, lying ill in a bed surrounded by the other conspirators, he successfully harangued them into carrying out their jerry-rigged plan of revolt. "Although he [Ryleyev] was my best friend," Aleksandr Bestuzhev told the Investigatory Commission, "for the sake of the truth I will not hide the fact that he was the chief instigator of the adventure; by enflaming everyone with his poetic imagination and fortifying them with his persistence" (Pokrovskii et al. 1925– , 1:444).

Ryleyev was able to profess contrition. At the end he underwent a religious conversion and expressed regret. He wrote a moving letter begging the forgiveness of his aristocratic opponent in the Northern Society Prince Obolensky and another begging Nicholas I to hang only him for the Decembrist affair (Ryleyev 1934, 517–18). But his doubts were few, his actions in the conspiracy and revolt firm. He spoke freely about his role to the Investigatory Commission and professed his ideals to the end. He denied the incontrovertible evidence that he was, with Pestel, the chief instigator of the plans for regicide, but otherwise refused to do anything to alleviate his fate and went to the gallows with religious fervor, begging his friends to forgive him for ruining them.

He behaved exactly like the heroes of his historical poems: champions of the people who go gladly to their death in the knowledge they have acted bravely for the common good and will be remembered in history as selfless martyrs in the cause of democracy. He envied the death of Byron in the Greek Revolution, and in his poem "On the Death of Byron" (1824; 1971, 95–97) he writes:

> "Druz'ia svobody i Ellady
> Vezde v slezakh v ukor sud'by;
> Odni tirany i raby
> Ego vnezapnoi smerti rady."

> "The friends of freedom and Greece
> Are everywhere in tears over his fate;
> Tyrants and slaves alone
> Rejoice at his death."

In his study of Ryleyev Walker concludes that "when the most compelling scenes in his poetry are examined in the light of his poetic biography, a death-wish is evident" (1969, 436).

Ryleyev was raised partly in Ukraine, whence a preference for heroes from Ukrainian history. He served in the army toward the end of the campaign of 1812 and established a record of poor discipline for speaking against military hypocrisy. From 1821 to 1824 he worked for the Petersburg Criminal Court, finally retiring after a frustrating failure to bring justice to ill-treated peasants. Typically, he preferred initiation into the lower-class "serious" German lodge Zum flammenden Stern to the Russian lodges dominated by elitist military officers and men of letters. From 1821 to 1823 he was active in the prestigious Free Society of Lovers of Russian Literature, Science, and the Arts, whose proceedings and journal he almost gained control of in 1823. He did succeed in exerting editorial influence on the official journal of the Society of Lovers of Russian Literature in 1823. After leaving the government he accepted the position of secretary of the Russian-American Company, founded to develop Russia's holdings in Alaska. There, under the protection of the liberal statesman N. S. Mordvinov, he was given free rein and time to develop his literary career. The Russian-American Company on the embankment of the Moika Canal became a favorite gathering place of poets and writers and the editorial headquarters of *Polar Star*. The Company also became the focus of the activities of the Northern Society. Ryleyev joined the Northern Society in 1823 and was elected to its ruling Duma in 1824 (Afanas'ev 1982; O'Meara 1984).

Born into a minor family of the petty gentry, Ryleyev was a natural democrat. He could not bear injustice. He saw himself as a champion of the downtrodden peasantry and of any lesser-born person who was not accorded respect in a city of aristocrats. In the years just before 1825 he and Bestuzhev debated with Pushkin over the latter's pretensions to aristocratic lineage, a debate that presaged the post-Decembrist schism between the Literary Plebeians and the Literary Aristocrats. He certainly preferred the plebeian journalists Nikolay Grech and Faddey Bulgarin to the poets of the Pushkin Pleiad, particularly after the latter abandoned *Polar Star* in favor of the new almanac *Northern Flowers*. He despised the Petersburg aristocracy almost as much as he hated the Romanovs, and not the least motivation for his conspiracy within a conspiracy was his dislike of the elite guards officers and privileged aristocrats who dominated the Northern Society.[3]

---

3. Indicative of his contempt for privilege and his fervid love of justice is the Chernov affair. In 1825 Ryleyev's cousin Mariya Chernova was jilted by a member of the prestigious Novosiltsev family, and Ryleyev decided to intervene on behalf of his kinsmens' "ruined" honor. Although the Chernov family attempted to downplay the scandal, Ryleyev pushed Mariya's brother K. P. Chernov into challenging Novosiltsev to a duel in which both men were killed. Ryleyev played the role of second in the duel to

He was prim and pious. In a study of the psychology of the Decembrists Yu. M. Lotman asserts that "the Decembrists were men of action." Theirs was an age of chatter, and they were as guilty of more talk than action as others of their class—even their plans for assassination were largely what Prince P. A. Vyazemsky termed "bavardage atroce"—but it would be a mistake not to see how ready they were to carry their ideas into "hasty action." Lotman distinguishes the Decembrists from the sophisticated, frivolous aristocrats by stressing that they "cultivated seriousness as a norm of behavior." He points to Ryleyev as an example of seriousness carried to the point of prudery. According to an anecdote told by Pushkin, when Baron A. A. Delvig invited Ryleyev to a house of prostitution, Ryleyev replied in an offended tone that he was married. "So what?" Delvig retorted. "Do you refuse to dine out simply because you have a kitchen at home?" (Lotman 1975a, 28–32).

Self-Sacrifice and Martyrdom

Ryleyev is prominent among the romantics drawn to the ideal of the assassin's dagger and the martyr's fate. In one of his first political poems, a savage satire against tsarist corruption titled "To the Favorite" (1820; 1971, 57–58), he warns the tyrant that "a worthy man" might "save his fellow citizens from evil fate": "Tyrant, beware!" At any moment there may appear "A Cassius, or a Brutus, or a Cato, the foe of Caesars!" Martyrdom for him was an actual, as well as a poetic ideal. In this he differs from most others, who understood that it is one thing to poeticize such ideals, quite another to sacrifice oneself for them. His poetry leaves no doubt that he desired to carry the ideal into reality. The hero of the *duma* "Ivan Susanin" (1823; 1971, 152–55), who saved the

---

such finely detailed extent that he was something like an accomplice in the affair, and he then turned Chernov's funeral into a demonstration against privileged aristocrats. Although there is some disagreement over whether Ryleyev wrote the verses read at the funeral—some believe the author was V. K. Küchelbecker—the poem certainly expresses Ryleyev's feelings. The poem calls on others to swear "by our honor and by Chernov . . . to show our hostility for the favorites . . . for the tyrants, ready to oppress us" (O'Meara 1984, 217–22). The affair is usually cited as an example of Ryleyev's defiance of public opinion, but it also suggests another facet of his personality. Granted that he successfully propagandized his own ideals, it is evident that the Chernov family sought to settle the affair quietly until he took up their cause, and that two men died needlessly. Ryleyev looked rightly to the general principle, but he missed the individual human implications of his quest.

first Romanov from marauding Poles, defies his vengeful enemies as he dies: "He who is Russian in his heart, bravely and boldly, / And gladly perishes for a just cause!" In "Volynsky" (1822; 1971, 164–67), about the Russian patriot of the reign of Anna in the early eighteenth century who was executed for his opposition to the German favorites of the court, the hero exclaims before his death:

> "Za istinu sviatuiu
> I kazn' mne budet torzhestvom!
> . . . .
> Ia posviashchal sebia dobru
> I veren pravde byl do groba!"

> "For sacred truth
> Even execution is triumph for me!
> . . . .
> I dedicated myself to good
> And to truth was true to the grave!"

Zhukovsky believed in Providence, Rayevsky in freedom. Ryleyev believed in fate—it was on the example of his poetry that Polezhayev turned the symbol of the star into his tragic expression of cruel personal fate. The words for fate (*sud'ba* and *sud'bina*, *uchast'* [lot], and the terrible fate designated by the word *rok*) appear far more often in his lexicon than is usual even for romantic poetry. The words for fate are usually linked with the words *prediction, foretell, foresee, omen,* and *portent*. In a "Memoir on Ryleyev" Nikolay Bestuzhev reported that Ryleyev once told him that his historical verse tale *Nalivayko* was a prediction of his own martyrdom in the cause of freedom. Bestuzhev was convinced that every work Ryleyev wrote was a "portent" (*predveshchanie*) (Azadovskii 1951, 7). *Nalivayko* (1824–25; 1971, 226–37) begins with a depiction of Ukraine enslaved by Poles, Turks, Tatars, Jews, Lithuanians, and others who exploit a people fallen from the glory of the ancient state of Kievan Rus. Its hero is the sixteenth-century rebel Nalivayko who raised the Cossacks to rebellion. The tale is not complete, but its thirteen parts show that the struggle for freedom is made glorious not by victory or failure, but by its inherent heroism. Nalivayko "foresees" that he will lose, but he is willing to sacrifice all to restore his people's native pride and set a heroic example for the future:

"Izvestno mne: pogibel' zhdet
Togo, kto pervyi vosstaet
Na utesnitelei naroda,—
Sud'ba menia uzh obrekla.
No gde, skazhi, kogda byla
Bez zhertv iskuplena svoboda?
Pogibnu ia za krai rodnoi,—
Ia eto chuvstvuiu, ia znaiu. . ."
                (1971, 233–34)

"I know: destruction waits
For him who rises first
Against the people's oppressors;
Fate has already chosen me.
But where, pray tell, and when
Was freedom purchased without cost?
I will perish for my land—
I feel this, I know it . . ."

In Ryleyev's poetry, fate—romantic fate—is not simply personal and individual. The fate of his heroes, and so his own fate, is raised to the level of national-historical tragedy. By welcoming his fate and dying for his land, Nalivayko ennobles his people. Ryleyev's poetry is rhetorical, imbued with the words and phrases of the eighteenth-century heroic epic and lofty civic ode.

Freedom, Rebellion, Conspiracy: Ryleyev's Mazepa

Ryleyev expressed his desire for martyrdom and his romantic belief in prescience most strikingly in his earlier historical verse tale *Voynarovsky* (1823–24; 1971, 185–225). The tale treats the Ukrainian Hetman Mazepa, who in the early eighteenth century attempted to free Ukraine from Russian rule by siding with Sweden's Charles XII in his war against Peter the Great. Mazepa's and Ukraine's hopes were ended when Peter destroyed Swedish power at the Battle of Poltava in 1709. *Voynarovsky* has been a frequent subject of study (Babinski 1974, and sources cited there; Khodorov 1975). It belongs to the tradition of the Mazepa theme in art and poetry—both Voltaire and Byron were attracted to the duplicitous Ukrainian "traitor." Ryleyev's response to Byron's Mazepa has been thoroughly examined, and so has his poem's relationship to Pushkin's historical verse tale *Poltava* (1828), written as a Russian response to Ryleyev's pro-Ukrainian view (Pauls 1963). The tale reveals a great deal about Ryleyev's feelings about treason and his involvement in the Decembrist conspiracy.

Mazepa was not an ideal choice of hero. In both his personal life and his political career he was a manipulator who more than once betrayed others—in love affairs, in friendships, in his family, and in his struggles with other potential leaders of Ukraine. Ukrainians have not accepted Mazepa as a national hero because in at least two instances he betrayed countrymen to Peter the Great, using the power gained thereby to advance his own ambitions. He supported Peter the Great through his entire career, and in the end he betrayed the Russian tsar too. To Pushkin, in *Poltava*, the motivation for Mazepa's treason was ultimately personal—he never forgot an insult inflicted on him many years before. In this sense, just as Ryleyev elevated individual heroism to national import, Pushkin lowered a cause of a historical event to personal frailty. For Ryleyev, faced with the task of championing Ukraine under the eye of both the censor and unreceptive Russians, Mazepa's motivations are ambiguous, never quite repudiated, never quite endorsed, yet heroic by implication, and in any case grand.

The formative theme of *Voynarovsky* is the struggle between democracy and autocracy. Mazepa is treated as a revolutionary of total conviction, a leader willing to betray his loyalty to Peter the Great in order to lead his people to freedom. The tale is narrated largely by the hero, Voynarovsky, the Hetman's nephew, a young idealist who has many doubts about the justice of Mazepa's cause but is persuaded to join him in treason. Voynarovsky tells his story in retrospect to a traveler through Siberia, the historian Georg Friedrich Miller. He is a lonely Siberian exile, an outcast reduced to an animal's existence as self-imposed penance for his treason. Although the tale is mainly about Voynarovsky, not Mazepa, the ideals of both are developed. Voynarovsky is led to revolt by his admiration for the more powerful Mazepa, his love for his country, and his desire for freedom. He loves Mazepa despite his awareness of his uncle's penchant for intrigue. He is totally under the man's influence save for one difference between them: Voynarovsky will sacrifice wife, children, and life, but he will not betray his honor; Mazepa will give even his honor for the cause of Ukrainian independence.

Mazepa's ideals and attitudes are expressed in his own words to Voynarovsky. As in *Nalivayko*, the words and phrases are elevated. Early in the tale Mazepa announces his faith in his cause and his conspiracy:

> "Ia chtu Velikogo Petra;
> No—pokoriaiasia sud'bine!...
> Uznai: ia vrag emu otnyne!"
> (1971, 204–5)

> "I revere the Great Peter;
> But—bowing to fate! . . .
> Know: I am his foe henceforth!"

For the land of his forefathers he is prepared to sacrifice his all:

> "No ia, no ia, pylaia mest'iu,
> Ee spasaia ot okov,
> Ia zhertvovat' gotov ei chest'iu."
> (1971, 204)

> "But I, but I, burning for vengeance,
> [Ukraine] to unfetter,
> Am ready to sacrifice my honor."

Mazepa knows that his plan to win independence for his people is risky, but he has decided to let fate decide, "Whether glory awaits me, or disgrace." He is convinced that his cause is "the struggle of freedom with autocracy," and he carries out the revolt without doubts (1971, 205). After the revolt has failed, Mazepa dies in terror and regret: "I see the dreadful Peter! / I hear his dreadful curses!" (1971, 211).

The tale's denouement suggests that the justice of a cause is decided by its outcome. Voynarovsky knows that Mazepa will be eternally cursed by his people. Himself he likens to Brutus, "the noble defender of Rome," but he believes that Brutus,

> "dostoin ukorizny
> Svobodu sam on pogubil—
> On torzhestvo vragov otchizny
> Samoubiistvom utverdil."
> (1971, 217)

> "deserves reproach:
> He it was who destroyed freedom—
> The triumph of his nation's foes
> By suicide assured."

Voynarovsky's attitudes—to both Mazepa and Peter—are also stated. He adores Mazepa and is prepared to support him to the end:

> "My v nem glavu naroda chtili,
> My obozhali v nem ottsa,
> My v nem otechestvo liubili."
>
> (1971, 209)

> "We revered in him the people's leader,
> We adored in him the father,
> We loved in him the fatherland."

But he does not understand his secretive hero and is not even certain Mazepa really wishes "To save the people of Ukraine from misery" (1971, 209). Still, whatever his doubts in the man, he has complete faith in homeland and freedom. He is prepared to bear any sacrifice for his native land, he will give even his children and wife, "Saving only honor for myself" (1971, 204).

And so, despite his doubts, despite even his distrust of Mazepa's allies and fellow-conspirators, he devotes himself to the cause:

> "Mazepe predalsia ia slepo,
> I, drug otchizny, drug dobra,
> Ia poklialsia vrazhdoi svirepoi
> Protiv Velikogo Petra.
> Akh, mozhet, byl ia v zabluzhdenii
> Kipiashchei revnost'iu goria,—
> No ia v slepom ozhestochen'i
> Tiranom pochital tsaria. . ."
>
> (1971, 205)

> "I gave myself to Mazepa blindly,
> And, friend of my fatherland, friend of virtue,
> I vowed terrible enmity
> Against the Great Peter.

> Ah, perhaps I was deluded,
> Overly hot from seething zeal,
> But in my blind enmity
> I deemed the tsar a tyrant."

In the end, just as Mazepa reconciles himself with death, so Voynarovsky, convinced that one rash moment destroyed his country, reconciles himself to his harsh fate:

> "Uvy! umru v sem tsarstve nochi!
> Mne tak sulil zhestokii rok."
> (1971, 206)

> "Alas! I shall die in this kingdom of darkness!
> Thus have I been condemned by harsh fate."

Linked with the words fate and prediction is the word hope. In the symbolic structure of *Voynarovsky* hope is the antithesis of terrible fate. When the Battle of Poltava is lost, Mazepa realizes "how powerless we are before fate":

> Odno mgnoven'e vse reshilo,
> Odno mgnoven'e pogubilo
> Navek strany moei rodnoi
> Nadezhdu, schast'e i pokoi.
> (1971, 208)

> One moment all decided,
> One moment did forever
> Destroy my native land's
> Hope, happiness, and peace.

In Siberia Voynarovsky willingly succumbs to "malevolent fate," accepts his banishment from his native land and lives without hope, consigned to die "in this kingdom of darkness": "Thus have I been condemned by harsh fate" (1971, 205–6).

Ryleyev and Bestuzhev, Hope and Friendship

Unmediated parallels between authors and their fictional characters are difficult to draw, but the biographical-allegorical parallels of *Voynarovsky* are as straightforward as Ryleyev's civic rhetoric. As Mazepa was a convinced rebel, so Ryleyev was a convinced Decembrist; as Voynarovsky was subject to doubt, so also was Aleksandr Bestuzhev. Like many intense idealists, Ryleyev was a self-centered person; his idealization of self in his heroes is an often remarked characteristic of his poetry. To the degree that Ryleyev's views were unabashedly political, his literary works are often intentionalist, biographical, allegorical. Under the influence of the censor, his works are also in many ways indirect and covert. The key to interpretation is again the word *hope*. If Voynarovsky's despair in his "kingdom of darkness" is a prescient expression of Decembrist fate, a valid literary indicator of Ryleyev's actual expectations in the years before the revolt of 14 December 1825, then clearly, hope was not enough. In his testimony before the Investigatory Commission, Bestuzhev said, "I made friends with Ryleyev . . . and we dreamed together" (Pokrovskii et al. 1925– , 1:433). The friendship between Ryleyev and Bestuzhev is central to the meaning of *Voynarovsky*.

Their friendship was axiomatic to the Soviet view of Decembrist solidarity, but because both men destroyed their papers before and after the revolt of 14 December, little is known about their relationship. Bestuzhev never once referred to Ryleyev in his post-December letters and diaries.[4] It should not be assumed that their friendship was as simple as political considerations have demanded. Ryleyev was, after all, the Decembrist who overwhelmed his comrades with his "poetic imagination." In the view of one contemporary who knew them well, the critic and journalist N. I. Grech, Ryleyev ruined Bestuzhev. Grech's attitude toward Ryleyev is hostile, but his assessment might still be telling. Ryleyev's "fanaticism," Grech reports in his *Notes on My Life*, "was powerful and contagious, and for this reason it is not surprising that the uneducated Ryleyev succeeded in carrying away men who were immeasurably above him in all respects, especially Aleksandr Bestuzhev." At the same time, Grech admired Bestuzhev, considered him "talented," "brilliant," "noble," believed

---

4. An exception would seem to be a statement in a published letter written in French by Bestuzhev to his brothers on 16 June 1828: "I received much from Ryleyev; did you receive too?" (Semevskii 1870b, 238). However, the original copy in the Bestuzhev family archives (Institute of Russian Literature, Fond 604, edinitsa No. 11 [5580]) shows that the word transcribed as "Ryleev" is actually the French abbreviation "Pburg."

that if Ryleyev had not led him to his ruin, he would have occupied an "honorable place in the first rank of Russian writers" (1886, 369, 393–94). Grech's opinion accords with the view that Ryleyev wielded power unwisely in the Northern Society and is supported by Bestuzhev's testimony that Ryleyev was the "chief instigator" of the Decembrist revolt.

Still, the poetry Ryleyev and Bestuzhev wrote to and about each other shows that their friendship meant a great deal to them. In the text of *Voynarovsky*, for example, hope is the antithesis of implacable fate, but in the verse dedication "To A. A. Bestuzhev" (1824; 1971, 185–86), who provided a biography of Voynarovsky to accompany the tale, hope is synonymous with Ryleyev's feelings about friendship. Ryleyev had come to hate and despise men; when Bestuzhev "suddenly appeared to me," the poet's trust was revived, "And once again the sky in its heights / Was brightly lit by the star of hope." The inter- and intratextual resonances of the Star of Hope are many. As with Zhukovsky and Pushkin, the poem moves from disenchantment to reenchantment—it begins at a low point of loss of hope and rises to renewal of faith. The word *hope* (*nadezhda*) interplays with the root of the words for faith, trust, belief, loyalty (*ver-*). Ryleyev's negative phrasing of the words for faith and trust seem to make faith antonymical to hope. But the positive outcome—the poet's recovery of belief—shows that the words are synonymous. Ryleyev is "undeceived"—dissuaded from his "lack of belief," that is, he learned again to trust in friendship.

Bestuzhev's response in 1829 to Ryleyev in his poem "Dream" (Bestuzhev-Marlinskii 1958, 2:502–4) is one of his best expressions of Decembrist fate among many post-December poems written in Siberia on such themes as regret, lonely exile, and the loss of friends and freedom. In the poem's first part "chance" holds "the golden stirrup" of freedom for the "frenzied horseman," who rides "the wild horse of fate.... Farther and farther, all hope is lost!" Horse and horseman race across the steppe, finally plunging in a nightmarish fall into an abyss.[5] In the second part the poet recovers his awareness chained to the bark of exile sailing through a gloomy icescape:

Ochnulsia ia ot strashnoi grezy,
No vse dusha toski polna

---

5. Bestuzhev's rich metaphoricization is indebted to Byron's poem *Mazeppa*, a treatment of a legend in the early life of the future Hetman according to which he was strapped naked to the back of a wild stallion and turned loose to be trampled to death in the steppes.

I mnilos', gnut menia zhelezy
K veslu ubogogo chelna.

I awakened from my terrible dream,
But my soul is yet with sorrow filled,
I dream, I'm bound by chains
To the oars of a wretched bark.

Whereas Ryleyev's dedication begins at a low point and rises to the heights of the bright Star of Hope, Bestuzhev's dream begins with heightened frenzy and falls precipitously into despair. The poet's "quiet heart is cold," "death is all around me," "And the stars' sparks of hope / Do not burn in the gloomy sky." Friendship, faith, and trust are absent from this poem; hope is denied. The progression of Ryleyev's treatment of the theme of friendship is reversed: after 1825 hope has become disillusionment. In relation to Ryleyev's *Voynarovsky* as a whole, however, the progression has been duplicated: Bestuzhev has experienced the same loss of hope expressed by Voynarovsky and predicted by Ryleyev in the epithet for exile, "kingdom of darkness." One moment destroyed Voynarovsky's—and Bestuzhev's—"Hope, happiness, and peace."

Romantic Prescience, Decembrist Fate

When he realizes that the Ukrainian cause is lost, Voynarovsky realizes also that he will be banished from his homeland. He experiences this realization as a "premonition" or "foreboding":

"Uvy! predchuvstvie sbylos':
Sud'by velen'em samovlastnoi
S tex por na rodine prekrasnoi
Mne pobyvat' ne dovelos'..."
                          (1971, 210)

"Alas! my prediction came true:
By order of despotic fate
My beautiful homeland since that time
I've never seen again..."

Be careful what you write, for what you write may come true. Ryleyev, known in legend as *le pendu,* is Mazepa, hanged for betraying Peter the Great. Bestuzhev, the admirer of Ryleyev, is Voynarovsky. Ryleyev's allegory is far more prescient than empirical logic is usually able to account for. In 1827 Bestuzhev was exiled to the same location in Siberia where Voynarovsky perished. And there, in Yakutsk on the river Lena, just as Voynarovsky tells his story to the explorer Miller, Bestuzhev found a way to tell Ryleyev's tale and his own to another visitor to Siberia, the German explorer Georg Adolph Erman.

In the late 1820s, Erman journeyed through Siberia on an expedition to measure the earth's magnetic field. There he became friends with Bestuzhev. The two men worked together on Erman's project, and in a later essay, "A Letter to Doctor Erman" (1830), Bestuzhev used his acquaintance with a representative of European science to inform his friends of his whereabouts and reaffirm his Decembrist ideals in a tour de force of Aesopic language expressing political views in the guise of scientific concepts (Alekseev 1930). Bestuzhev also confided his role in the Decembrist conspiracy to Erman and told a story similar to the plot of *Voynarovsky.*

In his retelling of Ryleyev's tale, as told to him by Bestuzhev, Erman indicated that he was expressing Bestuzhev's view of the conspiracy, his and Ryleyev's role in it, and his thoughts about the martyrdom of Ryleyev. "Alexander Bestujev," Erman writes in his *Travels in Siberia* (1850), "had been engaged in the conspiracy long before the outbreak of the revolution." He had joined readily "with those who were for raising [the Russian people] on a sudden from servitude . . . [and] resolved on extreme measures." According to Bestuzhev, it was important that "they hoped to get the better subsequently of some of their associates who were strongly suspected of selfish ambition." When the revolt failed, Bestuzhev was demoralized and underwent an immediate change of heart: "It is well known how the Emperor on that occasion, with a chivalrous contempt of death, awakened repentance in the more respectable of the insurgents and subdued the multitude. All felt as if proscribed by the moral power of the victory." Further,

> the fetters which he [Bestuzhev] afterwards bore in the citadel of St. Petersburg and in one of the fortresses of Finland, nay, the deaths of his friends, who fell by his side, under the hands of the executioner on the scaffold, had never been able to efface from the exile's memory that one passage in the night of his sufferings. He could not even today relate without shuddering how the Emperor came up to him . . . and with insupportable haughtiness of look told him of the loyalty of the deceased General Bestujev and the degeneracy of his son. (1850, 1:293–94)

If Erman's account reveals the profound effect the failure of the revolt had on Bestuzhev—an effect that Ryleyev anticipated in the form of Voynarovsky's remorse—it reveals even more about the similarity between the two and the heroes of Ryleyev's tale. "But the poems of Ruileyev and Alexander Bestujev," Erman writes, "appear still more decidedly to have been not so much the consequence of a noble spirit crushed at its first opening as the tragic harbinger of the calamities about to ensue. They worked together for three years . . . until Ruileyev snatched for himself alone the gloomily bright crown of a prophet and unchanging friend." And Erman pointed deliberately to *Voynarovsky* as an allegory of the respective fates of the two Decembrists:

> The origin of this piece can be explained only by supposing that, for some months before the poet's death, he knew, either from the sagacity of a sensitive and excited temper, or from some secret foreboding, how the threads of that web were to run, which he was assisting in the dark to weave. He beholds in spirit the dreams of the conspirators at an end, their plans wholly frustrated, their views stigmatized, his friend Bestujev expelled from society; he discerns beforehand every fine line and touch in the suffering of years, and finally, he sees himself in the hands of the executioner. (1850, 1:295–96)

According to Erman, "Bestujev received in the prophetic poem the name of his predecessor in banishment. . . . His friend's fate was next to his heart, and Ruileyev therefore left his own image in the background; yet he often gives vent to the feeling of a conspirator who knows his own ignominious end and yet goes onwards" (1850, 1:296).

It is easy to understand that Bestuzhev chose Erman to help ensure Ryleyev's immortality, just as Voynarovsky used Miller to make Mazepa's fate known to the world. In this sense, Bestuzhev served as something like an accomplice in Ryleyev's death wish, just as Voynarovsky was Mazepa's accomplice in rebellion. The elements of the respective attitudes and personalities of Ryleyev and Bestuzhev are thus consonant with their literary surrogates. Ryleyev's fanatic idealism, his powerful personality, his intrigues against "associates . . . strongly suspected of selfish ambition," his determination to seek the freedom of the Russian people even though he "knows his ignominious end." Bestuzhev's doubts, his loyalty to Ryleyev, his impetuous commitment to a risky venture (the wild horse of fate) as measured against his sworn duty to the tsar. The meaning of *Voynarovsky*, which Bestuzhev imparted through Erman, shows how much Ryleyev was willing to sacrifice in the face of his pessimistic evaluations of chances for success, and it shows that he sought martyrdom for himself while validating Bestuzhev's different motivations. These Decembrists understood each other in advance of the revolt, each knew how the other would behave.

Love of Death, Accomplice of Death

The Star of Hope has two referents in Ryleyev's biography. The most obvious of these is his coeditorship with Bestuzhev of *Polar Star,* a publication intended to express the political hopes of the Northern Society. The second is Ryleyev's Masonic lodge Zum flammenden Stern, the nominal successor to I. V. Lopukhin's lodge The Shining Star (Pypin 1916, 515). Ryleyev's lodge is described as a "serious" German lodge (Pypin 1916, 526). Correspondences between Ryleyev's shining Star of Hope and the symbolism of Baron de Tschoudy's Order of the Flaming Star are suggested by Ryleyev's use of the symbolism of the Star of Hope, including his plays with the words for hope and faith. He would have known Tschoudy's prescriptions for the Star of Hope in both the rite of initiation to the craft and the rite of elevation to the degree of Master Mason.

As a Master Mason, Ryleyev had access to the esoteric documents belonging to the Grand Lodge of Astraea and now preserved in the archives of the Institute of Russian Literature in Petersburg. He also had access to Lopukhin's explications of the symbolism of the Star of Hope: Lopukhin's treatise "On the Church Within Thee" was republished in 1810 as part of the revival of Freemasonry. With knowledge either of Lopukhin, or of Tschoudy directly, Ryleyev would have appreciated that as a Master Mason he was himself a Star of Hope, a shining example of friendship and virtue who so loves his brothers that he is "ready to perish gladly for [their] salvation" (Lopukhin 1924, 13). Ryleyev, the seeker of martyrdom, would surely have appreciated this virtue.

The signal-words of the symbolic Star of Hope are *hope, trust, faith,* and *friendship.* In Ryleyev's life and poetry they become *fate, prescience, martyrdom,* and *death.* Like many of his contemporaries, Ryleyev probably came to realize that Freemasonry was not the vehicle for revolution in Russia that it had been elsewhere, but he should not be counted among those who lost faith in the substance of the craft. He made philanthropy a chief component of his work in the Criminal Court and in the activities of the societies of lovers of Russian letters. He believed in the Masonic virtues of self-renunciation, altruism, and friendship. His life and poetry are replete with the seven Masonic virtues and three higher moral attainments.[6]

To Freemasons, love of death is not only the ultimate virtue, but the most dangerous. According to the teachings of Tschoudy and Lopukhin, death is to be loved and welcomed, for it is "the door to immortality, the entrance to eternal existence." Fear of death is overcome by love of death, and love of death is inseparable from love of one's brothers, humanity, and God. Death must be selfless, courageous, loving. According to one of the most authoritative Masonic encyclopedias, "To teach the doctrine of immortality is the great object of the Third Degree." To the Freemason, "death is . . . the symbol of initiation completed, perfected, and consummated" (Mackey 1924, 1:198). Love of death is tantamount, symbolically, to rebirth and resurrection, both the Resurrection of Christ and the resurrection common to most mythic systems. Indeed, the rite of initiation into the secrets of the craft is based on the symbolic death of the initiate, his rebirth and resurrection, and thereby his hope of overcoming fear of death and his attainment of faith in immortality. According to the authoritative *Internationaler Freimaurer Lexicon* "the act of rebirth falls into two stages. . . . The initiate dies. . . . Directly from this death comes a new life for all time forth." The initiate is "reborn into the light" (Lennhoff and Posner 1932, 1580).

According to Tschoudy's rites of the Flaming Star, the symbolic death and rebirth of the initiate is enacted as a major part of the initiation. In *Der Signatstern* the rite is basic to initiation into the First Degree of Apprentice Mason. The rite involves nine journeys in sequences of three around the "grave." The initiate is blindfolded and led around the interior of the lodge by three Wardens (*Vorsteher*). He is required to repeat the motto of the Order, "Memento mori." At the end of the second of the three triple journeys the Master of the Lodge symbolically strikes the initiate's head with a hammer, one of the seven tools of Masonic work; the initiate falls "dead" to the ground. He is then reborn (*wiedergeboren*) and led on the final journey around the grave. The grave is the

---

6. According to the surviving documents of the Grand Lodge of Astraea, the Russian Freemasons defined these virtues as *discrétion, obéisance* (sic), *les bonnes moeurs, l'amour de l'humanité, principalement des frères, persévérance ou courage, générosité, désintéressement*, and *l'amour de la mort* (Institute of Russian Literature, Razdel II, opis' 2, No. 105). Other texts substitute or add moderation and temperance to discretion, add patience to obedience and religion to good morals, and substitute hope or trust (*espérance*) for *persévérance* (No. 102; No. 104; see also No. 51). Discretion and moderation were hardly Ryleyev's virtues, but he prescribed faithfully to the others, especially morality, hope, and love of death.

grave of Hyram Abif, the legendary founder of Freemasonry during the building of King Solomon's Temple. At appropriate times the initiate must think of "the body of Hyram Abif." On the third journey the initiate must "know that Hyram Abif is dead," and he must "seek Hyram Abif." When the rite is completed the newly accepted Apprentice is given a ring inscribed with the logo of the Order, an initial "G" at the center of a Flaming Star and its motto, "Memento mori" (1866, 1:63–64, 66, 70, 71). Lopukhin describes the same motto and ring (1924, 19). According to *Allgemeines Handbuch der Freimaurerei*, the "G" stands for Geometry or *Meßkunst*, "the art of measurement" (1867, 3:325–26).

The symbolic death and rebirth of the initiate is common to most Masonic orders.[7] The implications of the symbolism are certainly commensurate with the personality of the idealistic Kondraty Ryleyev. Love of death and love of friends are inseparable from the poet's relationship to Bestuzhev, whose "fate," as Erman testifies, was "next to his [Ryleyev's] heart" even as he "snatched for himself alone the gloomily bright crown of a prophet and unchanging friend." One task of a Masonic brother is to be an accomplice in death—during the rite of initiation, at the actual death whenever possible, and thereafter in memoriam.

The importance of this duty to the Moscow Masons of the Novikov group is shown by a document preserved among their materials, according to which the sworn duty of a brother is to ensure the initiate's immortality. The document presents this as a sacred duty and stresses that immortality must be accomplished without jeopardizing or betraying the secrets of the craft and without revealing the brother's Masonic identity. The command to ensure remembrance of a brother was brought in the form of an instruction to Novikov and Lopukhin by Baron Schroeder from the Berlin lodge Zum den drei Weltkügeln. The instruction, written in German and signed with Schroeder's Masonic name Sacerdotos, warns that "in case of the death of an RC [Rosicrucian], his seal must be returned" and furthermore "every RC must for every moment of his life . . . ensure that not so much as a piece of paper [bearing the deceased brother's Rosicrucian name] fall into unfriendly hands. . . ." This must be done by "the use of secret writing [*mit den geheimen Schriften*]" because otherwise "the repose of the [deceased's] soul will be disturbed" and "great

---

7. Interestingly, a poet who shared Ryleyev's attraction to death and self-sacrifice, the symbolist poet Aleksandr Blok, introduced just these aspects of Freemasonry and the esoteric tradition into his poetry. See Altshuller 1982, 603–5; also Vladimirova et al. 1981.

harm can be done." Care must be taken "to impress this upon every Apprentice [*Junior*]" (Barskov 1915, 227; also Pekarskii 1909, 87).

That is, it is the duty of a Rosicrucian brother to protect the memory of a deceased brother, and to do so without betraying the secrecy of the order. The reference to secret writing signifies the need for knowledge of "Geheimschrift" (*tainopis'*). The need for secrecy is the first value impressed on every newly initiated Apprentice (Junior). Whatever means is used to revere a deceased brother, the brother's Masonic identity must not be betrayed. The provenance of Schroeder's instruction is not known. But it resembles Article 15 of Tschoudy's instructions in *Der flammende Stern*, according to which a member of the Order of the Flaming Star must assume a "Masonic name" so that his identity will not be betrayed in speech or writing, and Article 25, which instructs members how to immortalize the name of a deceased brother by "hieroglyphic signs" or "allegorical words" (1866, 2:160–61, 168–69).

If Ryleyev's writing of *Voynarovsky* and his relationship with Bestuzhev were guided or influenced by his Masonic beliefs, he was as devoutly committed to Freemasonry as to his Decembrist ideals. His use of the Star of Hope metaphor in his dedication to Bestuzhev must then be understood as a carrying of "the signs, the signals, and the words" of Masonic virtues into his poetry. He detected the efficacy of the Masonic way to immortality, and he appreciated the power of the word to transform personal ideals into literature and reincarnate both back into life. Logos is indeed gnosis: the word can be actual, as well as textual, discourse; the word is never so powerful as when it is hidden, indirect, secret. In the writing of *Voynarovsky*, followed by Bestuzhev's telling of the tale to Erman, Ryleyev succeeded in realizing the virtues of friendship and love of death in reality. By telling the story of Voynarovsky, and of himself and Ryleyev, Bestuzhev honored his duty of friend and accomplice in death.

4

Decembrist Repentance: "The Frigate Hope"

> We are called upon to say, this is how it was. Let time extract the good and evil from it.
> —Aleksandr Bestuzhev, "The Frigate Hope"

The role of accomplice in death is a heavy moral burden, and Aleksandr Bestuzhev's burden of conscience became heavier than he might have expected. Kondraty Ryleyev's verse tale *Voynarovsky* foretold a noble tragedy for the two conspirators, but the realization of the prediction, in the failure of the revolt of 14 December 1825 and the consequences of failure, was not fully heroic. Not, at least, for Bestuzhev, who had to face a painful dilemma. Just as Ryleyev turned to poetry to foretell the fate of the Decembrists, Bestuzhev found a way, in a prose tale titled "The Frigate Hope," to retell the story of Decembrist heroism and poetic immortality. His way was to confess—or obfuscate—a less-than-noble personal response to political failure. He carried the metaphor of the Star of Hope further along its path through Russian romantic literature and into a new maze of thaumaturgical puzzles.

Marlinsky and Marlinism

Aleksandr Bestuzhev (1797–1837) used the pseudonym Marlinsky once in the early 1820s to hide his authorship of a critical review; when he was permitted to resume his literary career in 1830, he did so under the same name. The younger Aleksandr Bestuzhev established himself in the early 1820s as a writer of historical prose tales and Byronic society "tales of men and passions," but he was better known as a devastating critic and leader of a widespread campaign for romantic aesthetics, a translator of European criticism, and coeditor with Kondraty Ryleyev of the literary almanac *Polar Star*. He is remembered for his ultraromantic style "marlinism" and as a brilliant conversationalist. He was a polymath: he made himself an authority on language, ethnography, political economics, aesthetics, history, art, philosophy, and the natural sciences. He was one of those rare linguistic chameleons who could speak foreign languages with native or near native fluency. He was admitted to an elite dragoon regiment thanks to his family's distinction and proved to be a brilliant staff officer; and at the time of his arrest in December 1825, he was an adjutant in the Winter Palace. He was a Freemason, and it is telling that whereas Ryleyev chose a lower-class lodge, Bestuzhev was initiated into the elite Russian lodge Michel l'élu.[1]

He was gifted, but his personality was flawed: he has been called a psychological chameleon who adapted himself to changing conditions with breathtaking rapidity. He was an aristocrat in his regiment, a democrat in the editorial office of *Polar Star*, a friend of the aristocrats of the Pushkin Pleiad *and* of their plebeian foes Nikolay Grech and Faddey Bulgarin. He was both rebel and escapist, conspirator and conscientious soldier. He did not simply change his views to suit the occasion—he was able to become what he came to believe. He was not a hypocrite or opportunist: his literary and political views remained consistent, and he was one of the most decisive leaders on Senate Square. But his desires to transform a new ideal into a new reality brought terrible grief to himself and to others.

His success in both his literary and his military careers is amazing. He was a social star, political activist, and, from 1823, a revolutionary conspirator. Bestuzhev astounded his contemporaries with his stylistic versatility—the metaphorical, hyperbolic style known as marlinism. In the 1830s his naval adventures, tales of the supernatural, passionate love stories, and exotic tales of the

---

1. Bakounine (1967, 62) identifies his lodge as Clef de la vertu, which is unlikely, since Clef de la vertu was located in far-off Simbirsk.

Caucasus made him Russia's most popular writer. He created in his poetry of the late 1820s the image of a lonely Siberian exile. When he was transferred to military duty in the Caucasus in the 1830s, he found that he was a hero to young Russian officers. He distinguished himself for bravery in the deadly Caucasian pacification campaigns and managed to win back his officer's epaulettes despite imperial disfavor. His frequent contacts with mountaineers suggest that he might have been a spy in the Caucasus. His reportage on the Caucasian campaigns, published in leading journals and newspapers of the 1830s, was pro-Russian, but he often betrayed sympathy and admiration for local rebels. He did in fact meet and become friends with the mountain bandit Mulla Nur, who became a leading character in his prose tale by that name. He was transferred to the worst hellholes of the region, assigned quarantine duty during cholera outbreaks, sent from battle to battle, subjected to constant surveillance.

By 1837 he was broken. In January of that year Pushkin was killed. The youngest Bestuzhev brother Pyotr, also in the Caucasus, was driven insane by brutal officers at a remote outpost. On the eve of 7 June Bestuzhev wrote his testament and ordered his papers burned. The next day he led a charge against Circassian mountaineers, dashed ahead, and disappeared into heavy gunsmoke. His body was never found. His final act thus became another legend. He was rumored to have used his contacts in the mountains to arrange an apparent death. He was believed to be alive and well and leading a new life as a mountaineer, or to have escaped abroad. Shortly after his death, Alexandre Dumas visited the Caucasus, heard the legends of "Marlinsky," and made him a romantic hero and published author throughout Europe.

"The Frigate Hope"

"The Frigate Hope" (1832, first published 1833) seems to be a straightforward naval adventure tale. Captain-Lieutenant Ilya Pravin commands the finest ship in the Russian fleet, the Hope. Like all Bestuzhev's heroes he is Byronic—possessed of lofty ideals, respected by his sailors, officers, and superiors, known even to Nicholas I for his devotion to duty, ship, and Russian national honor. He is also a dreamer, an idealist who is but a babe in crass Petersburg society: "He knew well the nature of the sea, but where could he have learned the character of men?" (Bestuzhev-Marlinskii 1958, 2:99). Chosen by highest authority to command a politically sensitive voyage, Pravin looks forward, in the year 1829, to a brilliant naval career. At this point, however, Pravin meets and falls in love with Vera, the young wife of an elderly court official. He begins to neglect the Hope and in long letters to his friend aboard the frigate, Lieutenant Nils Pavlovich Kakorin, he pours forth his feelings. For a time he becomes convinced that Vera is a coquette, and he returns to his ship to occupy himself with the difficult technical preparations for the voyage. But he discovers that Vera is serious and reciprocates his feelings. Passion has its way. On the eve of departure Vera boards the Hope. She has contrived, through her court connections, to have the ship put at her husband's disposal for a trip to England.

Again Pravin gives himself up to his affair with Vera, foolishly ignoring Kakorin's pleas to attend to his duty. And when Vera disembarks at Plymouth Harbor he is unable to resist the demands of passion. Even though a storm is rising, he abandons the Hope for a final rendezvous. The next morning the lovers are discovered by Vera's husband, and Pravin realizes he has compromised the woman he loves. Worse, at this moment the captain learns that his ship has been struck by the storm. Torn between his commitment to Vera and his duty to the Hope, he is unable to act: too late does he leave Vera and return to his ship. Injured in the attempt to do so, and tormented by the knowledge that his neglect has caused the deaths of his men and damage to the ship, he dies knowing he has failed both love and duty. His last act is to write a confession to the tsar in which he assumes full blame for his dishonorable behavior.

"The Frigate Hope" is a long tale, filled with witticisms and elaborated by subplots and digressions. It is structured on three levels for three different audiences: a conventional romantic adventure story aimed at the general public; an allegory of Bestuzhev's role in the Decembrist affair intended for more politically sophisticated readers; and a hidden text devised for those readers who could be expected to have special knowledge of the Decembrist conspiracy and could therefore be guided by allusions, including leads to external texts needed to decode the primary text. An analysis of this third level, which is shaped by calendarology, numerology, and cabalistics, reveals how the troubled mind of one Decembrist writer worked to use his fiction for extraliterary purposes—to express and perhaps exorcise deep feelings of guilt and justify his actions to posterity.

A Decembrist Allegory

The allegorical meaning of "The Frigate Hope" in relation to the author's biography is as readily apparent as Ryleyev's allegory of his and Bestuzhev's fates in *Voynarovsky*. Its meaning could hardly have been obscure to politically aware readers, who would have known that the sensational new author Marlinsky was the notorious Decembrist Aleksandr Bestuzhev. Pravin (root *prav-*, "right, true, correct") is a correct young man; Vera (root *ver-*) is faith, trust, belief; the Hope (*Nadezhda*) is hope and also in Russian something reliable, trustworthy (*nadezhnyi*). Here the conventional play between the words *hope* and *faith* becomes a full-fledged plot device. A young military officer, carried away by his passionate faith in an ideal, abandons his duty to tsar and country. Caught out in dishonorable behavior and struck by a storm at a crucial moment, he is unable to reconcile ideal and reality. In the end, all he can do is confess his guilt and accept blame.

A conventional romantic tale of love is thus raised to the level of social and political import. The allegory reads as an exposition of a Decembrist dilemma. Bestuzhev was not a Ryleyev or a Pestel; he was one of the Decembrists who were unable to reconcile the contradictions between their political ideals and their allegiance to a powerful state. Recall Doctor Erman's observation that Bestuzhev was morally shattered by Nicholas's victory on Senate Square. Doubt is one reason why so many of the conspirators were unable to act on the day of the revolt; it is why so many behaved badly under arrest and interrogation.

Bestuzhev was troubled not only by the contradiction between the ideals that made him a Decembrist and his duty as a military officer, but by his doubts about the plans of the impetuous Ryleyev. On its second level "The Frigate Hope" is the confession of a Decembrist who despite his convictions was unable to mend his torn loyalties. The fate of the hero Pravin parallels his own ambiguous role as a political conspirator—a role that as Ryleyev realized when he created the character of Voynarovsky, was not dissociable from doubt. Although Bestuzhev was typically treated in scholarship as a dedicated revolutionary (Ovsiannikova 1954), he participated with misgivings in the Northern Society and resisted Ryleyev's attempts to make him a more radical conspirator. His testimony before the Investigatory Commission, often self-serving, shows that he soon became "convinced of the lunacy of the adventure" and sometimes moderated Ryleyev's plans (Pokrovskii et al. 1925– , 1:433, 531, 444, 471–72). Like Pravin, he underwent a period of doubt. At the crucial moment—the implementation of the hastily contrived plan of revolt—he honored his commitment to his comrades. He was a decisive leader on 14 December—he led the key Moscow Regiment onto Senate Square and held it there until the tsar's cannons dispersed the rebels. But he acted without the convictions of a Ryleyev. And when the revolt failed he surrendered voluntarily and cooperated with the Investigatory Commission.[2]

As Ovsiannikova has shown, Bestuzhev successfully withheld information harmful to his brothers Nikolay and Mikhail and others (1954, 406–7), but even a cursory reading of his testimony shows that he was an amazingly cooperative witness. Bestuzhev did not surrender his ideals, but like the hero of "The Frigate Hope" he believed that his failure to reconcile commitment with duty brought tragic consequences to his country and friends. And like Pravin, caught in a situation that left no room for honor, he chose confession as the only way to recompense others for the consequences of his—and Ryleyev's—actions.

A Decembrist Confession

"Bestuzhev was completely frank in his testimonies," the Investigatory Commission concluded in its final summation, "he was the first to reveal the plans for regicide and the extermination of the imperial family" (Pokrovskii et al. 1925– , 1:473). When asked what persuaded him to join the secret society, Bestuzhev replied: "In joining the society, out of youthful delusion and my impetuous imagination, I thought thereby to be of use to my fatherland at a later date.... The lure of novelty and mystery played an equal part in this, and little by little seduced me into criminal ideas." Elaborating on this point, he stated: "From the age of nineteen I had begun reading liberal books, and this turned my head. For that matter, not possessing any positive conceptions of my own, I shouted into the wind, like all young men, without any purpose whatever. In 1822 ... I made friends with Ryleyev ... and we dreamed together, and with his fervid imagination he seduced me even further" (Pokrovskii et al. 1925– , 1:431, 433).

In placing blame on Ryleyev, Bestuzhev stated a fact. Recall his statement

---

2. A confidential letter written to the tsar following Bestuzhev's arrest is considered one of the most eloquent Decembrist statements about the social, political, and historical causes of the movement (Riha 1964, 2:298–300).

that Ryleyev was "the chief instigator" of the December uprising by "enflaming [his comrades] with his poetic imagination and fortifying them with his persistence" (Pokrovskii et al. 1925– , 1:444). Ryleyev, Bestuzhev said, recruited him into the Northern Society in 1824 (it has since been proved that the recruitment occurred in 1823; Ovsiannikova 1954, 412–13). Ryleyev influenced him to join the Northern Society's ruling Duma and attend meetings he might otherwise have avoided. Ryleyev used his friend's higher social standing to recruit new members (Pokrovskii et al. 1925– , 1:471–72). Ryleyev drew him into the most extreme activities—his conspiracy within a conspiracy to turn the Northerners to the Southern Society's plans to assassinate the tsar and establish a republic. It was through his offices that Ryleyev recruited the assassins Yakubovich and Kakhovskoy. He supported the plans to assassinate Alexander I and exterminate the imperial family or expel them from Russia. In true conspiratorial style, these aims of the "Ryleyev branch" of the Northern Society were kept secret from the majority of Northerners (see Lebedev 1954; Zakharov 1954). When Alexander I suddenly died, Bestuzhev helped Ryleyev persuade the reluctant Northerners to take advantage of the interregnum and carry out the revolt. All of this, Bestuzhev insisted, he had done without conviction that his cause was just:

> When I went after the Moscow Regiment I first prayed to God with hot tears—"If our cause is just, help us . . . if not, let Thy will be done." I now know His will—but the hand of God and the wrath of my Tsar bear heavily upon me. . . . I feel now that I have abused my talents, but that by my saber or pen I could still bring honor to my fatherland—to live usefully and die honorably for my Sovereign! (Pokrovskii et al. 1925– , 1:437)

The statement is self-serving—not the least reward for Bestuzhev's confession being that he was permitted to serve his tsar in the Caucasian campaigns and resume an active literary career. He truly was a psychological chameleon. Within hours after abandoning Senate Square he reported in full-dress uniform to the Winter Palace, where he apologized to Nicholas I for his "criminal" behavior (Syroechkovskii 1924, 228).[3]

3. In the 1860s the historian M. I. Semevsky won the confidence of the Bestuzhev family and in the next two decades published the letters, diaries, stenograms, and memoirs that have since been organized as the Bestuzhev family archives (Azadovskii 1951). In discussing a letter from Bestuzhev to his brothers in which he joked about his inability to say no, Semevsky notes: "It is very possible that in this jest A. Bestuzhev alludes to his loquacity during the investigation." Where Nikolay and Mikhail Bestuzhev were convinced they would be executed and therefore refused to cooperate with the Investigatory Commission, "Aleksandr, because of his lively and ardent temperament, went into detailed

Nevertheless, to assume that Bestuzhev confessed for gain or for fear is to simplify a complex moral dilemma. Imagine, for example, the dismay of his fellow Northerners, including his own brothers, when they learned their society had been subverted, without their knowledge, to plans for regicide. This was Bestuzhev's dilemma: if he remained loyal to Ryleyev, he could not exonerate his innocent comrades, he had either to sacrifice Ryleyev or doom the others. In this sense, by placing the blame on Ryleyev, Bestuzhev was playing his role of accomplice. When actually faced with death, Ryleyev defended himself—he denied knowledge of the assassination plans to the end, even in face-to-face confrontations with Bestuzhev and the two chosen assassins Yakubovich and Kakhovskoy (Pokrovskii et al. 1925–   , 1:437; also see Bestuzhev's testimonies nos. 8, 10, 11, 12, 15, 16, and Ryleyev's testimony, 1:194). But as the prescience of *Voynarovsky* indicates, Ryleyev knew in advance what his fate would be. It is not unreasonable to consider that when Ryleyev undertook such extreme measures as planning the assassination of the tsar he was fully capable of arranging to take the blame for his conspiracy within a conspiracy. All the more so when his belief in the virtue of self-sacrifice—the death wish that was a part of his psychological makeup—is also accounted for.

Whatever the case, regardless of Ryleyev's tacit or explicit consent, it is clear that Bestuzhev sent his best friend to the gallows, and he did so with the painful knowledge that he was ultimately responsible for his own actions. He did, after all, support Ryleyev's plans. All that can be said in his favor, therefore, is that having failed in an affair about which he had had much doubt, he was left with the knowledge that he and Ryleyev had compromised others. By blaming Ryleyev he succeeded in dissociating others from the extreme aspects of the conspiracy. He repeats throughout his testimony that his brothers and their fellow naval officer Konstantin Torson were ignorant of Ryleyev's assassination plans and rejected his plans to carry the imperial family abroad. Like Pravin, Bestuzhev lost his judgment and involved himself beyond hope. And like Pravin, he repented his behavior and attempted to ameliorate the consequences of his actions. When Kakorin suggests to the dying Pravin that "everything depends on the way we represent the affair to the authorities," the hero protests:

> "Do you really think, my friend, that I will stand for lying to excuse myself? In no way, never! Tomorrow I am going to make a report of this unhappy

---

explanations of the aims of the secret society and his part in it. His frankness was the reason his lot was eased: instead of penal servitude he was exiled to a settlement" (Semevskii 1870b, 245).

incident to the Emperor and the Admiralty—and everything as it was, without any concealment. You have forgiven me—it may even happen that the authorities will punish me less severely. But can I ever forgive myself—appease my own conscience for the death of men!" (1958, 2:162)

Unhappily, Bestuzhev did not enjoy the moral luxury of blaming only himself. In this respect the allegorical level of "The Frigate Hope" is dishonest: as the writer Marlinsky he represented the Decembrist affair in an allegory advantageous to himself even though the real Aleksandr Bestuzhev was neither as heroic nor as virtuous as his surrogate hero. He did not, that is, represent the full truth about himself to either the authorities or his readers.

Storms and Rebellions, Hints and Allusions

Bestuzhev's Decembrist confession is conveyed not only in these broad allegorical parallels, but on the tale's third level, in its system of covert motifs and encoded allusions. Meaning is harder to detect on this level. Some of this meaning is generally symbolic. In Orthodox hagiography, for example, Faith, Hope, and Love (the love story)—Vera, Nadezhda, and Lyubov—are saints martyred for their devotion to Truth (*pravda*, Pravin). It might be relevant here that the three saints are the daughters of St. Sophia (Wisdom), and Vera confides her love for Pravin in letters to her friend Sophie. In both naval and Masonic naval symbolism faith is often represented by an anchor, hope by a star. The Masonic encyclopedist A. E. Waite explicates a symbolism in accordance with which the virtues Faith, Hope, and Charity are subsumed under the ultimate virtue of Love (1970, 270). In an analysis of number symbolism in *The Divine Comedy*, Vincent Hopper explicates an esoteric system in which the triad of Faith, Hope, and Love is considered the true way to salvation (1938, 159). According to a study of Masonic symbolism by a believer in magic, "he who enters the Society finds the 'Lost Word,' but he must have first created in himself *Faith*, based on his own labor, and then *Love*, which will open for him the door to *Hope* of *Immortality*" (Papius 1911, 33–34). Although Bestuzhev was not a serious Freemason, he would have been aware of these and similar symbolic meanings from his work in the lodge Michel l'élu; certainly his brothers Nikolay and Mikhail, naval officers and Freemasons, could have made him aware of these symbols. More to the point, in his reworking of the triad Faith, Hope, and Love, Bestuzhev responded to Ryleyev's use of

Masonic symbols in his poetry. Recall, for example, from Ryleyev's poem "Signal-Star," "There with Hope abides / Faith, Friendship and Love."

The text of "The Frigate Hope" is saturated with plays on *hope, faith,* and related signal-words. The tale begins with a letter dated 1 July 1829 in which Vera describes the Peterhof Festival, the annual celebration at which the tsar customarily inspected the Russian fleet in the Gulf of Finland. In this letter to Sophie she describes Nicholas as "the hope and glory of Russia" (*nadezhda, slava;* 1958, 2:67). She emphasizes the word again by noting that "this word [hope] is worthy of preeminence" (2:68). Both the frigate Hope and the love affair are beset by unfavorable winds during the voyage to England (2:142). Pravin ceases to believe in hope ("*ne VERit nadezhde*"; 2:147) when he is unable to resolve his dilemma, and the seagulls abandon the Hope before the storm, thus presaging its unhappy fate (2:147). Bestuzhev observes in one of the tale's many philosophical digressions that a man who cannot reconcile divided loyalties is vulnerable to a fatal "belief [*VERa*] in evil" (2:147). Pravin regrets that he has not extracted an oath of loyalty (*VERnost'*) from Vera (2:148), and in another instance Kakorin reminds him that the Hope has been "entrusted" to him (*vVERennyi;* 2:150). On his deathbed Pravin calls himself a criminal because he "toyed with the tsar's trust" (*doVERennost'*), and he has no doubt that a jury would find him guilty (2:162, 155). This allusion to trust and punishment is developed into a motif when Kakorin observes: "God help the man who comes afoul of military judgment. . . . True, the Emperor knows Pravin personally . . . but he has no use for joking or partiality when it comes to duty" (2:161).

Other allusions have to do with storms threatening the Hope, and these are also developed into a motif. In keeping with romantic aesthetics, storms are often likened to rebellious will (*volia*). "Storm?" the hero declaims at one point, "What storm? What signifies this storm in comparison with all the rebellion in my breast?" (1958, 2:85). In one instance it is said that a belief in evil arises "involuntarily" (*neVOL'no;* 2:147), and the chapter in which Pravin abandons the Hope is structured on similes between the rising storm and the hero's growing willfulness. The chapter is even fitted with an epigraph from Juvenal: "Sic volo—sic jubeo—sta pro ratione voluntas!"[4] The fatal storm is anticipated earlier in the tale by a storm in which Pravin, before he has fallen under Vera's influence, acts quite differently, more decisively. Although the captain is ashore on leave, he unexpectedly boards the frigate, calmly explaining to his surprised and relieved officers: "I anticipated a storm and wished to share the danger

---

4. "As I want, as I command—let my will be its own reason!"

with you. I can provide you with new information about the weather because I have just been out there where your eyes cannot see in the night. A squall is even at this moment bearing down on us" (2:82–83). When the squall strikes, the ship is tossed and torn, but brought expertly to safety by her intrepid captain, who inspires his men with his calm decisiveness. When the Hope is threatened further by waterspouts, Kakorin asks, "Will you give the order, Captain, to treat these uninvited guests to a bit of cannon fire?" To this Pravin replies with an order to make two cannons ready, but not to fire, because "I do not wish to raise an alarm at Kronstadt" (2:84).

In terms of the tale as a Decembrist confession, these allusions to storms and rebellion ought to refer to the author's role on Senate Square. Instead, they are reminiscent of the decisive actions of Nicholas I. Nicholas had advance warning of the revolt, and he appeared unexpectedly on Senate Square to take personal command. He impressed witnesses with his decisive leadership and his reluctance to resort to force. Only at the close of the day did he order the cannons to open fire, and he rescinded the order several times. One of the reasons for his reluctance was his fear of raising an alarm at Kronstadt, the naval island-fortress in the Gulf of Finland where, he had been informed, a contingent of rebels was ready (Nechkina 1955, 2:107).

Nicholas is linked to the allegory of the frigate Hope in curious ways. The links are governed by the thaumaturgical practice known as calendarology, a skill that combines numerology with astrology. Calendarological systems can be based on standard calendars of various styles, on chronological records such as court or military calendars, or on personal diaries. Symbols are provided not only by the Zodiac, but by church calendars (Roman Catholic or Orthodox) and by the Jewish calendar (used by Freemasons and other orders). These thaumaturgical systems—known generically as "books of days"—are intricate, and rich with symbolism as well (Chambers 1967; for extensive materials on Russian calendars, see Rovinskii 1881–93).

In a study of "The Frigate Hope" V. G. Bazanov traces several of the tale's allusions he considers essential to his interpretation of it as an indictment of the "corrupt" regime of Nicholas I. Although the tale ends with the death of Pravin, Bestuzhev added an epilogue, which begins with an excerpt from the political newspaper *The Northern Bee,* dated August 1831:

> Kronstadt ... August. Yesterday the frigate Hope, under the command of Fleet Captain-Lieutenant Kakorin, arrived at the local yard from the Mediterranean. The beauty of the ship, the excellent order prevailing on

board, the healthy and vigorous appearance of the passengers attracted the attention of the authorities and all visitors to the ship. (1958, 2:166)

There are several such dated items in the tale. One item occurs at a crucial point in the plot, when Pravin and Vera seal their fate by deciding to sail to England together. Their decision "took place on 17 August 1829 at exactly one hour past noon. So at least it was noted with red pencil in Pravin's diary" (2:133). Taking this hint and its juxtaposition with the fictional notice about the return of the frigate Hope, Bazanov found an actual notice in *The Northern Bee* for 5 August 1831 (no. 174)—the same date on the Russian calendar (Old Style) as 17 August on the Western calendar (New Style), one year before "The Frigate Hope" was written: "The passenger ship Nicholas I is being held under quarantine at Drotningsgor near Karlskrona. All passengers aboard are in good health" (1953, 404). As Bazanov has shown, Bestuzhev was at this time a regular contributor to the newspaper, and once offered to sell "The Frigate Hope" to its publisher F. V. Bulgarin. A cholera epidemic (itself a politically sensitive topic subject to censorship control) was at its peak in 1831, and Bulgarin's newspaper regularly reported on the slow progress of the Nicholas I owing to quarantines between Lübeck and Petersburg (1953, 404–5).

Mysterious Voyage, Decembrist Hope

Bazanov's discovery shows that in allegorical terms the frigate Hope is Nicholas I. It also opens the way to the tale's hidden text and shows that the keys to this level are to be found in external texts pointed out by calendarological devices. For some reason, Bazanov did not pursue his discovery. Additional examination of the issue of *The Northern Bee* for 5 August 1831 shows that the report on the Nicholas I is followed immediately by a political report:

> Word has been received from Lisbon as of 13/1 July: "Until now complete silence has been maintained in our newspaper about what has been taking place here. This evening an addendum appeared in one newspaper in which is announced the cessation of military operations and the opening of communications between the city and a French squadron. At the same

time it is being trumpeted about that all points of contention between Portugal and France will shortly be resolved satisfactorily. On the 10th an English frigate entered the port of Belem. Perfect order now reigns in both city and port."

In the fictive report, order prevails on board the Hope when it returns to Kronstadt, and the passengers are in good health. Order prevails aboard the real Nicholas I despite the panic of the cholera epidemic. In the report from Lisbon perfect order reigns following a period of isolation.[5] These references to health, quarantine, and order might be called, in keeping with the ultraromantic aesthetics of marlinism, the Mysterious Voyage. Bestuzhev terms his tale's allusions puzzling when he has Pravin confide to Kakorin that "the puzzle as to why we alone have been left in the yard at Kronstadt, has now been explained. We are to deliver important papers to the Allied Admiral and the President [sic] of Greece" (1958, 2:85). What the voyage entails is not specified, but the reference to Greece has to do with the maintenance of order in the Mediterranean at the conclusion of the Greek Revolution and following the Battle of Navarino in October 1827. The uprisings in Spain, Italy, and Greece that excited the Decembrists in 1820 apparently still exerted their effect on Russians when Marlinsky wrote his tale in the early 1830s. Russians were also affected by revolutions in France and Poland in 1830.

Among other allusions in the tale is the quotation "pro teterrima causa omnis belli" (2:100), for the secret cause of all war does indeed figure into the motif of the Mysterious Voyage. The Peterhof Festival of 1829, at the start of the tale, was a celebration of the fact that the Allied Fleet of England, France, and Russia had recently destroyed the Turkish-Egyptian fleet at Navarino and thereby brought the Russo-Turkish War of 1828–29 to a victorious conclusion. War and rebellion are also hinted at by a third date marked in the tale, the date of the Hope's departure on its fatal voyage: "Exactly ten days after the date marked in red letters a wondrously beautiful frigate lifted anchor and set out into the open sea from the south anchorage at Kronstadt" (2:133–34). The date marked in Pravin's diary is 17 August 1829, "at exactly one hour past noon"; the date of the departure is therefore 27 August 1829 Old Style. On 27 August 1831, one year before the writing of "The Frigate Hope," the Polish Rebellion of 1830–31 ended when Russian troops took Warsaw. In the tale's

---

5. The report refers to order restored by combined French and English naval forces following a rebellion in 1831 in which Emperor Pedro of Brazil sought to depose Miguel of Portugal by supporting Portuguese Constitutionalists.

epilogue two characters, a diplomat and a young man, who turns out to be Pravin's younger brother, remark the beauty of a Polish and a Russian woman. The Russian beauty turns out to be the new wife of Vera's recently widowed husband. In response to the young man's admiration of the Russian woman, whom he first takes to be Vera, the diplomat chides: "Could it be, *mon cher,* that a bit of romantic smoke got in your eyes during the storming of Warsaw?" (2:169).

The Mysterious Voyage might involve more than these allusions to rebellions. Bazanov argues that they refer to a specific Decembrist event, namely the case of the Bestuzhev brothers' close friend Fleet Captain-Lieutenant Konstantin Petrovich Torson (1953, 404). Mikhail Bestuzhev recounted the Torson case twice in his memoirs. In the winter of 1823–24 Torson was assigned a project for the improvement of the Russian fleet and given command of the ship Emgeiten to be heavily armed as a test of Russian sea power. He and Mikhail Bestuzhev worked night and day on the difficult preparations of the ship, spending "millions of rubles" to perfect an idea they believed was essential to the defense of Russia. Then, just before the ship was to be inspected by Alexander I, "Torson suddenly received notice from the Minister that the ship had been assigned for a voyage by Grand Duke Nicholas Pavlovich and his wife to Prussia." Torson was obliged to stand by while his expensive armor was scrapped, the ship turned into a pleasure craft, and another officer given credit for "the beauty of the ship." When Torson threatened to complain to Alexander about this irresponsible action, he was pacified by being given authority to outfit two other ships for a voyage around the world, including a mission to the Mediterranean (Azadovskii 1951, 272–74, 299).

In Bazanov's view, the parallel between the Hope and the Emgeiten, combined with the allusions to health, quarantine, and the beauty of the ship, justifies an interpretation of "The Frigate Hope" as an allegory of "sick" Russia under tsarist rule. He points to other cases of arbitrary use of military ships for pleasure voyages and to Pravin's bitter criticisms of the Admiralty for failing to provide proper support during the difficult preparations for the voyage of the Hope (1953, 405). But while the tale does criticize the authorities, problems are at least partly resolved when Pravin threatens to complain to Nicholas I (1958, 2:109). Moreover, as Kanunova has pointed out in a refutation of Bazanov's interpretation, the Hope and Nicholas are the positive side of the allegorical equation, and it is Pravin, under Vera's influence, who allows the voyage of the Hope to be turned into a pleasure trip (1973, 141). Her argument is supported by the condition that far from being an attack on the tsarist system, the tale is filled with praise of Nicholas. Kakorin admires the tsar's impartial emphasis on duty; Vera calls him "the hope and glory" of Russia. "I hope you have heard," Vera enthuses, "that the Emperor loves the fleet. He has revived it, he has breathed Russian power into it and given it pure laurels at Navarino" (1958, 2:66).

Also relevant to a decoding of the hidden text is evidence regarding Torson's relations with the Bestuzhev family. Torson was like a brother to the Bestuzhevs: he participated with Mikhail and the older brother Nikolay in the preparation of Decembrist plans at Kronstadt and shared Siberian exile with them.[6] Mikhail was devoted to Torson in much the same way as Kakorin is to Pravin. This and the bitterness of both men over the Emgeiten incident had important consequences for their friendship. In one memoir Mikhail noted: "'It is time to put an end to all this,' [Torson] used to say . . . and finally . . . he revealed to me the existence of a secret society which aimed *to put an end to all this,* and initiated me as a member" (Azadovskii 1951, 274).

The Torson case provides other connections that help to finally explain the meaning of the Mysterious Voyage. Torson was the contact at Kronstadt for the Northern Society. By 1825 he and Nikolay Bestuzhev had organized elements of the Naval Guard Equipage to take part in the attempt to overthrow the autocracy. One of Ryleyev's plans called for the revolt to begin at Kronstadt, and it was Nicholas's fear of arousing just these elements, commanded by Torson and the Bestuzhev brothers, that made him reluctant to use cannons on Senate Square (Nechkina 1955, 2:107). Ironically, Nicholas did not know that Torson and the naval Bestuzhevs had rejected Ryleyev's plans on the sensible grounds that a revolt could be isolated on an island; neither did Nicholas know that elements of the Naval Guard Equipage were on Senate Square, not at Kronstadt. Ryleyev also hoped that Torson would perform an even more important task for the Northern Society. In June 1825 he proposed that Torson take command of a "reliable [*nadezhnyi*] frigate" to take the imperial family abroad after a coup. Returning to this idea later, he asked Torson, "Is it possible to have a frigate [ready at Kronstadt] with a reliable [*nadezhnyi*] captain and officers?" (Pokrovskii et al. 1925– , 1:182–83; Nechkina 1951, 171, 182).

Here, in the title of Bestuzhev's tale, is an explanation of the motif of the Mysterious Voyage—the health of the passengers and quarantines, the good order prevailing on board the Hope and the Nicholas I and in the Mediterranean, and the use of a military ship for pleasure cruises. The links are between the frigate Hope and Nicholas, the "reliable frigate" and the Nicholas I. These

---

6. In a letter to Torson's wife in 1832 Bestuzhev sent "cordial greetings to all three of my brothers [in Siberia], for I consider Konstantin in no other wise" (Semevskii 1870a, 520).

links form a complex of connections ratified by the dating of events, which in their turn correspond to actual rebellions, voyages, and quarantines. The connections are structural, as well as semantic-stylistic, for Bestuzhev has reversed the equation between hope (*nadezhda*) and trust (*vera*) established by Ryleyev in his dedication to *Voynarovsky* and used this semantic reversal to construct a tale based on hope as the antithesis of trust. In "The Frigate Hope" the heroine Vera—faith, belief—turns out to be the unreliable side of the equation and the Hope proves to be reliable (*nadezhnyi*).

Calendarology and Conspiracy

On its third level "The Frigate Hope" becomes even more complex, for it reveals Bestuzhev's troubled memories of some of the most radical aspects of the Decembrist conspiracy. The keys to the code are again calendarological. As has been seen, the date 17 August 1831 leads to the issue of *The Northern Bee* for 5 August 1831 by converting from the New Style to the Old Style calendar (that is, by subtracting twelve days). The date of the real report from Lisbon provides another key—13/1 July. Bestuzhev was used to this calendarological practice—the substitution of one calendar style to signal the date of another. In a letter of 16 June 1828 from Yakutsk to Nikolay and Mikhail at Chita, he made this suggestion: "Prièz [*sic*] madame *** au moins qu'elle écrive la date comme ça: 18 VII/1 28 quand vous portez bien, et *ordinairement* quand vous sérez [*sic*] malade, en replacant le numéro de moins pour M et en hout [*sic*] pour N" (Semevskii 1870b, 234; emphasis in the original).[7] The text of the letter as printed does not explain why the suggestion contains so many errors. (Was Bestuzhev careless? Are these misprints? Are they part of the code?) It has not been possible to determine what is meant by "madame ***," although it might be assumed that she was a woman in charge of the mail. It is not clear why the word *ordinairement* is emphasized. Although the letter was dated 16 June, Bestuzhev chose the date 1 July for his illustration. His suggestion refers to health. He meant political health: his brothers should use an encoded date to warn him if they are in political danger. In the same letter he used another allusion common to political danger: ". . . but the real hospitality

---

7. Thus, in curiously written French: "Request that madame *** at least write the date this way: 18 VII/1 if you are well and *ordinarily* if you are ill, placing the number in small for M[ikhail] and in large for N[ikolay]."

is frigid in this land of 40 degrees frost, it is not just for show [il n'y a que l'étalage]."[8] Such allusions based on health and weather appear throughout the correspondence and memoirs of the Decembrists (and not only the Decembrists). In a letter to his brothers dated 16 August 1828 Bestuzhev used an allusion to quarantine as a reference to the problem of communicating under the watchful eye of the government. Referring to difficulties of correspondence, he noted that "I am now firmly convinced (that is, formally notified) that all letters to Chita pass through the Petersburg quarantine" (Semevskii 1870b, 238).

The date 13/1 of the report from Lisbon, which uses the device of indicating both Old and New Styles, suggests two referents in the text of "The Frigate Hope." The first of these—1 July—is important because I. A. Yakubovich proposed to assassinate Alexander I at the Peterhof Festival on 1 July 1825. He made this proposal to Ryleyev and Bestuzhev, and when he did, they persuaded him to postpone his plan and place his services at their disposal (Nechkina 1955, 2:108). The text of "The Frigate Hope" contains two hints that might refer to Yakubovich's assassination plan. The tale begins at the Peterhof Festival on 1 July, and Vera immediately characterizes Pravin with a quote from Shakespeare: "Nature might stand up / And say to all the world 'This was a man!'" (1958, 2:68). That is, Pravin is likened to Brutus as the only murderer of Julius Caesar motivated by the welfare of Rome rather than personal ambition. Bestuzhev believed that his and Ryleyev's motives were pure, and they distrusted many of their fellow conspirators. Recall Doctor Erman's report that the two Decembrists "hoped to get the better subsequently of their associates who were strongly suspected of selfish ambition" (1850, 1:293). It is possibly relevant, too, that a masked ball was one of the main events of the Peterhof Festival, and Vera describes it in detail, mentioning that it took place at Marly Pavilion (whence the author's pen name). Yakubovich counted on a mask to make his escape after killing Alexander. More generally, other Decembrist plans called for them to gain access to the tsar by wearing the uniforms of common soldiers and representing themselves as a change of guard (Nechkina 1955, 2:112). A variant of the plan of 14 December 1825 called for Bestuzhev to wear the uniform of a Polish officer and represent himself to the soldiers as an emissary sent from Warsaw to rescue Grand Duke Constantine, rumored to be held in Peter-and-Paul Fortress by the "usurper Nicholas." In a privately delivered letter dated 14 December 1828 Bestuzhev recalled the fatal day three years

---

8. Reference is apparently to possible discovery of letters sent back and forth through a friendly courier between Bestuzhev in Yakutsk and his brothers sentenced to hard labor at Chita.

before and added: "On New Year's I will attend a masquerade dressed as a Pole" (Semevskii 1870b, 246, 248).

The second date—13 July—obsessed many Russians after the Decembrist affair. It is the date in 1826 when Ryleyev and the other four Decembrist leaders were hanged. Bestuzhev had particular reason to be obsessed with the date, of course, and lest there be any doubt that he remained mercifully ignorant of how fatal his testimony had been, he somehow obtained a copy of a secret report of the Investigatory Commission in which his testimony figures prominently. The report was found among Bestuzhev's effects after his death in 1837. He had ordered it burned, and it was in fact partly burned, but the intact pages (9–32 plus eight unidentifiable pages), which are in the Bestuzhev family archives, show that the Commission praised him for his cooperation and recommended that his testimony be used to determine the sentence of Ryleyev. One finding after another throughout the report is substantiated by a reference to Bestuzhev's testimony.[9] His shock when he read the report can be easily imagined. He had to bear the blame for Ryleyev's death and the knowledge that he had been rewarded for his cooperation. Now he learned that his behavior would someday become known to posterity.

One last date appears in the text of "The Frigate Hope." Immediately after the fictional notice about the arrival of the Hope, Bestuzhev describes the opening night of the new Alexandrine Theater in Petersburg, noting correctly that the theater opened on 31 August 1831 (1958, 2:166). The description matches a report of the opening in *The Northern Bee* for 3 September 1831. The text of "The Frigate Hope" does not seem to yield evidence of a systematically encoded calendar corresponding to actual political events such as the Decembrists' assassination plans.[10] Instead, Bestuzhev hints at some of the dates, emphasizes the date of the Peterhof Festival plan in which he was personally involved, and points to external texts featuring two other fatidic dates that

---

9. The document, titled "Fragment from an Investigatory Report on the Decembrists" (Institute of Russian Literature, Fond 604, edinitsa No. 8 [5557], 11. 70–85, "Otryvok iz sledstvennogo dela o dekabristakh"), is a similar but not identical secret version of two published (but specially distributed) reports (which also differ from each other in some essentials), one subtitled "Attached to the Supreme Criminal Trial of the State Criminals" (*Donesenie* 1826a), the other "By Highest Authority" (*Donesenie* 1826b).

10. The tale begins on 1 July 1829 and ends on the night of the opening of the Alexandrine Theater, 31 August 1831. Pravin resolves to take Vera on the voyage of the Hope "on 17 August at exactly one hour past noon" and marks the date and time in his diary in red pencil. The Hope leaves Kronstadt ten days later, on 27 August 1829, and returns to its home port shortly before the date of the arrival of the Nicholas I reported in *The Northern Bee*, 17 August 1831.

were very much on his mind, 14 December 1825 and 13 July 1826.[11] To this he adds the semantically significant allusions to Brutus, masked balls, quarantines, and so forth—all of this in close connection with the allusions to storms and rebellion that constitute the motif of the Mysterious Voyage. What seems to be important to him is not the assassination plans per se, but the painful fact that he was the first to reveal them to the Investigatory Commission and thereby doom Ryleyev. The tale thus becomes not a reconstruction of a reality—the Decembrist conspiracy—but a confession of personal culpability.

Troubled Conscience, Moral Ambiguity

"Thus everything is relative in this world," Bestuzhev remarks in an authorial aside in "The Frigate Hope." "Lightning is something to be wished for when it reveals the lost path. But terrible is the dawn when it reveals the scaffold to the condemned. The former shines like a lamp at a revelry; the latter is to the criminal like the blade of an axe" (1958, 2:141). And at the end of the epilogue he replays this motif: "But does there exist in this world even one thing, to say nothing of one word, one thought, in which evil has not been mixed with good? The bee suckles honey from the Deadly Nightshade, while man brews poison from it. Wine invigorates the body of a sober man and kills the very soul of a drunkard. Tacitus, that teacher of charity, was to blame for the *noeud* [strangulation knot] in the terrors of revolution" (2:170–71). The ultimate meaning of "The Frigate Hope" is that it contains its author's hidden confession of his feelings of guilt and reveals a terrible moral ambiguity. Many of Bestuzhev's thoughts and feelings are evident on the tale's second, allegorical

---

11. The date 31 August might be a further hint at the Decembrists' assassination plans in that on 12 September 1824—twelve days after 31 August—the Decembrists of the Southern Society planned either to seize Alexander I or assassinate him during a scheduled inspection of the Russian army at Bobruisk (Nechkina 1955, 2:21–22). This was the first of several assassination plots not carried out by the Decembrists. The others were planned for early May 1825 during Alexander's inspection of the Third Infantry Corps, First Army, at Belaya Tserkov; at Peterhof on either of the two dates of the Festival, 1 July or 22 July 1825; again at Belaya Tserkov in early May 1826; and, with the new tsar as target, on Senate Square, 14 December 1825 (Nechkina 1955, 2:112–13, 126–31). Regarding the so-called Belotserkov Plans, the conspirators had to be able to predict the tsar's whereabouts, and they chose the inspection at Belaya Tserkov because it was a scheduled annual custom (Nechkina 1947, 442; Schilder 1904–5, 4:336, 344, 349). The formula for this timing became "on the first night after the arrival of His Highness at the pavilion of the Alexandrine Park in early May" (Sablin 1906, 27).

level; a system of definite links and suggestive associations is revealed by referents to external texts that supply keys to the text on its third level. The tale is thereby more than a simple allegory; it is an encoded confession of a man caught in a moral cul-de-sac. Under the influence of a powerful friend, he participated in a conspiracy against the state he had sworn to protect; in his attempt to make amends for his behavior, he sacrificed the same friend. To the end of his life he could not avoid a terrible double burden of guilt, nor could he lessen the pain of his ambiguous dilemma. "We are called upon to say," he declares in the final words of his epilogue, ". . . *this is how it was. Let time extract the good and evil from it. A resident by the shore of the sea is horrified in the evening at the sight of a shipwreck, but on the morn gathers the remains from the wreckage, builds a frail craft, fastens it together with the bones of his brothers, and singing a carefree tune, sets forth into a stormy sea*" (2:171; emphasis in the original). There was no way for Bestuzhev to justify his actions as a revolutionary; there was no way he could alter the consequences of his actions or exorcise his guilt over Ryleyev. All he could say to posterity was, "*This is how it was. Let time extract the good and evil from it.*"

5

Decembrist Fate: Pushkin and Bestuzhev

And the stars' sparks of hope
Do not burn in the gloomy sky.
—Alexander Bestuzhev, "Dream"

In the years 1823 through 1825 Aleksandr Pushkin, banished for writing radical poems, carried on a correspondence separately and jointly with Kondraty Ryleyev and Aleksandr Bestuzhev. The three men debated some of the most important literary and social questions of the romantic period. Some of the results appeared in print in Bestuzhev's "Glances," which prefaced the three issues of the literary almanac *Polar Star* and in Ryleyev's essay "Some Thoughts on Poetry." Pushkin intended to rebut both Decembrists in several essays, the point of which exercise was nullified by the failure of the revolt of 14 December 1825. One of the most controversial questions of the debate was the character and quality of the first chapter of Pushkin's *Eugene Onegin*. To Ryleyev and Bestuzhev, Pushkin's novel in verse was a rejection or misinterpretation of Byron and Byronism.

The first prose tale Bestuzhev published on his return to literature as the new authorial persona Marlinsky in 1830, "The Test," was a rebuttal to Pushkin's *Eugene Onegin,* a positive treatment of the Byronic hero that Bestuzhev intended as a reply to what he considered Pushkin's negative treatment. Among many questions argued by the three writers in the early 1820s was the very nature of romantic poetry. Their most heated arguments had to do with the different attitudes of aristocrats and plebeians toward court, autocrat, and "magnate-patron." To the two Decembrist poets, with their commitment to a lofty civic poetry, Pushkin seemed overly frivolous in both his poetry and his life. Bestuzhev never once mentioned Ryleyev's name in either print or his correspondence after 1825. Pushkin seldom mentioned Bestuzhev and Ryleyev in his correspondence and literary works. A number of his literary works were written with Marlinsky or marlinism in mind, but only once did he indicate an overt response—his use of a quotation from an early story by Bestuzhev as an epigraph to his short story "The Shot" (1830). Bestuzhev, however, was as if obsessed with Pushkin, often mentioned him in his letters, quoted his poetry constantly in his literary works. "The Frigate Hope" is especially notable for the frequent overt and covert references to Pushkin, which make it an importunate "message to Pushkin."

Two Lives, One Bark, and a Storm

Aleksandr Pushkin and Aleksandr Bestuzhev were almost the same age, they frequented the same social and literary circles, their careers ran at the same pace through the romantic movement in its peak years, they died violently in the same year. But apparently they never met. In the late 1810s–early 1820s when one was in Petersburg, the other was usually out of town. When Pushkin returned from his punitive transfer to the south and his confinement to his estate at Mikhaylovskoye, Bestuzhev was in prison awaiting exile to Siberia. When Pushkin visited the Caucasus in the 1830s, the two men sought but did not find each other. A well-known painting of Pushkin and Bestuzhev at Kamenka, the Ukrainian estate where the Southern Society held many of its meetings, reflected the mistaken notion that the two men participated in meetings together there, but Bestuzhev is not known to have visited Ukraine (Alekseev 1930, 241–42). A fragment purported to have been censored from Pushkin's "Journey to Arzerum" (1835) describes a melodramatic meeting on a Caucasian military road in 1829 (Mart'ianov 1885), but the fragment has been proved to be a forgery (Maikov 1899, 382–85; Alekseev 1930, 247–48).

The Decembrist conspiracy was very much on Pushkin's mind after 1825, too. He felt pain because he had expressed strong revolutionary ideas in his poetry, but had failed to stand with his Decembrist friends on Senate Square. He expressed this in the image of himself in the poem "Arion" (1827) as a "carefree singer" aboard the bark of the Decembrist movement and sole survivor when the frail craft is struck by a sudden storm. He sent his affirmation of solidarity with the exiled Decembrists in his "Message to Siberia" (1827); and in his "Exegi monumentum" (1836) he had the Decembrists in mind when he asked to be remembered for calling for mercy for the fallen. His verse tale *The Bronze Horseman* (1833) is in part an allegory of the revolt of 14 December 1825, he includes his hero Onegin among the Decembrists in the encoded "Decembrist chapter" of *Eugene Onegin;* his historical view of Russian rebellion was expressed in the novella *The Captain's Daughter* (1836). He signaled that he was responding to Bestuzhev's "Test" and "Frigate Hope" by prefacing his prose tale "The Queen of Spades" with a "Gambler's Song," a parody of one of Ryleyev and Bestuzhev's anonymously circulated "Agitational Songs." Never once after 1825 did Pushkin say, write, or do anything that in any way would diminish or demean the Decembrists, but he had literary and other differences with Bestuzhev that obliged him to reply to the Decembrist's message.

For his part, Bestuzhev read versions of Pushkin's lyric poems while in Siberia and used their imagery in the poem "Dream" and other poetry of Decembrist fate and lonely exile. He used similar imagery in the romantic motif of the storm of fate in "The Frigate Hope" and elaborated it in the curious conclusion to the tale's epilogue. The tale's allusions and hints are often so pointedly aimed at Pushkin that they make the message to Pushkin almost as urgent as the Decembrist confession. The message involves the same matters of troubled conscience, personal fate, failure, and exile. It centers on the theme of Napoleonic fate and continues an argument about the poet and the court begun in the earlier debates of 1823–25. The message is conveyed by the same thaumaturgical skills that form the hidden text of the tale.

Analysis of these textual and extratextual connections can begin with Pushkin's use of the romantic image of the bark in his 1827 lyric poem "Arion" (1937–59, 3:58). Together with Bestuzhev's "Dream," Pushkin's "Arion" belongs to the tradition of fate symbolized by bark and storm. In "Arion" a bark and its crew are destroyed by a storm and its carefree singer survives to contemplate the tragedy:

> Nas bylo mnogo na chelne;
> Inye parus napriagali,
> Drugie druzhno upirali

> V glub' moshchny vesla. V tishine
> Na rul' sklonias', nash kormshchik umnyi
> V molchan'e pravil gruznyi cheln;
> A ia—bespechnoi very poln—
> Plovtsam ia pel ....

> Many were we aboard the bark;
> While some drew taut the sail,
> The others did readily ply
> Deep the mighty oars. In the calm,
> On rudder bowed, our skillful helmsman
> In silence steered the laden bark;
> And I—with carefree faith filled—
> To the sailors I sang . . .

Suddenly the laden craft is struck by "roaring wind." "Both helmsman and sailor were lost!" Only the poet—"a secret singer"—is cast ashore, there to "sing my former hymns" and wring his garments dry "In the sun beneath the cliff."

Pushkin used the same imagery and symbols common to such poems as Zhukovsky's "Traveler" and "Sailor," Rayevsky's "Autumn," Polezhayev's "Song of a Drowning Sailor," and Ryleyev's "Signal-Star." The same images appear in Bestuzhev's "Frigate Hope": craft, sailor, steersman, storm. The established background of Pushkin's poem is that Pushkin freely adapted the ancient Greek legend of Arion, the survivor of perfidy at sea, preserving only the central metaphor of the bark struck by a storm from which Arion alone is saved. The imagery peculiar to Pushkin's treatment of the symbolism—the "skillful helmsman," the singer "with carefree faith filled," the "secret singer" who survives—is seen as a device to get by the censor and as Pushkin's covert reaffirmation of his allegiance to the surviving Decembrists in exile (Gorodetskii 1970, 111–12; Meilakh 1958b, 361; Rozhdestvenskii 1966, 149). Soviet scholars used to see the line "I sing my former hymns" as "the weightiest and most important line" of the poem, "a declaration of the poet's fidelity to the Decembrists' liberationist ideas and strivings, and to their politico-artistic creed" (Blagoi 1967, 159).

Walter Vickery (1976) and Gerald Mikkelson (1980) disagree, each insisting that the Soviet interpretation reads too much into the line. They see the image of the carefree singer as Pushkin's statement that whatever his sympathies and his modest claim to a place on the Decembrist bark as a passenger, he was, to his regret, a mere fellow traveler. The poem's subdued ending, in which the singer is cast ashore after the calamity to dry his clothing in the sun beneath the cliff and sing his former hymns, does not justify the interpretation that the poet had unequivocally accepted the Decembrist creed. Pushkin had serious reservations about the efficacy of armed rebellion and regretted the consequences of 14 December 1825. Mikkelson concludes from a sophisticated analysis of "Arion" that Pushkin "wished to convey his sympathy, his moral support, his faithfulness to the Decembrists as contemporaries, as friends." But he also "experienced horror before the specter of the gallows, relief, and even despair for the chances of his kind ever effecting positive change in Russia, at least through violent means" (1980, 12). These complex feelings, and not his ideological allegiance, are what Pushkin expresses in "Arion."

Although "Arion" was not published until 1830, copies of it reached the Decembrists in Siberia shortly after 1827. A copy apparently also reached Bestuzhev, who was exiled alone to Yakutsk, for the poem "Dream" (Bestuzhev-Marlinskii 1958, 2:502–4) is as indebted to "Arion" for phraseology associated with the image of the bark as it is to Ryleyev's dedication to *Voynarovsky* for the metaphor of the Star of Hope. The dual structure of "Dream" is important. In the first part the poet dreams of a frenzied ride on a wild horse; in the second part, following a nightmarish plunge over a cliff into an abyss, the poet recovers to find himself chained to the oars of a bark sailing through a dismal icescape. Whereas Pushkin saw himself as a carefree singer who survived the Decembrist storm to contemplate the fate of his lost friends, Bestuzhev saw himself as an impetuous Decembrist who cast away all care to ride, without control, the wild horse of rebellion into an abyss of destruction, and as a survivor doomed to row the bark of exile through a gloomy north. In contrast to Pushkin's restraint in "Arion," the tone of Bestuzhev's more elaborate poem is intense:

>I sluchai, preklonniaia temia,
>Derzhal mne zolotoe stremia,
>I, gordo brosiv povoda,
>Ia poskakal tuda, tuda! . . .

>And chance, bowing its mane,
>Held for me its golden stirrup,
>And, proudly casting down the reins,
>I raced away to there, to there! . . .

Like Ryleyev in *Voynarovsky*, Bestuzhev uses the words *chance (sluchai)* and *fate (sud'ba)*. In this poem, however, the symbols are animated by the metaphor of the wild horse and made frightening by the outright madness of the ride to freedom. The poet gave himself mindlessly to fate and cast away all hope of control over his own destiny:

> Letim—sorval brazdy shelkovy
> Neukrotimyi kon' sud'by,
> . . . .
> Ia obezumel, vozdukh svishchet—
> Vse vdal' i vdal', nadezhda proch'!
>
> We fly—the silken reins are torn
> By the wild horse of fate,
> . . . .
> I'm in a frenzy, the wind whistles—
> All is far, so far away, hope is lost.

The rider is free and rebellious but hope is lost, and inevitably the horse hurls itself over the cliff and into an abyss of water and rocks. Thunder roars above his head and a storm rages all around, but sight and sound are drowned in the terror of the plunge into the depths.

Bestuzhev's wild horse is not like Pushkin's well-steered bark, but the poet does see similarities in their fate after the failure of the Decembrist revolt. He expresses this solidarity by using the same phraseology to create a similarly subdued tone of regret:

> Ochnulsia ia ot strashnoi grezy,
> No vse dusha toski polna,
> I mnilos', gnut menia zhelezy
> K veslu ubogogo chelna.
>
> I wakened from my terrible dream,
> But my soul is yet with sorrow filled,
> I dream, I'm bound by chains
> To the oar of a wretched bark.

The poet finds himself sailing through a gloomy icescape. His rebellious feelings are gone, he is sad, he is surrounded by death:

Zabven'ia tok menia leleet,
Mechta usnula nad veslom,
I vremia v tikhii parus veet
Svoim miritel'nym krylom.
Vse mertvo u menia krugom.

The flow of oblivion lulls me,
My revery drowses over the oars,
And time wafts the silent sail
With its soothing wing.
Death is all around me.

Whatever the differences in their respective commitments to the Decembrist affair, Pushkin and Bestuzhev express like feelings of regret and resignation. The Decembrist has not escaped—his bark is the hopeless exile to whose oars he is chained. But the metaphors are identical: bark, sail, oars, storm, noise, cliff, shore. "Arion" also shares with Ryleyev's dedication of *Voynarovsky* and Bestuzhev's "Dream" the structure of rise and fall first developed by Zhukovsky. For Ryleyev in the dedication, loss of hope becomes revival of faith— "And once again the sky in its heights / Was brightly lit by the star of hope." When the motif is extended into the tale, hope is destroyed by implacable fate. For Pushkin the carefree singer is struck by a catastrophe that he alone survives to contemplate. For Bestuzhev hope rises to a frenzied quest for freedom, and then is cast into an abyss of destruction—"And the stars' sparks of hope / Do not burn in the gloomy sky."

Two Fates, One Frail Craft, and a Shipwreck

Hope, or rather lack of hope, is strongly marked in Bestuzhev's "Dream." In this respect, as also in the imagery of the bark, the poem is a landmark along the path from Baron de Tschoudy's Order of the Flaming Star to Lopukhin's Masonic tracts and the rich metaphoricization of the Star of Hope by Zhukovsky and other romantic poets. This is one context in which the elaborate motifs of ship and storm in "The Frigate Hope" must be understood. So far as the relationships between "Dream" and Pushkin's "Arion" are concerned, the ambiguous ending of "The Frigate Hope," with its motif of storm and shipwreck, reveals even more about the tale as a message to Pushkin. The ending is Bestuzhev's final comment on his role in the Decembrist affair and after: "We are called upon to say only, *this is how it was.* Let time extract the good and evil from it. A resident by the shore of the sea is horrified in the evening at the sight of a shipwreck, but on the morn gathers the remains of the wreckage, builds a frail craft, fastens it together with the bones of his brothers, and, singing a carefree tune, sets forth into the stormy sea" (2:170–71; emphasis in original).

The ending shares with "Arion" the symbolism of frail craft, storm, and survivor; it shares with "Dream" the images of bark and survivor; it is the culmination of the tale's theme of ship, storm, and destruction. The word *bark* (*cheln, chelnok*) is not used, but the metaphoricization is close to "Arion," for it is based on a shipwreck in a storm and an uninvolved witness cast ashore to "sing a carefree tune."[1] The ending recalls Pushkin's line, "I sing my former hymns," and echoes Pushkin's carefree singer: "And I—with carefree faith filled— / To the sailors did sing."[2]

In "Dream" Bestuzhev seemed to say that whatever the difference between his and Pushkin's commitments to the Decembrist affair, their fates were similar. But in "The Frigate Hope" he has separated their fates, and the structure of the closing paragraph shows that he has done so by drawing two parallels. The first half of the ending, with its curious allusions to executions, fits Bestuzhev's fate—his conscience, troubled by his memories of Ryleyev. The second half, with its subtext in "Arion," is aimed at Pushkin. For himself, the compromised Decembrist leader, he can only say, "*this is how it was.*" To Pushkin, the poet who did not join his friends on Senate Square, he says, in effect: do not flatter yourself that you were aboard the Decembrist bark, you were "a resident by the shore of the sea," an uninvolved witness standing safe on dry land. You were horrified at the sight of the ship's destruction, but on the morning after you gathered the remains of the wreckage, built a frail craft, fastened it together with the bones of your brothers, and "singing a carefree tune," set off again into the sea. Bestuzhev has rudely cast Pushkin over the side of the Decembrist craft, just as Arion was cast from a ship in the legend. The key statement is "sing a carefree tune," for it implies that the resident by the shore

---

1. The Russian word is *pripevaiuchi*, a gerund denoting unconcerned, absentminded singing, and more generally a carefree state of mind.

2. Bestuzhev seems to have read not the canonical version of "Arion," but an early variant. Where Pushkin has the epithet "laden bark" (*gruznyi cheln*) in the final version, he has "frail bark" (*utlyi cheln*) in the variant (Pushkin 1937–59, 3:593). Bestuzhev uses the same epithet: "frail craft" (*utlaia lad'ia*).

of the sea has already forgotten the calamity. You did not sing your former hymns and sadly contemplate the fate of your comrades, Bestuzhev tells Pushkin. You left the scene without even a thought for their fate. You are indeed "with carefree faith filled."

The indictment is strong. It shows that the differences between the aristocratic Pushkin and the Decembrist Bestuzhev were sharp. The reproach has to do with Bestuzhev and Ryleyev's resentment over a boast by Pushkin in the early 1820s about his six-hundred-year-old ancestry (Shaw 1967, 1:222–23, 251, 295–96). It also raises the question of Pushkin's rapprochement with Nicholas I in 1826 and the tsar's promise to be the poet's benefactor and personal censor. Especially, it expresses a common Decembrist view of Pushkin that was for a long time not mentioned in the established view of the poet's solidarity with the Decembrists, namely that many saw Pushkin's position as Nicholas's court poet as betrayal. One expression of resentment of Pushkin can be found in the memoirs of I. I. Gorbachevsky, a radical member of the Society of United Slavs. Gorbachevsky's accusations were consistently excised from editions of his memoirs (1963, 337–39), but were traced to the original manuscript by N. Ya. Eydelman, who reproached Pushkinists for suppressing it and thereby failing to defend Pushkin from what Eydelman concluded was unfounded slander (Eydelman 1979, 143–68). According to Eydelman's full version of the censored text, Gorbachevsky reported that members of the Southern Society were ordered by the Supreme Council not to associate with Pushkin because he was an informer to the secret police. Gorbachevsky and, in his opinion, other members of the Southern Society considered Pushkin a gossip and a hypocrite (1979, 147–49).

Gorbachevsky's testimony is not justified, but that is not the point. The point is that Pushkin was not the indubitable Decembrist ally he has been made to seem. Many considered him a frivolous person whose love of gossip made him a risky guest at Decembrist gatherings. If Bestuzhev ever heard the gossip, he probably would not have given it credence, but it should be kept in mind that the relationship among Pushkin, Ryleyev, and Bestuzhev in the early 1820s was shaped by the Decembrists' sense that Pushkin's frivolity did not accord with their civic faith in the lofty mission of poetry. The scholar Yury Lotman is right: the Decembrists were as a rule "serious" men who frowned on the worldly aristocrats of the Pushkin Pleiad (1975a, 28–32). In addition, by the time Bestuzhev had written "The Frigate Hope" his own return to literature under the benevolent auspices of Nicholas's forgiveness had already begun to turn into the nightmare of systematic humiliation that legend says drove him to his death in battle. The earlier arguments with Pushkin about the role of the poet and the magnate-patron were very much on Bestuzhev's mind in 1832.

The troubled relationship between the two writers is not without irony. Bestuzhev was apparently unaware of Pushkin's humiliation under the patronage of Nicholas I. And when he did learn that they shared this similar predicament, together with the already fully regnant legend that Pushkin was driven to his death, and perhaps even murdered by order of Nicholas I, it was too late to apologize. Five years before Pushkin's death in the duel, in a letter to Ksenofont Polevoy, a leading plebeian journalist, Bestuzhev wrote: "About Pushkin I shrug my shoulders. . . . Has the time yet come to sing a requiem for his soul? I have always considered him to be a characterless person, if not even an immoral one—*Mais c'est plu qu'un délit, c'est une faute*" (Polevoi 1861, 333). When he received the news of Pushkin's death, he did have a requiem sung for Pushkin's soul, and he wrote of it in a letter of February 1837: "I cried then as I am crying now . . . cried for a friend and comrade in arms, cried for my very self; and [the priest's chant] seemed to me to be not only a remembrance but a premonition. . . . Yes, I sense that my death will be just as violent and unexpected, that it is already close at hand" (Bestuzhev-Marlinskii 1958, 2:673–74). In the next few months before his own death Bestuzhev expressed envy that Pushkin had found peace and prayed that he too would be delivered from official persecution. So he did finally overcome his resentment of Pushkin.

Napoleonic Fate

Despite Bestuzhev's ambiguous attitude toward Pushkin, their fates were connected in his mind. In "The Frigate Hope" Pravin calls himself "a stern Slav, as Pushkin puts it," and he uses another line from *Eugene Onegin* to describe a friend: "In duels a classicist and a pedant" (1958, 2:89, 93). A cynical wit in the tale parodies the main epigraph to *Eugene Onegin*—"We hasten to live, and tarry to marry"—and the same character pretends that Russian national honor has been offended because Pushkin (in *Onegin* again) "has found only three pairs of shapely feet in all Russia" (2:102, 106). When he courts Vera, Pravin quotes lines from Pushkin's Byronic verse tale *The Captive of the Caucasus,* and the tale's narrator praises the smooth beat of Pushkin's lines (2:131, 140).

Many of the allusions to Pushkin are lodged in the theme of Napoleon. The theme is introduced in "The Frigate Hope" with an allusion taken from Pushkin. During a visit to the Hermitage Pravin contemplates a work of art and imagines to himself the great historical personages who might have viewed the work before him. Among the great persons who come to mind is Napoleon, whose "lightning-swift glance might have once fallen upon it while he was ranting about conquering the world." The work of art has survived, those who viewed it have passed on, and Pravin recalls a phrase from the Persian poet Sa'adi (2:116), used by Pushkin as the epigraph to his verse tale *The Fountain at Bakhchisarai* and, with reference to the exiled Decembrists, in the last stanza of *Eugene Onegin*. Where are Pushkin's friends and Pravin's historical personages now? "Some are no longer, others have gone their way!"

The theme of Napoleon, having in this way been anticipated, is then developed at length in a digression on Pravin falling in love. Once again a conventional romantic theme is raised to the level of great historical import. Here, however, hyperbole is used to parody Bestuzhev's own ultraromantic style. Pravin is like all young men in love, yet there is more passion in him. Some men die where they were born, others hurl themselves through life like a comet. In this respect Pravin is like Napoleon: "Thus, to Napoleon's lot fell the muddy road whose first verst was the battery at Toulon, and the last the island of St. Helena." Napoleon was like "a gigantic eruption of the volcano revolution." Napoleon was fate, Napoleon was heart, represented by his grave "stamped with the mysterious hieroglyph of terrible fate!!" Little wonder that the author rises to such hyperbole, for "the example of Napoleon is everywhere apt, his name fits every occasion, it is like the all-meaning number 666 of the Apocalypse." Young lovers like Vera and Pravin are like the triumphant Napoleon—each love letter is another great victory, but the lovers forget that Napoleon, too, suffered defeat. Finally, when called to a halt by an imagined reader, the narrator sums up the Napoleon theme by shifting the comparisons to Pravin's fate. "The nature of all lovers in general is the same as Pravin's in particular: As it is wont to be [*kak byvalo*] with others, so it was with him [*tak bylo*]" (2:123–25). That is, in anticipation of the tale's conclusion, "*this is how it was [tak bylo].*"

Bestuzhev's treatment of the Napoleon theme is linked to Pushkin's version of the theme in his poem "To the Sea" (1824; 1937–59, 1:331–33). In "To the Sea" Pushkin pondered the fate of Napoleon in images of sea, storm, clouds, and cliffs; in "The Frigate Hope" Bestuzhev uses similar epithets—"crimson clouds," "forbidding steeps of Saint Helena," and "gray waves of the ocean" (2:124). Both men metaphorize Napoleon's fate in the image of the cliff that symbolizes fate or its gloomy aftermath. They use the image to symbolize their own fates in "Arion" and "Dream." According to F. Z. Kanunova, who has compared Pushkin's treatment of the Napoleon theme with Bestuzhev's, both writers were drawn to the image of the passionate Napoleon whose well-laid plans and strong will carried him up the "steep cliffs" of victory and whom fate plunged into the "abyss" of defeat. Both authors portray Napoleon the great historical personage whose astounding deeds are ephemeral. In Pushkin's poem "To the Sea" Napoleon is finite in comparison with the eternal sea; in "The Frigate Hope" Napoleon is petty in comparison with art (Kanunova 1973, 154–61).

Kanunova also links Bestuzhev's treatment of the theme of Napoleon with Pushkin's in "The Queen of Spades." In her view, Count Tomsky's teasing warning to the heroine Lizaveta Ivanovna that the hero Germann "has the profile of a Napoleon and the soul of a Mephistopheles" (Pushkin 1937–59, 8:244) is history's opinion of Napoleon himself. Here, however, Kanunova has missed an important point, namely that both authors deal with a third Napoleon, the demonic Napoleon. Bestuzhev's Pravin is like Napoleon because he is carried by his passion to the heights of love and glory and is dashed to destruction by the storm of fate. Pushkin's Germann is like Napoleon because his grandiose dreams of wealth are destroyed by chance and fate. Bestuzhev's demonic Napoleon is expressed in the author's allusions to numerological phenomena—"the mysterious hieroglyph of terrible fate," "the all-meaning number 666 of the Apocalypse." Similarly, Pushkin links Napoleon with Mephistopheles, and thus with his tale's numerological-cartomantic phenomena—its mystique of fate, magic cards, and "cabalistics."

Fateful Dates and Calendarology

Thaumaturgical connections, both links and associations, between "The Frigate Hope" and "The Queen of Spades" are numerous. Among these are the calendarological hint in Pravin's diary that his fatal decision to run off with Vera was made "on 17 August 1829 at exactly one hour past noon" (Bestuzhev-Marlinskii 1958, 2:133) and the date "7 Mai 18★★" appended to the enigmatic quotation that serves as the epigraph to chapter 4 of Pushkin's tale: "Homme sans moeurs et sans religion!" (1937–59, 8:243). Bestuzhev's hint opens the way to the tale's third level—the link between the ship the Nicholas I and the tsar Nicholas I and then leads to the fatal dates

14 December and 13/1 July. In the case of Pushkin's epigraph, scholars have searched for years for the source of the quotation and the reason for its apparently unrelated date. Pushkin believed in his "fatidic dates" (to use Vladimir Nabokov's term); he kept careful record of dates in his diaries. He did not use dates or other numerical phenomena without careful intent. This is nowhere truer than in "The Queen of Spades" with its "secret of the three cards"—the trey, the seven, and the ace—and its thorough use of the "magic," "cabalistic" numbers 3, 7, and 1.

The fatal Decembrist date that troubled Pushkin most was the same date that troubled Bestuzhev—13 July 1826. The poet Anna Akhmatova, who believed that Pushkin was obsessed with the execution of the Decembrists, has shown that Pushkin spent years wandering through Petersburg in search of the graves of the five martyrs (1977). Pushkin often discussed the execution of the Decembrists, and he almost always related it to his problems with Nicholas I. He had difficulty reconciling the imperial order of execution with the hope he placed in the new tsar and the special relationship conferred on him by Nicholas. In a letter of 14 August 1826 to P. A. Vyazemsky, Pushkin said that he welcomed the impending coronation even though "the hanged are hanged" and "penal servitude for 120 friends, brothers, comrades, is horrible" (Shaw 1967, 1:314). In his autobiographical notes of the 1830s Pushkin remarked: "NB the Emperor who now reigns is the first who had the right and opportunity to execute regicides or thoughts of regicide; his predecessors were obliged to be tolerant and forgiving" (1937–59, 13:291). Pushkin did not condone Nicholas in this comment. He meant that Nicholas was the only Romanov in recent history who had not gained the throne through intrigue and assassination within the dynasty, and therefore felt no impulse to forgive the rebels who attempted to overthrow the autocracy from without. Catherine the Great became empress by conspiring with the murderers of her husband Peter III; Alexander I condoned the murder of his father Paul I by not punishing the assassins, and was therefore obliged by his troubled conscience to be "tolerant and forgiving."

Yury Lotman has examined Pushkin's remarks about Nicholas and the execution of the Decembrists in a study of the theme of mercy in Pushkin's verse tale *Angelo* (1833), and he points to two factors: Pushkin's pride that he "called for mercy for the fallen" in his "Exegi monumentum" (1836) and his belief that the Decembrists were executed not for regicide, but for "thoughts of regicide." Lotman quotes Vyazemsky's letter to Pushkin in which he called the Decembrists' assassination plots "atrocious chatter:"

All of it remained in words and on paper, because there were no regicides in the conspiracy. I do not see them on Senate Square on 14 December, just as I do not see a hero in every warrior on the field of battle.... Crosses of St. George are not given for intentions alone and in the hope of future deeds: so why carry out an execution in advance? This places prattle about murder (*bavardage atroce,* as I termed it when I read everything said about it in the report of the commission) on the same level with an assassination actually committed. (1973, 11–12)

Pushkin was apparently not privy to the innermost secrets of the Decembrist conspiracy. B. S. Meylakh has demonstrated that Pushkin was not a member of either society, and probably was not aware of the plans that Bestuzhev knew in such detail and revealed to the Investigatory Commission (Meilakh 1958a, 345–46; Meilakh 1958b, 294; also see Vatsuro and Meilakh 1966). This is so even though Pushkin's Lyceum comrade I. I. Pushchin, a Decembrist who, as it happens, recruited Ryleyev and Bestuzhev, visited Pushkin at his Mikhaylovskoye estate in 1825 and reported in his memoirs that he confided the existence of the conspiracy to him (1979, 54–55).[3] After 1825, however, the dates and other details of the Decembrist plans became generally known. Pushkin knew enough after 1825 to detect the significance of the dates in "The Frigate Hope," along with the tale's allegorical confession and the allusions directed at him. Certainly Pushkin did his own pondering about the fateful implications of the date 7/13.

Pushkin and Bestuzhev were not alone in their preoccupation with the date 13 July 1826. Nicholas, who kept track of every detail of the findings of the Investigatory Commission, also, it seems, appreciated fatal dates and numerical ironies. He personally chose the date for the execution, and in a letter to his mother of 12 July 1826 he indicated that it was important to him that the hanging take place at exactly 3:00 A.M. (Oksman 1926, 475). The execution did not take place on time—it was botched and took another two hours to complete, an event that the surviving Decembrists never forgot (Kotliarevskii 1908, 186–91). But the choice of date and time suggests that Nicholas the Hangman possessed the cruel sense of irony for which he is reputed. The numbers 3, 7, and 1 were prominent among the Decembrist plans and programs, and the tsar could not have missed their appearance throughout the

---

3. It is the most probable case despite Nechkina's reminder that Pushchin was the contact between Pushkin at his estate at Mikhaylovskoye and Bestuzhev and Ryleyev in Petersburg, and Pushkin did in fact set out for Petersburg just prior to 14 December (Nechkina 1955, 2:103–4; Nechkina 1937, 298). Eydelman (1979, 286–305) is less certain in this matter.

Decembrists' testimonies. Not only the first date of the Peterhof Festival—7/1 (=7/13 New Style), but the 17 principles of the Society of United Slavs and, in accordance with the Pythagorean numerological system practiced by the United Slavs, the symbols for the 8 Slavic tribes, 4 great seas, and 1 Society that add up to 13 (Bogdanovich 1871, 6:480). Especially noticeable was "the dread number 13!!!" that appeared in the Decembrists' testimonies as the number of members of the imperial family who, by Pestel's count, would have to be exterminated (Porokh 1954, 140; Sablin 1906, 34, 31).

These and other numerical and coincidences of dates would not have been missed by Pushkin when he saw the calendarological indicators in "The Frigate Hope." Dates are powerful forces in the thaumaturgical practices of numerology, astrology, and alchemy, and they bear great symbolic meaning in both secular and church calendars. Dates are also chosen with great care for imperial announcements and other events of court calendars. Pushkin's superstition about dates and other numerical phenomena is a frequent subject of Pushkin studies. In his commentary to *Eugene Onegin* Vladimir Nabokov speculates about the significance of a letter that Pushkin began, but did not complete or mail, to Alexander I sometime between early July and late September 1825. Pushkin wrote the letter at a time when he was sending an elaborately coded series of letters to friends he had recruited to help him escape abroad by feigning a potentially fatal aneurism (Shaw 1967, 293). In the letter, Pushkin spoke of a rumor that offended his honor, to the effect that "I had been taken to the secret chancellory and whipped," a rumor known to have been originated by the adventurer Fedor Tolstoy. Pushkin then added: "I became despondent. I dueled—I was 20 in 1820. I pondered whether I would not do well to commit suicide or to assassinate V [. . . .]." (Shaw 1967, 1:255). Pushkinists have speculated that the abbreviation stands for "Votre Majesté"— Pushkin was confessing thoughts about an attempt on the tsar's life. In Nabokov's view, however, the remark "I dueled—I was 20 in 1820" indicates that the confession refers not to Alexander, and not only to Tolstoy, but to another possible opponent in a duel of 1820, Kondraty Ryleyev (Nabokov 1964, 2:430–34; also Tsiavlovskaia 1983, 139–46).

Nabokov, whose family owned the former Ryleyev estate at Batovo near Petersburg, believed that Pushkin and Ryleyev fought a duel at Batovo in early May 1820. In their childhood Nabokov and his cousin used to reenact duels à la Pushkin-Ryleyev at Batovo. The Nabokov family believed in "the legend of Batovo," known also as "the legend of *le pendu*." Taking a cue from the fact that Pushkin once gave the date of his departure from Petersburg, in accordance with his decreed administrative transfer to the south, as 6 May 1820 and marked it in another place as 9 May 1820, Nabokov reasoned that the poet left the *city* of Petersburg on 6 May, sidestepped to Batovo to fight with Ryleyev, and left the *district* of Petersburg on 9 May. The duel therefore occurred on either 7 or 8 May. Nabokov argues that Pushkin could not have mistaken the date because he never erred about his "fatidic dates." Nothing is known about the duel, there is no evidence other than the legend of Batovo to indicate that it took place. But in a letter to Bestuzhev, Pushkin said that he fought a duel with Ryleyev, adding jokingly that he envied Ryleyev's poetry so much that he wished he had killed him when he had the chance (Nabokov 1964, 2:430–34; Tsiavlovskaia 1983, 172–73).

Nabokov does not mention the date in "The Queen of Spades" or the epigraph "Homme san moeurs et sans religion."[4] This is unusual, because Nabokov was himself attentive to connections between dates and numbers, and the date and epigraph seem to fit the legend of Batovo. For that matter, the fate of Pushkin's hero Germann, who risks and loses all on a game of cards, is a similar rehearsal of the fate of the fanatic idealist Ryleyev. Such an interpretation would be perfectly logical: the epigraph expresses the character of the calculating hero Germann, who "has the profile of a Napoleon and the soul of a Mephistopheles," and it also matches Ryleyev, the revolutionary conspirator. The interpretation would also provide an explanation for the date, which is appended to the epigraph with no apparent reason. However, this possible solution to a puzzle that has preoccupied Pushkinists for over half a century is discounted by new evidence. According to Gareth Williams (1981, 216–19), the long-sought source of the epigraph is a verse satire by Voltaire titled "Dialogue d'un Parisien et d'un Russe." As Williams notes, when the Russian asks whether it is possible to find a genius in society, the Parisian replies that were a genius to appear, society would unite to destroy him. A genius is the most hated and feared figure in society because he is independent, sufficient unto himself, arrogant. Were a genius to appear, cabals of mediocrities would rise against him. Above all, a genius according to Voltaire is "Sans doute il est sans moeurs et sans religion" [without doubt, he is without morals and without religion] (1820–26, 14:175). Williams ascribes the date of the epigraph to Pushkin's departure from Petersburg on 6 May 1820, "7 Mai" then being the

---

4. Among the fateful associations possibly on Pushkin's mind when he added the date "7 Mai 18★★" to his epigraph is the court calendar date when in the official military newspaper *Russian Invalid* it was reported that "His Imperial Majesty . . . in his presence in Petersburg on the 7th day of May 1826" announced that the investigation was almost concluded (*Russkii invalid,* 12 May 1826). In other words, anyone in any way involved with the Decembrists and who had not been arrested could draw an easy breath.

first day of the poet's banishment from society for his verse satires against Alexander I. He suggests that Pushkin "no doubt attributed his exile to the sort of intrigue described by Voltaire" (1981, 218).

Williams does not mention Nabokov's speculation on the legend of Batovo or Tolstoy's calumny that Pushkin had been whipped in the tsar's secret chancellory. Nabokov notes that the letter to Alexander I is incoherent even for a draft and speculates that Pushkin might have jumbled references to Tolstoy and Ryleyev. Ryleyev might have heard the rumor, repeated it with sympathetic intent, and unwittingly incurred Pushkin's wrath for spreading the rumor. But the letter, like the epigraph, is more in keeping with the sort of intrigue described in Voltaire's satire on the relationship between the poet-genius and the society he disdains. It seems more probable, therefore, that the epigraph refers not to Ryleyev, but to Pushkin's view of himself as a poet-genius tormented by society, hated and feared because he is independent, arrogant—"A man without morals and without religion."

Given that "The Queen of Spades" was written when Pushkin was suffering under court patronage and the social intrigues that eventually impelled him to his death in a duel to defend his honor, the epigraph certainly evokes his attitude toward Nicholas. All the fatal connections, both associations and links, lead in this direction. The fallen genius Napoleon was a man without morals and without religion, and so is the Napoleonic-Mephisthophelian Germann. Pushkin's ambiguous relationship with Nicholas, involving as it did his belief that Nicholas should have but did not show mercy to the Decembrists, is relevant. Regardless of whether or not the epigraph refers specifically to Ryleyev, the Decembrist's fate was an event that obsessed Pushkin and was very much on his mind when he read Bestuzhev's "Frigate Hope" and when he wrote "The Queen of Spades." But the epigraph most likely expresses Pushkin's view of himself as a poet alienated from society and troubled by his relationship to Nicholas I.

The theme of the genius isolated and destroyed by society is common throughout world literature. The theme is almost synonymous with the name Voltaire. It comes immediately to mind in connection with the fate of both Pushkin and the genius with whom he is most often compared—Mozart. It is a favorite romantic theme—Byron, Shelley, and for that matter the many Byronic heroes ruined by crass society in Bestuzhev's tales. In a study of the influence of Freemasonry on the German romantic concept of fate, Josef Ferd analyzes many German romantics and their Masonic works. Ferd stresses the importance of the theme of the genius's fate, dramatized in the martyred romantic hero, and explicates the theme in relation to Masonic morality. In his view, Masonic symbolism is present in the theme as it is treated by Tieck, Jean Paul, and Achim von Arnim, and in Schiller's *Braut von Messina* and Goethe's *Wilhelm Meister* (1909, 192–99). Ryleyev's heroes are the epitome of romantic martyrdom, and his death on the gallows made him an actual martyr—the ultimate victim of political power. Pushkin subscribed to the legend of *le pendu*, and his attitude is revealed by other links and associations involved in Bestuzhev's message to Pushkin.

Good, Evil, and the Jester's Death

Thanks to the careful order in which Pushkin left his manuscripts and papers, Pushkinists have a clear and deliberately cultivated image of Russia's national poet. Pushkin scribbled and drew caricatures as he wrote. While he wrote the several works in which Decembrism or rebellion are a theme, he brooded and scribbled. Among these intriguing bits of graphic evidence are sketches of the hanged Decembrists, gallows, and ropes (Efros 1934). Similar scribblings are extant in the margins of Pushkin's Russian edition of Walter Scott's novel *Ivanhoe*. Especially intriguing is a many-times-scribbled phrase that has been deciphered as "I ia by kak shut na" ("And I like a jester would have on") or "I ia by kak shut vi[sel]" ("And I like a jester would have been ha[nged]"). Scholars have worked for years to interpret this phrase, for it shows that Pushkin brooded about the possibility that had he joined the Decembrists on Senate Square, he might have been hanged with them (Tsiavlovskaia 1983, 178–86; Tsiavlovskaia 1975; Krestova 1963; Gorodetskii 1964).

The source of the metaphor was identified by Lidya Lotman, who read *Ivanhoe* and there found the jester Wamba, in the scene in which Wamba trades jibes with King Richard the Lion-Hearted on the theme of the balance between good and evil. Lotman notes that at the bottom of the paper on which Pushkin likened himself to a jester he drew a small set of scales. She shows that the Russian, French, and English texts of *Ivanhoe* all contain elaborations of the idea of "weighing" and "balancing" good and evil events, and that an interpretation of good and evil "affects the 'balance' of the scales of morality" (1981, 54–55). She points out additionally that Pushkin incorporated the English saying "Necessity is the mother of invention" into his collection of Russian folk sayings at the time he read *Ivanhoe*. The saying occurs when Wamba is threatened with the "jester's death"—to be hanged upside down—

and escapes his predicament with the wit of a jester's "inventive mind" provoked by "necessity." Pushkin incorporated Wamba's predicament and developed the theme of a balance between good and evil in several works of the 1830s. He used the notion of necessity in "The Queen of Spades," in Germann's remark that "I am not in a position to sacrifice the necessary in hope of obtaining the superfluous" (L. Lotman 1981, 55–59).

Lotman believes that Pushkin was drawn to the jester metaphor at two points of his life. In the years after 1825 he applied the jester's death to himself in relation to the Decembrists. He believed that his "carefree" behavior before 1825 made him unworthy to die with the Decembrists. And in the 1830s, aware of the traditional comparison of the court poet with the court jester, he used the metaphor to express his resentment toward Nicholas I. Well known here is Pushkin's reaction to the title of Kammerjunker conferred upon him by Nicholas, a rank usually given to young men and considered by Pushkin beneath the dignity of his six-hundred-year-old ancestry (as compared, for example, to the less distinguished lineage of the Romanov family). Pushkin likened his new court uniform to a jester's suit and swore on several occasions that he would not allow Nicholas to turn their relationship from that of tsar and poet to king and jester (1981, 55–59).

The gruesome image of the jester's death was an especially apt metaphor for the botched execution of the Decembrists. Bestuzhev certainly found it apt, for Scott's metaphor of scales on which good and evil are weighed is the source of the curious allusions to good and evil at the end of the conclusion to "The Frigate Hope." "But does there exist in this world even one thing, to say nothing of one word, one thought, one feeling in which evil has not been mixed with good?" the narrator asks in his summation of the tale. "The Deadly Nightshade offers honey to the bee, but man brews poison from it. Wine invigorates some men and kills the very soul of a drunkard" (Bestuzhev-Marlinskii 1958, 2:170). Bestuzhev also read *Ivanhoe*. His prose tale "Tournament at Reval" (1825) is an adaptation of the tournament in Scott's novel. The connection between the theme of good and evil and execution was as firm in his mind as it was in Pushkin's. Tacitus preached mercy and was to blame for the use of cruel methods of execution in the terrors of revolution. A traveler welcomes light on his path in the dark, but "terrible is the dawn when it reveals the scaffold to the condemned man" (2:141).

Pushkin and Bestuzhev: Psychological Exorcism

Literary creativity can be a healing process. In his expression of ambiguous feelings and painful matters of conscience, in his confession of his not fully honorable role in the Decembrist affair and its aftermath, even in his less-than-frank attempt to justify himself before posterity, Bestuzhev perhaps found comfort, if not peace of mind. The writing of "The Frigate Hope" was in this sense a psychological act, the use of art as revelation of and attempted liberation from a troubled psyche. Bestuzhev aimed his confession at two readers—posterity and Pushkin. To him, posterity and Pushkin may very well have been the same. In their time it was Bestuzhev, not Pushkin, who was Russia's most beloved writer. But Bestuzhev must have realized, as their contemporaries did, that Pushkin was already Russia's chosen national poet. Bestuzhev was very much like his image of Napoleon in that he flew through the heavens of Russian romanticism like a comet. Posterity did in fact make this judgment of him: within two years after his death his already fading reputation was likened to a falling comet. Today he is, like Dumas and Hugo, popular among adolescent readers of old-fashioned adventure tales. Pushkin, not Bestuzhev, has spoken to posterity, and Bestuzhev had every reason to believe this would be so. This is why he quotes or refers to Pushkin throughout his tale.

For his part, Pushkin did not respond as obsessively to Bestuzhev as Bestuzhev spoke to him. Pushkin's sin was, after all, one of omission not comparable to Bestuzhev's sin of commission. When the impulsive Pushkin set out for Petersburg in 1825, the sensible Pushkin told him to turn back. The carefree singer of "Arion" had different burdens to bear and a different behavior to justify to posterity. But Pushkin did have burdens to bear and actions to justify, and when he finally responded to Bestuzhev's message—in the writing of "The Queen of Spades"—he chose to use similar thaumaturgical skills.

6

Numbers and Numerology: Pushkin's "Queen of Spades"

> How complex "The Queen of Spades." Layer on layer.
> —Anna Akhmatova

The European esoteric tradition was introduced into Russian culture by the Moscow Mystic Masons or Rosicrucians primarily in the symbolism of the Order of the Grand Architect of the Universe. Vasily Zhukovsky and other romantic poets transformed one of its most prominent symbolic systems into a rich poetic metaphor, the Star of Hope, capable of expressing diverse aesthetic and personal meaning. In the poetry of the Decembrist romantics, particularly Kondraty Ryleyev, the esoteric tradition proved to be an equally capable vehicle of political conspiracy and propagation of revolutionary ideals. Ryleyev's use of the Star of Hope and other Masonic symbols to predict his fate became in the works of Aleksandr Bestuzhev an instrument of allegorical confession and painful psychological exorcism. In his prose tale "The Frigate Hope" the Star of Hope is conjoined with thaumaturgical devices to create an encoded text containing hidden allusions to the innermost secrets of the Decembrist conspiracy. "The Frigate Hope" demonstrates that it is possible to use complex thaumaturgical devices to construct a literary work. It was left to

Aleksandr Pushkin to prove that it is possible to use complex thaumaturgical devices to create a literary masterpiece.

Numbers are the most obtrusive feature of "The Queen of Spades" (1833; first published 1834). The ways they are used throughout the tale have intrigued readers for over a century and a half. It is impossible to avoid numbers in the tale, particularly the key numbers 3, 7, and 1, which derive from the "secret of the three cards" on which the tale is based. The very first word in the text is "once." Various forms of the word *one* appear throughout the text, together with various forms of the words for other numbers. There are numerous references to time ("at nine in the morning"), day ("at the ball on Friday"), dates (that enigmatic "7 Mai 18★★"), and time sequences ("three days later . . ."). Attention is drawn thrice to the old countess's age, and in the boudoir scene at the start of chapter 2 she is surrounded by three maids. We are told that it has been "seven years" since the death of one of the old woman's contemporaries; the heroine Lizaveta Ivanovna is warned that her secret suitor, the hero Germann, has "at least three evil deeds on his conscience." Pushkinists have debated the function of Germann's favorite saying: "No! calculation, moderation and industriousness: these are my three trusty cards; this is what will triple, multiply seven-fold my capital and bring me peace and independence!"

Numbers in "The Queen of Spades": The System 3–7–1

The three key numbers appear in various ways and forms in the text of "The Queen of Spades" and are accompanied by other numbers: 2, 4, 5, 6, 8, 9, 10, 12, 17, 20, 30, 40, 50, 60, 70, 80, 87, 100, 275, 47,000, 50,000, 94,000, 300,000, "a half million," and "millions." Many of these numbers readily correspond to the three key numbers, but others do not seem to fit or even appear to violate a pattern. Why does an event occur at five in the morning instead of so very nicely at three or seven? Why "two days later" and "about two days later" when the time sequences have otherwise been so neatly established as "three days later" and "not three weeks had passed since . . ."? Why does the clock strike two, and why does Lizaveta Ivanovna read "two more pages" instead of three? Why is the old countess eighty-seven instead of, perhaps, seventy-seven? Why 275? And especially, why does Germann gamble 47,000 rubles when 33,000, 37,000, or 77,000 would have done so nicely? These anomalies have been either ignored or explained by some nonnumerical logic.

In fact, every number that appears (or is hidden) in the text of "The Queen of Spades" is used in accordance with a system 3–7–1 originating in the Cabala or in numerological systems derived from the Cabala and known generally as cabalistics. Perhaps one of the sharpest differences between Pushkin and his romantic contemporaries is that he valued credibility. In its psychology of obsession with a supernatural secret, "The Queen of Spades" is one of Pushkin's most credible works. Its story is all the more credible because its numerical logic is unimpeachable.

Pushkin keenly appreciated numbers and the potentials of numerical and numerological practices. He was first of all a poet whose sense of metrical tact made him acutely aware of numerical patterns. He said in his verse tale *The Little House in Kolomna* (1830) that he delighted in numbers: "How fun it is to guide one's lines / With ciphers precisely row by row" (1937–59, 5:84).[1] His earliest indication of interest in the cards he chose for his tale is in the fragment of an unfinished work to be titled "Faust" (1825), in a scene resembling the "Hexenküche" of *Faust I*. Where Goethe's monkey begs Mephistopheles to help him win at dice and the witch performs an incantation based on the numbers one through ten, Pushkin's fragment features a card game in which a queen and an ace are punted (1937–59, 2:380–82; see also Bem 1934–35, 390–94).[2] Pushkin was superstitious and greatly attracted to dream interpretations and folk divinations (Izmailov 1937, 156–58). He indulged in cartomancy, which figures in *Eugene Onegin* and *The Captain's Daughter*. He attributed his decision to turn back from Petersburg prior to the Decembrist revolt to encounters with bad omens. He was an inveterate gambler whose library contained numerical probability tables (Modzalevskii 1910, nos. 1059, 1070, 1429). As an Apprentice Mason, Pushkin was required to learn the symbolism of the Grand Architect of the Universe—"the signs, the signals, and the words." His initial work when he was entered in the Kishinev lodge of Ovid in 1821 required him to master three skills: alchemy, numerology, and the Cabala. It seems that he did not master Masonic skills at this time—he was more interested in the pre-Decembrist Union of Welfare (Druzhnikov 1991,

---

1. For thorough analyses of the role of thaumaturgical phenomena in the formation of verse metrics, see Butler 1970 and Fowler 1970a and 1970b.

2. Pushkin's interest in science has been exhaustively surveyed (Alekseev 1972). An interest in the esoteric aspects of numbers is provided by a brief explication of an Arabic numerical scheme in his collection *Table-Talk* (1937–59, 12:157). His upbringing in the Russian Orthodox Church gave him access to bibliomancy and calendarology. He was familiar with calendarology and astrology from the symbolically numbered Bryusov (Bruce) Calendars, which were forty-seven pages long, with each page devoted to numerological, calendarological, astrological, and other thaumaturgical phenomena (Rovinskii 1881–93, 2:392–434, 5:87–86).

112). But he would certainly have learned during his initiation ceremony that numerology is considered not only an art and science, but a theosophical system and a thaumaturgical skill.

"The Queen of Spades" is not anomalous to Pushkin's creativity. He is well established as a poet of "sacred play" as Dutch philosopher Johan Huizinga has defined the tradition (Erlich 1964). When Isaiah Berlin divided literary history into hedgehogs (the stern, serious literature of Dante, Milton, Dostoyevsky) and foxes (the witty sophistication of Shakespeare, Cervantes, Voltaire), he included Pushkin among the foxes (1957, 8–11). Further, Pushkin was a consummate player of literary games; it is not without reason that Sergey Davydov identifies Pushkin as the literary predecessor of the great modern master of gamesmanship Vladimir Nabokov (1983, 170). Simply stated, Pushkin would not be Pushkin were it not for the wit of such works as *Eugene Onegin, Count Nulin, Little House in Kolomna*, or his *Tales of Belkin*. Just as he would not be Pushkin without the profound thought of such verse tales as *Poltava, Angelo*, and *The Bronze Horseman*.

"The Queen of Spades" is one of Pushkin's most thoroughly studied works; the tale joins *Eugene Onegin* and *The Bronze Horseman* as striking examples of scholarship leading consistently to well-verified interpretations.[3] As far as numbers are concerned, however, the scholarship is still beset by certain misunderstandings and errors. The numerological, cartomantic, and calendarological systems have not been fully decoded; their origins have not been traced. The questions therefore remain, What is the numerological system 3–7–1 and how does it work?

A numerical combination in "The Queen of Spades" should be considered valid only when it can be shown to be operative in the text. Pushkin consistently validates his use of numerical combinations by specifying them in the text of his tale, often drawing attention to them by using them in obtrusive ways. In accordance with the rules of numerology, numbers are interpreted by their lowest denominations: 47,000 is 47; 50,000 and 50 equal 5; 300,000 equals 3. There are two methods of combining numbers in the system. Numbers are joined by simple association or are derived from arithmetical operations. Examples of the first method are 17, 47, 275, and so on as they actually

---

3. The most exhaustive study of the tale, including a definitive examination of the numbers, is an article by Vinogradov (1936). Among the most productive studies of the cards and numbers are two articles by Chkhaidze, in which he correctly verifies the discovery that the key numbers originate from the system of tally for the game of faro (1960, 1973); Weber's innovative study of the tale as a parody of Masonic rites and practices (1968); and Rosen's psychological account of the magic of the three cards (1975).

appear in the text. Pushkin's validation of this method can be found in the cell "number 17" of the Obukhovsky Hospital where Germann ends his days. The joining of one and seven is explicit in that 17 is the sole number given in figures in the text (the only other numbers as numbers—not given as words—appear in the date of the epigraph to chapter 4, "7 Mai 18**"). Examples of the second method, of which there are three types of combination by arithmetical operation, are 1 + 1, 3 + 1, 7 + 1; 3 x 3 = 9 or 3 x 7 = 21; and 3 x 7 + 1 = 22. These three types of arithmetical operation are basic to the skill of numerology, which, as can be seen, admits addition, multiplication, and addition and multiplication together. Pushkin explicitly validates these types in such references to time sequence as "Not three weeks had passed since . . ." (3 x 7) and "Three days after the fatal night, at nine in the morning . . ." (3 x 3 = 9). He validates the latter usage again in the outcome of the first punt of the cards: "To the right lay the nine, to the left the trey." He validates other numbers and combinations of numbers both overtly and covertly, and almost always in a way that entices the reader into a maze of ironic, distancing, and never disappointing discoveries.

Pushkin knew the rules specified by numerological and other thaumaturgical systems. He does not use subtraction or division, because addition and multiplication increase the "power" of numbers, whereas subtraction and division diminish such power. He takes advantage of the system's flexibility, but he does not resort to numerical combinations that have no symbolic significance in the thaumaturgical system 3–7–1. The combination 3 x 7 + 1 = 22, for example, is an especially powerful operation of the Christian Cabala, which derives from and runs parallel to the system of the Jewish Cabala, based on the combination 3 + 7 + 12 = 22.[4] Christian Cabalists, under the influence of Lullism, replaced the Jewish number twelve with the Christian number one for the Unity and substituted the operation 3 x 7 + 1 to achieve the same powerful number 22. They preserved the order of the numbers: three and seven first, one last. This explains why the old countess instructs Germann to play the cards in the order trey, seven, ace. In the esoteric tradition with its devout obligations to the Cabala, the numbers 3, 7, and 1 are magic, "cabalistic." They are basic to Masonic symbolism and to such cartomantic systems as the Tarot and, not incidentally, the system of tally for the card game faro on which "The Queen of Spades" is based. (For studies of cartomancy and numerology, see Cavendish 1967, Seligmann 1948, and Wilson 1971.)

---

4. The Jewish system is based on numerical values corresponding to the twenty-two letters of the Hebrew alphabet in three groups: mother letters, double letters, and single letters.

The combination 3 x 3 = 9 is another numerological operation believed to have great thaumaturgical power. According to the Masonic encyclopedist Albert Mackey, the number nine, known as the "Triple Trinity," is one of the most powerful "Masonic numbers" (1924, 2:513). No matter what number is multiplied by 9 it can be manipulated back to 9. Thus, 9 x 9 = 81 (8 + 1 = 9), 9 x 8 = 72 (7 + 2 = 9), and so on. 9 x 371 = 3339 (3 + 3 + 3 + 9 = 18 [1 + 8 = 9]), and so on for any number multiplied by 9. In a basic numerological schema such as,

$$09\ 18\ 27\ 36\ 45\ 54\ 63\ 72\ 81\ 90$$

it can be seen that the first numbers in the pairs reading forward and backward are in sequence from 0 to 9 and the second numbers in the pairs, again reading forward and backward, are in reverse sequence from 9 to 0:

$$0\ 1\ 2\ 3\ 4\ 5\ 6\ 7\ 8\ 9$$
$$9\ 8\ 7\ 6\ 5\ 4\ 3\ 2\ 1\ 0$$

The pairs read the same backward as they do forward (09, 18, 27, and so on). Each pair when added yields 9 (0 + 9 = 9, 1 + 8 = 9, 2 + 7 = 9, and so on). When the number nine is added to or subtracted from any number, both results work back to the same number: 371 + 9 = 380 (3 + 8 + 0 = 11 [1 + 1 = 2]); 371 − 9 = 362 (3 + 6 + 2 = 11 [1 + 1 = 2]). Such is the stuff of pre-Cartesian esoteric logic. This is what makes numerology enticing to gullible victims of charlatans, ever-hopeful gamblers, and authors of tales of the supernatural. The system is also a source of authentic knowledge for literary scholars, a new way of looking at some kinds of texts.[5]

A mark of the excellence of modern esoteric studies is that such esotericists as Yates and Scholem deal carefully with numerical-numerological and other coherent systems. In this they differ from those scholars who were prone to such careless formulations as, "It is generally known that the number such-and-such symbolizes such-and-such." When numbers are analyzed without reference to a specific system, any number—or word, letter, color, card, graphic figure, fish, bird—can be said to represent or symbolize virtually any concept or phenomenon. The system 3–7–1, for example, can generate many arithmetically related numbers and combinations such as 3 x 3 and 3 x 7 + 1. But it does not yield such numbers as, say, 12 x 12 = 144, and it should not

---

5. Those of Rabelais, for example, or of Dante, Milton, or Spenser, or Fielding's *Tom Jones*.

be indiscriminately associated with such different systems as, say, Pythagorean geometric numerology or Swedenborg's system.[6] The system 3–7–1 cannot be dissociated from its rules, and any interpretation of the numerological character of "The Queen of Spades" must be governed by *this* and not some other system or by some vague reference to a meaning not permitted by the system.

The numerological system 3–7–1 derives from the Christian Cabala, thus from the Bible, and it has well-established traditional links with such related systems as astrology, calendarology, and alchemy. The one is the One God, the three the Holy Trinity, the seven, among other things, the days of the week, the seven visible planets, the seven liberal arts, or the sum of the triad and tetrad. Its symbolism can be enlarged, or changed, or adapted to other purposes by a particular author. But the basic system and its rules cannot be changed without corrupting it.

Illustrative here is the all-important queen of spades. When Pushkin added the main epigraph, "The queen of spades signifies secret ill-will," to his tale, he identified the provenance of this symbolism—*The Modern Divination Book*. He did so in the first place because in other systems the queen of spades represents death, misfortune, betrayal, and scores of other possible phenomena, and in the second place to signal his reader that he intends to associate the system 3–7–1 with the playing cards system. Pushkin is not the first to associate these two systems, but "The Queen of Spades" yields some ingenious combinations derived from the association—for example, with the number of fifty-two cards in the playing deck. Nor should it be missed that the queen of spades is alien to the system 3–7–1 in the same way that any demonic symbol is alien to the Judaic and Christian symbolism of the Cabala.

Pushkin's applications of the numerical rules of the system 3–7–1 can be deciphered from the tale's text. There are no exceptions to the rule of numbers in the tale—what seem to be anomalies (the numbers 2, 4, 5, 6, 8, 275, 47,000, etc.) are well established in the system's symbolism. The logic, however, is disguised, misrepresented, or hidden—the "code" must be "broken." The system 3–7–1 is not simply a subject of Pushkin's tale. It performs specific structural, thematic, and stylistic functions and arranges the tale's allusions. The system can be clarified by analyzing these functions in two categories: the narrative and the stylistic.

---

6. Swedenborg's numerological system, explicated in his chief work *Arcana Coelestia*, has only slight similarities with Pushkin's tale. His "Apocalyptic," "Cabalistic" numbers are 2 through 10, 12, 20, 30, 50, 70, 100, 144, 1,000, 10,000, and 12,000 (1918, 193–98).

Numerical Governance: Narrative Structure

The functions of the numbers 3, 7, and 1 can be most readily detected in the narrative structure of "The Queen of Spades." When the tale is analyzed for the simple mechanics of its organization—the basic compositional arrangement—it can be seen that it is organized into seven parts (six chapters and a conclusion). Less apparent than this organization is that each of these seven parts is divided into three plot units defined by their narrative functions: a scene, an event, an anecdote, an exposition, or the development of a theme or motif. The plot units of chapter 1 are the opening scene, which introduces the gambling theme, establishes the atmosphere of high society ennui, and provides an initial statement of Germann's calculating yet romantic character, the first part of Tomsky's anecdote about his grandmother's receipt of the secret of the three cards from Count Saint-Germain, and the second part of the anecdote in which Chaplitsky recovers his losses at faro with the help of the old countess and her marvelous secret.

The plot units of chapter 2 are the scene in the countess's boudoir; the exposition of Lizaveta Ivanovna's miserable life as the countess's ward; and this lonely young woman's growing fascination with Germann's covert courtship. Similarly, chapter 3 begins with the secret courtship correspondence leading to the final letter in which Lizaveta Ivanovna arranges a rendezvous with Germann, which gives him access to the mansion. The focus then shifts to Germann's lonely vigil outside the mansion, his stealthy invasion after Lizaveta Ivanovna and the countess depart for the ball, and his sinister vigil in the old woman's bedroom. The chapter concludes with the confrontation between Germann and the countess, his ritualistic pleas for the secret, and the old woman's death. Chapter 4 begins in Lizaveta Ivanovna's bedroom with her remembrance of the ball and Count Tomsky's teasing warning about Germann's Napoleonic-Mephistophelean personality and the three evil deeds on his conscience. This scene is followed by the confrontation between Germann and Lizaveta Ivanovna where she learns that he courted her only to gain access to the old woman and her secret of the three cards. The chapter ends with an exposition of Germann's morbid thoughts as he leaves the mansion via the secret staircase.

The three plot units of chapter 5 are the scene of the countess's funeral; Germann alone in his quarters, frustrated by his failure to obtain the secret of the three cards; and the nocturnal visitation in which the ghost of the old countess reveals the secret of the three cards and stipulates the three conditions restricting its use. Chapter 6 begins with the exposition on Germann's obsession with his possession of the secret of the three cards; it moves on to introduce the professional gambler Chekalinsky and his establishment; it concludes with the three punts of the three cards on three successive nights, ending with Germann's fatally wrong "pull" and loss of his chance for fortune. And finally, the conclusion disposes of the fates of three characters: Germann has gone insane; Lizaveta Ivanovna has married the son of the old woman's steward and succeeded to her wealth; Tomsky has been promoted and will soon marry (Shaw 1962).

One narrative prose tale is organized into seven parts, each composed of three plot units, for a total of twenty-one numerically arranged divisions. This structure can be depicted graphically in the following scheme:

1	opening	anecdote-countess	anecdote-Chaplitsky
2	boudoir scene	Lizaveta's life	courtship
3	correspondence	vigil/invasion	confrontation/death
4	ballroom scene	confrontation	Germann's departure
5	funeral scene	Germann alone	Countess's visitation
6	obsession	Chekalinsky's	three punts
7	Germann's fate	Lizaveta's fate	Tomsky's fate

The tale is, however, no rigid mechanical construct. The principle 3–7–1 is used not only to unify the narrative—to build a solid plot foundation—but also to vary it, to transform a numerically devised structure into a graceful tale. The use of the principle to vary the narrative can be appreciated especially in chapter 1. The opening is followed by dialogue that prompts Tomsky to tell his anecdote. The anecdote prompts dialogue that in its turn prompts Tomsky to tell his second anecdote. The guests then depart with their usual banal conversation, thereby duplicating the atmosphere of ennui of the opening. In effect, the opening and two absorbing stories are framed by lively dialogue, and the chapter begins and ends in a monotonous social milieu. The chapter is thus organic in the romantic idealist meaning of the term: it is urbane, sprightly, and natural; the author shows, not tells, the weary manners and worldly wit of Petersburg high society.

Chapter 2 develops in the same dynamic way. The scene is set (first plot unit: the countess is attended by her maids and Lizaveta Ivanovna), and Tomsky arrives with his empty chatter and his teasing of Lizaveta Ivanovna; Lizaveta Ivanovna is left alone with her thoughts about her dull life with the old countess, interrupted by Tomsky's chatter as he departs; Lizaveta Ivanovna, again alone, recalls Germann's first appearance on the street outside her window and his subsequent courtship, which is continued from his point of view and ended by his arrival on the street where Lizaveta Ivanovna first saw him ("That moment decided his fate!"). Again the parts are framed, and the chapter circles back, this time in a loop from the end to the start of the third part.

The principle 3–7–1 also controls the relationship between the "real" and "supernatural" events that have preoccupied readers of "The Queen of Spades." Does the ghost of the old countess visit Germann and give him the secret of the three cards, or is there some credible explanation for this and other supernatural aspects of the work?[7] As a general rule of governance, the tale's first three chapters deal with rational, credible events; it is only in the second three that events become, or seem to become, supernatural. The tale's basic compositional pattern would therefore seem to be 3–3(1). This mechanistic structure is not realized, however, for some irrational events are shifted to the first three chapters, and some credible events to the second three chapters. One shift occurs at the juncture of the 3–3 pattern, between chapters 3 and 4. The courtship correspondence that comprises the chapter's first plot unit is a credible event—Germann seduces Lizaveta Ivanovna into inviting him to her room at night. The other two plot units—Germann's invasion of the mansion and the confrontation with the countess that causes her death—are also real, but they are told in a sinister tone and in scenes that evoke the supernatural. Similarly, the first two plot units of chapter 4 (the ballroom scene and the confrontation in Lizaveta Ivanovna's room) deal with credible events, but the third unit (Germann's morbid thoughts about his predecessor on the secret staircase sixty years earlier) converges with the tale's supernatural chapters. A similar rearrangement of real and supernatural events occurs in a match between chapters 1 and 6. The second and third units of chapter 1 (the two parts of Tomsky's anecdote) treat incredible events, whereas the corresponding units of chapter 6 are rational (the intense but credible exposition of Germann's obsession with his secret of the three cards and the introduction of Chekalinsky). Both shifts occur in a graceful pattern: between the center chapters 3 and 4 and the first and last chapters.[8]

N. D. Tamarchenko has made a number of ingenious discoveries about the narrative logic of "The Queen of Spades." Noting the division of the tale into

---

7. The essentials of the debate are provided in a review of the first debate over this issue by Izmaylov (1937, 159–60).

8. For a debate on the structure and time sequences, see Vinogradov 1936, 75, 114–25; Stepanov 1962, 200–206; and Lezhnev 1966, 179–80.

its 3–3 arrangement (the six chapters minus the conclusion), he defines it as "a device of dual synchronic return" from beginning to middle and back to beginning. The tale's real and supernatural events parallel each other in their positioning within the two basic divisions in an arrangement from front to back for chapters 1 through 3, back to front for chapters 4 through 6, the arrangement thus providing a great deal of "compositional irony." The parts themselves are organized in events by threes. In chapter 3 Germann kneels to beg the old countess for the secret, gets to his feet, bends down to whisper in her ear, causing her great anxiety. In chapter 4 he bows to the ground before her coffin, gets to his feet, and bends over the coffin again to see her wink at him. In this way the reader is led through a pleasingly recidivist arrangement of narrative parts, thanks to which motifs and plot events are played, replayed, and interplayed back and forth in a carefully achieved but dynamic pattern (Tamarchenko 1971, 53–60).

To his analysis may be added the same pattern in the concluding plot unit of chapter 6: when Germann mispulls the queen of spades instead of the ace, he leans forward stunned and leans back, leans forward again to see the queen of spades wink at him, and falls back from the table. This pattern is anticipated by the dialogue frames of chapter 1: the guests prevail on Tomsky to tell his anecdote, they respond with disbelief, if they are not convinced by the second part of the anecdote, they certainly must want to believe, and of course Germann does come to believe. The pattern is also preceded by the event that disturbs the countess's funeral. Germann approaches the coffin, he looks at the old countess's body and she seems to wink at him, he falls prone on his back, Lizaveta Ivanovna falls in a faint.

Tamarchenko's decoding of the narrative arrangement (first three chapters forward, second three backward) can be combined with the additional division of chapters into plot units and illustrated graphically as follows:

Chapters 1 through 3   →   1–2–3   4–5–6   7–8–9
Chapters 6 through 4   9–8–7   6–5–4   3–2–1   ←

It can be seen in this way that parts of the first three chapters reading forward match significantly related parts of the second three chapters reading backward. For example, the introduction to the gambling milieu at the start of chapter 1 (1,1) matches the denouement in the three punts of the cards at the end of chapter 6 (6,9). Tomsky's first anecdote about the Parisian gambling milieu (1,2) interplays with its corresponding second part in chapter 6, Germann's entry into Chekalinsky's gambling establishment (6,8). Germann's enticement by the knowledge gained from the second anecdote that the old countess once shared the secret of the three cards (1,3) is echoed by his obsession with his possession of the secret (6,7). Tamarchenko's illustrations to his decoding of Pushkin's "compositional irony" work out in the gambling scene, too. Germann's first punt of the cards on the first night is a test of the secret which he must have attempted with some trepidation. On the second punt on the second night he is confident. On the third night he is supremely confident, and cruelly disabused by his mispull of the third card. Chekalinsky's reactions mirror Germann's perfectly. On the first night this experienced professional gambler is amused by Germann's unexpected decision to gamble. On the second night he is made nervous by his loss. He meets the third punt on the third night with visible anxiety, and is barely able to hide his relief when Germann plays the wrong card.[9]

Numerical Governance: Style

Russian literature enjoys a strong tradition of rhythmic, poetic, often musically composed prose styles. Gogol, Leskov, Andrey Bely, and the Ornamentalists

9. The narrative potentials of the system 3–7–1 are so numerous that it sometimes seems that the numbers three, seven, and one really are magic. It is possible to rearrange the plot in any number of combinations, the result being a like number of different tales. These combinations can be visualized by positing that each of the three plot parts of the seven chapters is a card. The twenty-one cards can then be laid out in seven horizontal and three vertical rows as follows:

1	2	3	4	5	6	7
1	4	7	10	13	16	19
2	5	8	11	14	17	20
3	6	9	12	15	18	21

It can be seen in this way that the position or positions of a card or combination of cards can be "shuffled" to the position or positions of another card or combination of cards. The sequences of any given combination can be reversed in relation to the sequences of its corresponding combination. The story can then be rewritten in the resulting new order. For example, were the story to be reworked by beginning at the end, the result would be a gradual revelation of the events leading to Germann's downfall. At the beginning of the tale a young man named Germann goes insane, a young woman named Lizaveta Ivanovna inherits a fortune, a Count Tomsky marries and is promoted. By the end, and only by the very end, do we learn of Germann's frustrated social aspirations, Lizaveta Ivanovna's despair, and the origin of Germann's obsession with the secret of the three cards in an anecdote told by Count Tomsky. Such a version could be written—or numerologically rewritten. Despite the mathematically controlled structure of "The Queen of Spades," it is indeed one of Pushkin's most open-ended works, and perhaps one of the most open-ended masterpieces of world literature.

of the 1920s come to mind here, to say nothing of the ornate style known as marlinism. Pushkin's prose style, like his poetry, is restrained; the style is simple, terse, unadorned, laconic. Analysts like V. V. Vinogradov have noted the patterning of sentences in threes and the ternary rhythms of key passages (1936, 583–617). Vinogradov's work on rhythms in the tale has been disputed, primarily by A. Z. Lezhnev (1966), but Pushkinists generally accept his analyses.

In another ingenious study of the tale N. I. Mikhaylova has demonstrated that the rhythms are even more pervasive in the text of the tale than Vinogradov believed (1974, 18–19). When the old countess nags Lizaveta Ivanovna during the carriage ride, her abrupt questions correspond to the bumping of the wheels over the cobblestone pavement. When Germann *descends* the secret staircase, his thoughts about his "lucky" predecessor *ascending* the staircase some sixty years before are broken into segments by pauses (indicated in every case but the final pause between "mistress" and "had" by commas), each segment constituting a single emphatic thought utterance:

> On this very staircase, he thought, perhaps, some sixty years before, to this very same boudoir, at this very same hour, in an embroidered caftan, coiffeured a l'oiseau royal, pressing his three-cornered hat to his heart, crept a lucky young man, long ago decayed in his grave,—and the heart of his aged mistress had this day ceased to beat! (1937–59, 8:245)

Mikhaylova notes that the segments of Germann's thoughts correspond to each step down the staircase. There are twelve segments, therefore twelve steps. She traces this to a common "twelve-step" staircase (1974, 19). If it is considered that Germann pauses to think on the second step (the narrative interpolation "he thought"), there are thirteen steps.

Is it possible to govern a style in virtually every respect by a numerical-numerological system? Pushkin uses numerical combinations to arrange the style of sentences and clauses. A typical sentence is constructed from a single subject and three verbs: "Tomsky *lit* his pipe, *puffed* [on it], and *continued*." In other instances sentences are composed of one subject and three verb clauses: Lizaveta Ivanovna "*never spoke* with him, *had not heard* his voice, *had never heard* of him. . . ." When the countess decides to turn to Count Saint-Germain for help with her gambling debts, she does so in three decisive steps: "She *resolved* to resort to him, *wrote* him a note, and *begged* him to come to her posthaste." The same syntax constructed from one noun and three verbs is used to describe Germann's introduction to the gambler Chekalinsky: "Chekalinsky *shook* his hand in friendly fashion, *begged* him not to stand on ceremony, and *continued* dealing." In some instances syntax is constructed from three nouns and three verbs: "*Champagne appeared,* the *conversation became animated,* and *everyone took part* in it."

The governance of style by three is a common rhetorical device of French neoclassicism and of folklore, but Pushkin's usage far exceeds these conventions. When Lizaveta Ivanovna sits down to write her first reply to Germann, she does so in a sentence composed of three nouns and verbs: "She *sat down* at the *desk, picked up* a *pen, paper*—and *fell to thinking."* Three short-form adjectives are used to describe Germann's first letter to Lizaveta Ivanovna: "It was *tender, respectful,* and *taken* word for word from a German novel." When Lizaveta Ivanovna asks the teasing Tomsky where Germann could possibly have seen her, Tomsky replies with three locative phrases: "*in church,* perhaps, *on an outing!* . . . perhaps *in your room.* . . ."

One of the most important statements in "The Queen of Spades" is the sentence in which the three cards are metaphorized:

> "No! calculation, moderation and industriousness: these are my three trusty cards; this is what will triple, multiply seven-fold my capital and bring me peace and independence!"

The utterance has been analyzed many times for its psychological importance because it indicates that Germann is fixated on the three numbers (the third by implication) (Kashin 1927, 33–34; Slonimskii 1959, 521–22; Izmailov 1937, 158; Vinogradov 1936, 588 n. 2; Rosen 1975, 255–56). In the Russian original the first one-word exclamation is followed by twenty-one words:

> "Net! raschet, umerennost' i trudoliubie: vot moi tri vernye karty, vot chto utroit, usemerit moi kapital i dostavit mne pokoi i nezavisimost'!" (1937–59, 8:235)

In addition to the verbs for two of the key numbers (*utroit, usemerit*), the utterance has one other verb (*dostavit,* "bring"), for a total of three. The sentence has seven nouns: calculation, moderation, industriousness, cards, capital, peace, independence. The utterance is divided into an initial strong exclamation

("No!") followed by three syntactic segments marked off by pauses ("... calculation [*raschet*] ... these are [*vot*] ... this is [*vot*] ... "). The cards will bring about three rewards in three ways: they will triple Germann's capital, multiply it sevenfold, and bring him peace and independence. And the utterance is personalized three times: "*my* three trusty cards," "*my* capital," and "bring *me*." Germann's saying is thus a covert validation of the cabalistic formula 3 x 7 + 1 = 22.

Said otherwise, the sentence seems to be a validation of two of the numbers (3 and 7), but is actually a cleverly disguised validation of the system 3–7–1 in its entirety and, not incidentally, a remarkable example of how style can be governed by numerical combinations. Many of the debates over numbers in "The Queen of Spades" have been hopelessly confused by Pushkin's omission of one of the numbers where all three numbers ought to appear. *It needs to be repeated, therefore, that there are no exceptions to the tale's numerical logic and that Pushkin often hides the presence of a number or disguises it.* In a study of the ace in the tale, Davydov (1989b) has systematically refuted arguments against the seeming inconsistencies of Pushkin's numerical usages and discredited numerous incorrect interpretations arising from lack of understanding of the system. In his analysis of the passage just cited, for example, he has shown that the seemingly absent ace (*tuz*) is present not only by implication, but in the sentence's phonetic structure, moreover, exactly at the point where, in the original Russian, the words "triple" and "multiply seven-fold" overlap: "Vot chto utroi*TUS*emerit moi kapital" (122; also 1987, 265).

The same precise ordering of syntax in accordance with the key numbers can be seen in another sentence that intrudes on the reader's consciousness:

> *Odnazhdy*—eto sluchilos' *dva dnia* posle vechera, opisannogo v nachale etoi povesti, i za *nedeliu* pered toi stsenoi, na kotoroi my ostanovilis'—*odnazhdy* Lizaveta Ivanovna, sidia pod okoshkom za pial'tsami, nechaianno vzglianula na ulitsu i uvidela molodogo inzhenera, stoiashchego nepodvizhno i ustremivshego glaza k ee oknu. (1937–59, 8:234)

> *Once*—this happened *two days* after the evening described at the start of this story, and a *week* before the scene on which we have stopped—*once* Lizaveta Ivanovna, while sitting at the window at her embroidery-frame, chanced to glance out on the street and caught sight of a young engineer standing motionless and gazing at her in the window.

The sentence attracts because it begins with "Once," associates it with "week," and underscores the association by resuming an interrupted thought by repeating the word "once." The number three seems to be absent, but is present by implication (or has been hidden): the event "two days after" occurs on the third day of the story. Seen in relation to thaumaturgical practice, this and the tale's other usages of the number two instead of the expected three are commensurate with the system 3–7–1. According to René Le Forestier, the number two, falling as it does between "the Spiritual Unity" and the Trinity, is "le nombre de confusion" and is used to mislead (n.d., 58).[10] The sentence is complex for Pushkin—its start, interruption, and resumption, and its use of participles. Like the utterance about the three cards, the construction of this sentence is triadic. The initial "once" is followed by the interpolation, which is followed by the resumption. In the third segment Lizaveta Ivanovna's actions are described with three verbs: she is "sitting," she "glanced," and she "caught sight of." The participial clauses are also triple: Lizaveta Ivanovna is "sitting," Germann is "standing" and "gazing." There are thirteen nouns in the sentence, and seven words are numbers ("two"), number-derivatives ("once"), or units of time ("day," "evening," "week," "at the start"). The fact that the sentence is composed of forty-six words—just one word less than the important number of Germann's capital of 47,000—suggests that Pushkin might have erred for once.

Another reason for the confusion over arrangements of words by number is that scholars have correctly counted four, rather than three words in a sentence or clause, but have not seen that the four words are commensurate with the system's combination 3 + 1. In fact, the governance of syntax by the numerical combination 3 + 1 is used more often than the simple governance by three. A good example of the combination as a stylistic determinant can be found in Surin's complaint, at the start of the tale, over his luck at cards: "I play mirandole, never get excited, nothing is allowed to distract me, and still I lose!" Here three statements are made in three different ways—a positive, negative, and

---

10. Davydov has questioned some of my analyses of numbers and other phenomena hidden in the text of Pushkin's tale (1987, 264; 1989b, 120–21), but agrees with my emphasis on the consistency of Pushkin's numerical logic: "Trusting Pushkin, I would like to insist on the flawlessness of the poet's cryptographic method" (1989b, 122). Many of his findings coincide with my own, particularly his analysis of this passage (1989b, 121). Davydov does not subscribe to the rules of numerology, and thus does not appreciate the role of numerical combinations. In addition, he finds exceptions to my analyses by discovering the number two where I have found threes. Given the function of the number two as a number of "confusion," I believe that my analyses are valid.

passive verb—and then contrasted or contradicted by the exclamatory concluding clause. The same construction can be found in the dialogue that follows the first part of Tomsky's anecdote of the three cards:

> "Chance!" said one of the guests.
> "Tall tale!" Germann remarked.
> "Could it possibly be marked cards?" added a third.

This dialogue has often been cited as an example of a simple governance by three (the unnamed speakers are even numbered), but in fact these protestations are followed immediately by a disclaimer: "'I think not,'" Tomsky replied haughtily." Again three syntactic units are counterpointed by a fourth: said-remarked-added-*replied*.

In chapter 2 it is said of the old countess: "The countess, of course, did not have a mean soul; but she was willful . . . stingy and immersed in cold egoism." In this sentence a negative statement is followed by three attributives that seem to contradict but actually confirm the first: "The countess . . . did not have . . . *but* she was willful . . . stingy and immersed . . ." The opening scene of the same chapter, in the countess's boudoir, also has a remarkable usage of the combination 3 + 1: "Three maids surrounded her. One held a jar of rouge, another a box of hairpins, the third a tall cap . . ." Here a simple sentence sets a scene (three maids surround the old countess) and is immediately followed by a tripartite sentence verbalized by the numbers one and three. The entire scene is arranged this way. Three main characters take part in the scene—the countess, Lizaveta Ivanovna, and Count Tomsky. The countess is attended by three maids. In a few moments Lizaveta Ivanovna will be left "alone" (*odna*, the feminine form of the word for one). Later on, the countess will ring a bell, and one Kammerdiener will run in one door and three maids in another.

The combination 3 + 1 is validated five times in the text of "The Queen of Spades." Just as one Kammerdiener and three maids run into the room, so one countess was previously surrounded by three maids. Later in the tale, when Germann hides in the same room, three maids enter, followed by the old countess. The combination is stated twice in quick succession when Tomsky remarks in his anecdote that "She [the old countess] had *four* sons, *including* my father," and immediately adds that "all *four* were inveterate gamblers, but not to *one* of them did she reveal her secret." The number present in these two remarks is four, but the numbers actually operative are 3 + 1. Quite often the combination sets up a contrast or contradiction. One example of this has been noted in the description of the old countess's personality. A similar description can be found in a picture of her life: "The countess *did not have* the least pretension to beauty . . . but *preserved* all the habits of her youth, *observed* strictly the fashions of the seventies, and *took* just as long *to dress*." Here one verb is used to make a negative assertion, and this is contrasted by three positive verbal statements. The numbers three and one in this usage of the combination are accompanied by the third number in the denomination "seventies."

In most instances the combination is realized by parts of speech, and sometimes it is the grammatical form of parts of speech that makes the combination. One common syntactical pattern of this kind is based on a combination of adverbial participle clauses in contrast to regular verbs: "While *sitting* at her work place, she [Lizaveta Ivanovna] *felt* his [Germann's] approach, *raised* her head, *looked* at him . . ." This combination of three regular verbs and an adverbial participle is often varied: "Lizaveta Ivanovna *stood up, began* to gather her work . . . upon again *glancing* out on the street, she again *caught sight* of the officer."

A frequently argued example of the role of three is Germann's plea to the old countess for her marvelous secret of the three cards in the name of three generations of his descendants. This usage is repeated later at the countess's funeral when it is reported that three generations of her descendants are present. In fact, the combination 3 + 1, not the simple three, is operative here. "Not only *I*," Germann pleads, "*but* my *children, grandchildren,* and *great-grandchildren* will bless your memory." At the funeral, the three generations are first described as "the relatives in deep mourning," and this entity is then elaborated into "children, grandchildren, and great-grandchildren." The statement is ironic: the sexually deprived parvenu Germann will never have the three generations of descendants reserved for privileged members of high society like the old countess.

The confrontation scene is a remarkable arrangement of words, sentences, and sequences in numerical successions. To begin with, it is comprised of nine pleas by Germann. The old countess responds at first by not responding, then by taking fright at his pleas not to take fright, then by protesting that the anecdote of the secret is a joke and falling into frightened silence. Her response to his threat with a pistol is to die of fright. Her responses—as opposed to her nonresponses—are therefore three. Germann reminds her of the secret, asks her if she is able to give him the secret, argues in three ways that her grandsons are too frivolous to make use of the secret, whereas he in three ways knows how to make good use of it. He then launches into a long triadic plea. He begins with a sentence composed of four "if" clauses: "*If ever* . . . your heart has known the feeling of love, *if you* remember its raptures, *if you* have but once smiled at the cry of a newborn son, *if anything* human has ever beat in your breast . . ." He follows this with his plea in the name of "the feelings of a spouse, lover, mother—in the name of all that is sacred in life" (3 + 1). He suggests that her possession of the secret might be accompanied "by a terrible sin, by the loss of eternal bliss, by a satanic pact," and then declares that "I am prepared to take your sin on my soul" (3 + 1). He completes the plea with his promises that not only he, but three generations will bless her memory (3 + 1). He intersperses these pleas with three pleas to "reveal your secret to me!" This elaborate plea is composed in entirety of seventeen verbs and thirty nouns.

The System 3–7–1 and Marlinism

This practice of governing style in accordance with numerical operations is not unprecedented. Bestuzhev uses the numbers to arrange syntax throughout one of his most hyperbolic digressions in "The Frigate Hope." In fact, he elaborates his previous uses of the numbers into a virtual orgy of threes, sevens, and ones. When the Hope departs on its fatal voyage, he launches on another digression on the fate of his hero Pravin (Bestuzhev-Marlinskii 1958, 2:136–40). When Pravin hears a cannon salute from Kronstadt, he thinks of it as "these sounds, these wondrous hieroglyphs, these fleeting forms of smoke." It seems to him at first that "the fatal sounds have been transformed into hieroglyphs," then that "these hieroglyphs have unwound themselves into wondrous corporeal images," and finally that they merge with "the eternal sun and the eternal waves." The author himself then surrenders to a revery about his three favorite subjects, the eyes of a beloved woman, the sea, and the sky. The digression echoes the tale's themes of storms and rebellion, and of the hieroglyph 666 of Napoleon's fate, for it is filled with references to fate, cannon shots, sea, storms, and rebellion. The allusions are again directed at Pushkin, for a reference to "the seventh shot of *Freischutz*" (Carl Weber's opera of fate and seven magic bullets) is anticipated by a reference to "the seventh chapter of Onegin," and the digression concludes with praise of the smooth beat of Pushkin's lines (2:135, 107, 140).

Words do not simply appear a significant number of times in the text—they are used singly and in combinations to control sentence structure. "There are three objects I can watch for hours on end," Bestuzhev writes, "they are the eyes of a beloved woman, they are God's sky, and the blue sea . . . (which are) the three worlds, that is, feelings, thoughts, and the visible world." The digression as a whole is structured on a pairing of the three objects with the three worlds: eyes are described with metaphors of sight, sky with thoughts, sea with feelings. Sentences are composed of three clauses, or three verbs, nouns, adjectives, or epithets in sequence. There are *three things* the author loves to gaze at—"the *eyes* of a beloved woman . . . God's *sky* / and the blue *sea*." The author's eyes catch things "*in a single instant, in a single glance,* even *in a single blink* of the eye." As is the case with Pushkin's "Queen of Spades," Bestuzhev constructs whole sentences in accordance with the numbers. One sentence contains seven nouns and three proper names:

> But curious is the eye [1] of every person [2]: a wondrous, albeit unpublished novel [3] hides within it; its every glance [4] is a chapter [5], now in the manner [6] of a Gil Blas, now in the manner [7] of a Don Quixote or a Rob Roy.

The sentence begins with a statement that is then elaborated in three clauses, the third of which is composed of three similes based on three literary figures. The original Russian sentence is composed of thirty words. Here and throughout the digression Bestuzhev has carefully counted his words. But he has not simply counted for the sake of a sum plus a sum. Like Pushkin, he has used the system 3–7–1 to create pleasing sentences with gracefully varied syntactical parallels and sequenced epithets.

Bestuzhev is known as the Victor Hugo of Russian romanticism; the style of the later Marlinsky became so ornate that it is little wonder that it came to be called marlinism. He has here used numerical techniques to enhance his syntactic ingenuity. The grace of his numerically controlled style can be seen throughout the digression, as in another sentence composed of nine (3 x 3) nouns and, again, one statement elaborated by three adverbial clauses (*skol'ko*, "so many"), each extended by a relative (*kotoryi*, "which") or participial subclause ("never executed"):

> And then, such a swift weave [1] of intentions [2], inventions [3], snares [4], adventures [5]; so many evil plots [6] never executed, so many words [7] which will never be uttered, so many miraculous ideas [8] which dissolve into nothingness [9]!

Another sentence is structured on eight active verb infinitives and twenty-two nouns:

It is sweet *to contemplate* in beloved eyes [1] the play [2] of light [3] and shadows [4], that is, of feeling [5] and thought [6]; *to remark* how expands and contracts the pupil [7], in which as on the Homeric shield [8] of Achilles all of nature [9] is sketched; *to follow, to divine, to catch* the sparks [10] of passion [11]; *to pierce* the fog [12] of sorrow [13] and by their mood [14] *to read* in the depths [15] of the soul [16] conceptions [17], tendencies [18] hatreds [19]; *to observe* how the world [20] acts upon a dear person [21] and how she as if acts on the world [22].

The numerical combinations here are 7 + 1 infinitive verbs and 21 + 1 nouns. The first verb ("to contemplate") is the basic statement, and the subsequent seven verbs elaborate it. The first noun, given as an epithet ("in beloved eyes"), is the subject; the subsequent twenty-one nouns elaborate qualities of the eyes. In accordance with his romantic idealist division of world-reality into three concepts, nouns and verbs are oriented to visual, emotional, and intellectual aspects or objects.

The passage is saturated with numerically controlled sentences. One sentence, a description of the author's generation, is composed of twenty-two words, of which eight are nouns and three affirmation of existence verb infinitives (*est'*, "there is, there are"). The eight nouns are correlated in accordance with the combination 7 + 1: *pokolenie* (generation) is elaborated by seven objects. The nouns are modified in a variegated arrangement of seven adjectives or demonstrative and possessive pronouns. The sentence introducing Pravin's three favorite objects contains thirteen words in the original; three words are nouns, three are verbs: "*There are* three objects [1] at which I *can gaze* for hours [2] on end, without *noticing* their [swift] race [3]." An exclamation by Pravin contains seventeen words organized syntactically into three negative interrogatives ("are they not?") and structured on seven nominal and pronominal subjects: Are not "sounds," "wondrous hieroglyphs," "fleeting images"—"ourselves in the eternity of the world"? The digression has not only three beloved objects and three worlds in one sentence, but "*one* instant, *one* glance, and *one* quiver of an eye" in another. It features an exclamation of nine words, three of which are nouns: "Peaceful luminary! you know not our storms and whirlpools!" One sentence is a double exclamation of the three objects: "Eyes, sky, and sea; sea, eyes, and sky!"

Bestuzhev and Pushkin both found an effective stylistic device in the system 3–7–1, and each applied it to his own expressive needs. Both writers seem to have enjoyed playing a numerical-stylistic game, and to a great extent the practice is a game. Bestuzhev enjoyed arranging sentence after sentence in many variations of the system's combinations. It is easy to imagine Pushkin's Mozartian delight in sacred play while he ordered and arranged his style by the numbers and the combinations of numbers. Truly, "How fun it is to guide one's lines / With ciphers precisely row by row." Just as important, however, is that the arrangements, even when they are obtrusive, are meant not to be consciously "known," but heard, seen, and felt. They are pleasing rhythms, "precisely row by row." In this sense, thaumaturgical practice is literary practice, just as the strict rules of metrics are poetic creativity. In this sense, too, "The Queen of Spades" is an authentic cabalistic text: cabalistic documents are not meant to appeal to reason. Instead, they convey ineffable meaning intuitively, secretly, by arcane means. Quite often, cabalistic texts are incantations—repetitions and patterns are an essential device by which meaning is to be spontaneously conveyed, but not literally "grasped" (Seligmann 1948, 343). This can be demonstrated by turning to other aspects of "The Queen of Spades" and the system 3–7–1.

7

Thaumaturgy in "The Queen of Spades"

That moment decided his fate.
—Aleksandr Pushkin, "The Queen of Spades"

Aleksandr Pushkin's prose tale "The Queen of Spades" has mystified generations of readers. Not the least reason for this is its mixture of serious meaning with verbal and numerical games that amuse and deceive the reader. The tale also mystifies because it is open-ended. Pushkinists solve puzzle after puzzle in it, but inevitably new questions arise and old questions remain unsolved. Anna Akhmatova once exclaimed: "How complex 'The Queen of Spades.' Layer on layer" (Chukovskaia 1976, 21). Each new reading of this short, deceptively simple tale yields new meaning.

Germann is a calculating yet imaginative gambler who lusts for wealth; he is a parvenu who covets acceptance in high society and transgresses moral bounds to gain entrance. Germann is a cad who takes advantage of the sentimental heroine Lizaveta Ivanovna at the time of her greatest romantic need. Lizaveta Ivanovna is a Cinderella who, not incidentally among the tale's many ironies, learns from the abuse, gains the old countess's wealth, and thereby achieves the status sought by the man who used her. Germann and Lizaveta

Ivanovna are abject examples of sexual deprivation and social inferiority. This is a tale of cold, indifferent high society and its aristocratic conventions; it is a re-creation of the speech, the manneredness, the social and cultural milieu (*byt*) of Nicholaevan Russia in the 1830s. Where Ryleyev elevated personal bravery to the level of great historical significance, Pushkin may be said to have lowered the themes of heroism and love to the level of what happens to a plebeian lout who aspires to aristocratic privilege. The work belongs to "that other" Russian literature of the phantasmagoric Petersburg theme. This is a story of chance and risk versus fate and calculation, and of cruelly ironic failure. The supernatural events of this tale are enhanced by remarkable psychological credibility. This is a tale of cards, numbers, dates, environmental accoutrement, jargon, and "the spirit of the time."

Like *Eugene Onegin*, "The Queen of Spades" is also a message to friends—it is meant to entertain members of a social "in-group" who would immediately understand allusions that had no meaning for other contemporaries and have had to be recovered by scholars since Pushkin's time. Like *The Bronze Horseman*, it has Decembrist meaning. It is a game of mystification. The enticing details of the work have been traced to seemingly every possible literary, biographical, and historical source, some convincing, others probably coincidental, many speculative. Analysts have discovered, and probably will continue to discover, many more curious things about this work. Scholars have offered as many interpretations of this tale as of any work by Pushkin, and the curious thing is that some interpretations please even when they are wrong and others do not satisfy even when they are right. Akhmatova spoke truly: "The Queen of Spades" is complex, layer on layer.

Mystification, Ambiguity, Multiplicity, Irony

"The beauty of ["The Queen of Spades"] is not that it has a single specific meaning hidden in it," J. Douglas Clayton has noted, "but that it has a multiplicity of more or less obvious aspects." The tale is "a nacre of ambiguous associations and resonance of detail, in which various patterns or planes of understanding are overlaid on the narrative at once to produce a highly complex statement" (1971, 204, 199–200). The literary sleuths who have for over a century and a half sought the "hidden meaning" of "The Queen of Spades" have provided ingenious interpretations. In an attempt to interpret the supernatural aspects of the tale, Diana Burgin neatly articulates how Pushkin was able to incite so much speculation:

> In order to make the supernatural tale credible, to suspend momentarily the reader's disbelief, Pushkin employs the narrative device of mystification. He plays upon certain events and characters in such a way as to make them seem strange and mysterious when they are not, and, conversely, he de-emphasizes or mocks those mystifying and supernatural events ... which are clues to the real mystery. Using the device of mystification as a veil for his supernatural mystery, Pushkin creates in the reader ambivalence about the reality of irrational occurrences, so that he can, with ample justification in the text, interpret the story several ways. (1976, 56)

The device of mystification can be taken one step further, for no sooner does what seems to be important in the tale turn out to be insignificant, and the deemphasized important, than the process is reversed—the important that turns out to be unimportant is again given import, and what has been ridiculed, only to be suddenly revealed as serious, is again shunted aside by irony.

The reader of this tale plays its author's game at great risk and great reward. Pushkin confounds his readers with a false lead, then rewards them with an unexpected find that amuses even when it is irrelevant. Similarities to a tale by Balzac lead to an atrociously phallic joke on an atrociously phallic joke in Sterne's *Tristram Shandy*. The mention of Mephistopheles provokes attempts to fit "The Queen of Spades" to Goethe's masterpiece, and along the way Pushkin's interest in the "Hexenküche" is discovered (Bem 1934–35). Pushkinists have searched for answers to questions raised by the tantalizing references to Count Saint-Germain, Casanova, Swedenborg, and Napoleon, as well as rumors that Count Cagliostro is relevant to the tale. Explications of similarities with Stendhal transform a tale of high-society insouciance into an indictment of tsarist absolutism according to which Germann carries the class struggle into the camp of the aristocrats (Gukovskii 1957), but we are at least convinced that these are two classic treatments of the parvenu in world literature. Pushkin does not fail to reward. Searches for the sources of the tale's epigraphs provide new ironies, or no apparent connection at all, and an obvious source—Voltaire's verse about a man without morals and without religion—is missed despite years of research.

Searches prompted by Pushkin's revelation that the prototype of the old countess was Countess Natalya Petrovna Golytsina, known as "la princesse

Moustache," reveal that she did in fact meet Count Saint-Germain in Paris and punt against the Duc d'Orleans at Versailles; and that she was ugly, not beautiful, in her youth, and it was her daughter (or sister) who was known as "la Vénus moscovite" (Belousov 1965). Golytsina outlived her contemporaries, became a social fixture, and tyrannized her relatives, servants, and companions. Inspection of her mansion on a side street off Nevsky Prospekt shows that the interior does not match the description in Pushkin's tale. Neither does the mansion provide the boudoir in the detailed description of one of Pushkin's seductions offered by P. V. Nashchokin (Bertenev 1925, 46–47), who testified that Golytsina did in fact entertain lovers (and for that matter also possessed the secret of the three cards). A lifelong search for the mansion provides a probable, and most interesting, location, including the secret staircase and a delicious answer to the question, to whose boudoir did the staircase lead? Further searches lead to further discoveries, but more new questions are raised (Raevskii 1976b, 315–20; also 1976a). And incidentally, perhaps even irrelevantly, did Pushkin ever ascend (and descend) that secret staircase? Who else ascended (or descended) those thirteen (or twelve) steps?

Scholars have searched gambling stories in many literatures and found correspondences in numerous minor Russian tales and plays, and in Balzac and in Karl Heun's tale "Der holländische Jude" (Vinogradov 1936, 75–86, 87–88), Hoffmann (Lerner 1929, 141–48), and Hugo (Tsiavlovskii 1936–38, 738–43). B. V. Tomashevsky proved that Pushkin took the name of his hero from Balzac's tale "L'Auberge rouge" (1927, 246), and Lerner, taking note of Pushkin's expressed admiration of another tale by Balzac "La Peau de chagrin," found tantalizing correspondences of plot and gambling argot (1929, 142; also Vinogradov 1936; Gregg 1966). Nabokov found similarities with a novel by the Swedish writer Clas Johan Livijn (1964, 3:97), which he mistakenly credits to its German translator La Motte-Fouque (see Clayton 1974; Davydov 1989b, 133).[1]

Tomashevsky has emphasized the literary importance of aphorisms about the superfluous and the necessary in relation to Germann's self-assessment: "I am not in a position to sacrifice the necessary in hope of attaining the superfluous" (1956, 174), and Elizabeth Stenbock-Fermor has traced the saying to aphorisms of Beaumarchais, Voltaire, and Buffon (1964, 121). An assessment of the atmosphere that led to the Decembrist revolt, by the French envoy Noailles, may

---

1. For a summation of possible sources of "The Queen of Spades," see Debreczeny 1983, 204–9. Bitsilli, who did brilliant work showing the links among the hints and allusions in "The Queen of Spades," was the first to find some of the tale's most important literary sources (1932).

or may not be relevant to "The Queen of Spades": "Russians are generally concerned with and seek in everything the superfluous without having even the necessary. . . . A young Russian officer, armed with his knout, subject of an abusive sovereign, surrounded by his own slaves, talks to you of the rights of peoples, of liberty, like a citizen of the United States!" (Florinsky 1955, 2:735–36).

In a discussion of Pushkin's reference to Mephistopheles, M. P. Alekseyev notes that an engineer of Pushkin's acquaintance, a Russified German like Germann, translated *Faust* into Russian (1972, 86, 108–9). Clayton has suggested another association with the name of Armand Herman, who presided over the guillotine for Robespierre (1971, 211). J. Thomas Shaw points out that no one seems to have noted another resonance in the name in the tale itself: Germann and Saint-Germain (1962, 125). Davydov, taking attentive note of "the shapely foot of a young beauty" stepping from a carriage, decides that the tale is really about Pushkin's well-known foot fetish, but misses the hint about whose foot is at hand (1987, 267). Little by little, Pushkinists discover more and more and clarify their discoveries of ironic resonances that are this open-ended tale and its many interpretations.[2]

Key Word Repetition: Numerical Combinations

Numbers and numerological-numerical combinations are powerfully enhanced by the repetition of key words. This aspect of the tale is most readily demonstrated by word counts. The authoritative text of "The Queen of Spades" can be found in the Jubilee edition of Pushkin's complete collected works (1937–59, 8:225–52).[3] Pushkin did not preserve the original manuscript

---

2. The tale resonates with so many legends of Petersburg that it might be relevant that the actress and singer Nimforoda Semenova, mistress of Pushkin's cousin the Grand Master of the Grand Lodge Astraea Count V. V. Musin-Pushkin-Bryus, treated her ward much as the old countess treats Lizaveta Ivanovna. Semenova's niece Sonyushka Birkina shared with Pushkin's heroine the unhappy lot of having to dress like an aristocrat on a small allowance. Pushkin was a frequent guest in the "luxurious" home of his cousin's mistress, and he knew Birkina (Karatygin 1928, 1:356). For that matter, even though Musin-Pushkin-Bryus was known to be good for a bon mot, he was considered a frivolous fop, and in this was very like the wastrel Tomsky.

3. The basic word counts provided here are based on the authoritative edition; they have been checked against the word tracings in the *Dictionary of Pushkin's Language* (Vinogradov 1956). The authoritative text corresponds to the text of the tale's first publication in 1834.

of his tale; he left only one small draft of his calculations of Germann's winnings. This is unusual practice for Pushkin: he usually left several carefully prepared drafts and castoffs of his works, with the intent of showing the process of his creativity as he wanted posterity to perceive it.

The basic words for the number one—*odin, raz, pervyi, pervye, vpervye* (one, once, first [sing.], first [plural], first of all)—appear exactly fifty-two times in this tale of a card game. There are an additional twenty-one usages of the word *one* in its higher denominations or words to which it is morphologically related—*desiat', sto, odnazhdy, naedine* (ten, hundred, once, alone)—for a total of seventy-three. The Russian word for three (*tri*) appears twenty-one times in the text (3 x 7). All forms of the number three—*tri, tretii, troika, utroit* (three, third, trey, to triple)—appear thirty-three times. Of these, the word for the trey (*troika*) appears nine times (3 x 3). The number three appears three more times in the text in higher denominations or in a morphological derivative. Chaplitsky in the second part of Tomsky's anecdote is said to have lost "about three hundred thousand" to the notorious gambler Zorich; "more than thirty cards" are on the table when Germann arrives for the first time at Chekalinsky's; and Germann imagines his predecessor on the secret staircase carrying a three-cornered hat (*treugol'naia shliapa*). The total usage for the number seven—*sem', semerka, sem'desiat', usemerit* (seven, the seven, seventy, [to multiply] seven-fold)—is thirteen. The count of words for the basic numbers is as follows:

1	52x	
10, 100, etc.	21x	73x
3 (all forms; basic forms 21x)	33x	
3 (larger denominations, derivatives)	3x	36x
7 (*sem', semerka*, "seven, the seven")	13x	
2 (*dva, vtoroi, udvoili*, "two, second, doubled")	17x	
4 (including 47, 94, and quatre)	9x	
5 (*piat', piatyi*, "five, fifth," 50, 50,000)	7x	
6 (including 60)	5x	
8 (including 87)	3x	
9	3x	

As can be seen, all numbers except six appear a significant number of times in relation to the system 3–7–1 or its association with the playing cards system.

The words for time also appear with significant frequency:

minuta, minutno, "minute, by the minute"	13x
chas, "hour"	13x
totchas, seichas, "immediately, now"	7x
den', segodnia, "day, today," *jour*	17x
piatnitsa, sutki, "Friday, full day"	3x
nedelia, "week"	4x
let(o), "year"	7x
god, "year"	3x
vek, stoletie, "century"	3x
vremia, "time"	13x
pora, "it is time"	3x

Among these time usages, the count of four for the word "week" seems to be an anomaly. In fact, it is central to the numbers 3, 7, 1 of the Christian Cabala, and Pushkin demonstrates his awareness of this by associating the number four with the number seven in the amount of the "modest capital" Germann inherits from his father and finally resolves to use as his first stake—47,000 rubles. The numbers four and seven are associated in the system 3–7–1 and other numerological systems because they validate the ancient tertiary-quaternary relationship ($3 + 4 = 7$). The combination is not dissociable in cabalistic systems from the numerological combinations $1 + 1, 3 + 1, 7 + 1$.

Other curious numerical and numerological relationships are apparent in the counts of words for numbers. The number eight appears all three times in the old countess's age. Twice she is said to be in her eighties; once Germann, who appears to have no knowledge of her precise age, calls her an eighty-seven-year-old woman. This unexplained association might possibly validate the combination $7 + 1 = 8$, which seems to be validated again in the sentence in which the seven and one are linked: "Once—this happened ... a week before the scene on which we have stopped—once." By appearing three times in the text the number nine validates the cabalistic combination 3×3 again, and the combination is validated still again by the other counts of nine and combinations of nine with three. The cardinal and ordinal forms of the number five occur five times and the number appears again in the higher denominations 50 and 50,000. The number five appears thrice again: in the day Friday, in the number assigned by calendarological systems to the month in the date "7 Mai 18★★," and in the number 275, which is the standard limit at Chekalinsky's gambling establishment. The total count for the number five is therefore 10 ($7 + 3$ [$=1$]). The number 275 associates the number five with the key number seven, as does the fifth day of the week. Seven is also associated here with the number of cards in the playing deck. The relationship between *chas* (hour), excluding *chasy* (clock), and its derivatives *totchas* (immediately) and *seichas* (now) is 13 + 7, while the relationship between *den'* (day) and *segodnia* (today) and their associated words is 17 + 3. The seven and three usages of the two words for year (*let[o], god*) add up to 10 (=1).

A word count also reveals other consistent usages of the numbers and number combinations explicit or hidden in the text of "The Queen of Spades." The word for countess (*grafinia*) appears fifty-two times; other words used repeatedly for the old countess—*babushka, starukha* (grandmother, old woman, and "grandmaman")—appear thirty-seven times; the incidental references to the old countess—her given and patronymic names, "old witch," "the deceased," "your radiance," "benefactress," "lover," and so on—are thirteen. The heroine is called Lizaveta Ivanovna forty-seven times; Mademoiselle Lise, Liza, and Lizanka seven times; and by other terms—"ward," "dreamer," "blind accomplice," "poor girl," and so on—twenty-one times. Germann's name appears ninety-seven times in the text, a number close enough to the number ninety-four of the second punt to justify suggesting that Pushkin might have miscounted once again. The tale features three main characters and seven subsidiary characters (Guards Officer Narumov, Duc d'Orléans, Count Tomsky, Count Saint-Germain, the countess's late husband, Chaplitsky, Chekalinsky). The number of all other figures in the tale, from Richelieu and Casanova, the servant, the Kammerdiener, the storekeeper on the corner, the three maids, the butler, the sleeping servant, and on through Dante, Montgolfièr, Mesmér, Mephistopheles, and Swedenborg, is fifty-two.

Those words in the tale which can be considered significant—that is, words which are thematically and semantically symbolic—are also used with numerically significant frequency:

igrat', "to play, to gamble" (all forms)	47x
taina, "secret" (all forms)	17x
okno, okoshko, "window"	17x
zerkalo, zerkal'tse, "mirror"	17x
lesnitsa, "staircase"	10x
stupeni, "steps [of staircase]"	3x
bit', "to beat, to win," *ubit'*, "to kill"	13x
mertvaia, smert', konchina, "dead, death, demise"	10x
umer, umerla, umiraiushchaia, "died, died, dying"	7x
iavliat'sia, "to appear"	9x
za/trepetat', "to tremble, shake, quiver"	7x

schastie, "luck" (all forms of root *schast'*-)	9x
schastie with *sluchai*, "chance"	13x
sud'ba, fortuna, rokovoi, "fate, fortune, fatal"	3x

All forms of the verb *igrat'* include verbal, nominal, adjectival, and participial forms of the root *igr-*. The meanings of the words derived from this root range from the verb "to play," meaning "to gamble," to the verbs "to win" and "to lose" to the nouns for "winnings," "losses," "game," "gambler," and so forth.[4] The words for window are significant in the tale because things are seen through a window or scenes take place while a character is seated in or at a window. The verb "to appear" signifies an apparition, as the ghost of the old countess. The stairs and staircase are important as points of access to and exit from the countess's mansion. The verb for tremble or shake (used in both the imperfective and perfective aspect (*trepetat', zatrepetat'*) signifies moments of suspense or agitation, and might have additional significance if Pushkin was aware that in the esoteric tradition numbers represent "vibrations" of natural and supernatural forces or the "emanations" of the Cabala.[5] The count of all words for luck—*schastie, uchast', schastlivyi, nechaianno* (luck or happiness, lot or fate, lucky, by chance)—is nine, the powerfully lucky Triple Trinity. When all forms of the basic root *(s)chast-* are counted with the word *sluchai*, "chance," the unlucky number thirteen is achieved. These and the other words for luck and chance in the sense of fate (*sud'ba*) and the word for terrible fate in the adjective *rokovoi* (fatal) correspond to the symbolism already seen to be important to Ryleyev and Bestuzhev. The words for hope (*nadezhda*) and faith (*vera*) do not seem to appear a significant number of times, and do not seem to be used in any semantically or symbolically significant way in the tale.

All forms of the basic verb *bit'* (to hit, to beat)—*b'ete kartu, chasy probili, serdtse zabilos'* (beat the card, the clock struck, the heart began to beat)—appear seven times. The verb *ubit'* (to kill, to murder) appears three times. All other forms—the noun *ubiitsa* (murderer, killer) and the short-form verb *ubita* (killed or beaten)—appear three times. It is difficult to count the verbs *bit'* and *ubit'* separately because they occur as a play on the double meaning of the verbs: Chekalinsky tells Germann, "Your queen is beaten" ("Vasha dama ubita"), and the utterance has the ironic meaning, "Your lady [the old countess] is killed." The basic noun *taina* (secret) appears ten times; all other forms—*tainyi, tainstvo,*

---

4. Excluded from the count are two usages that do not have the meaning "to gamble": "to play a role" and "toys" (*igrushki*).
5. According to Cavendish, "Numerology is simply an extended study of vibrations" (1967, 63).

potaennyi, tainstvennost' (secret [adj.], mystery, hidden [adj.], mysteriousness)—appear seven times.[6] If there is any word in the tale that should be expected to appear fifty-two times, it is the word *karta* (card). Instead, the noun appears thirty-five times and the adjective (*kartochnyi*) once, for a total of thirty-six times. The cartomantic significance of this count might be that thirty-six is the number of the cards in the deck of Russian divination cards (Guberti 1881, 326–27).[7]

Allusions, Associations, Links

When "The Queen of Spades" is examined in terms of its semantic-thematic links, numerical combinations again prove to be operative. The functions of numerically controlled allusions, associations, and links have already been seen in Bestuzhev's use of calendarology in "The Frigate Hope." Pushkinists have pointed to the importance of repetition of semantic-thematic links in Pushkin's tale (Bitsilli 1932, 557–58; Stenbock-Fermor 1964). According to Vinogradov, who calls them "allusions," these links are crucial to the structure of the tale because they lure the reader into following the signals or "hints" from one narrative part to another. Numbers arrange scenes and propel events (1936, 585). To this it might be added that they show the way among the tale's many themes—chance, outsider, seduction, greed, revenge, sacrilege, madness, the supernatural—and from one level of this sophisticated tale's multiple layers of meaning to another.

Examples of this type of usage have already been seen in the arrangement of scenes and in Germann's ritualistic pleas for the secret of the three cards, repeated later in the funeral scene. An example of the combination 3 + 1 can be found in chapter 2 where Lizaveta Ivanovna first catches sight of Germann. She sees him three times through the window as he stands "motionlessly" on the street, and she returns to look for him after lunch, only to find him gone this time. In the next chapter, in the part dealing with the secret courtship,

---

6. Excluded from this count is the adjective *tainyi* in its meaning of "privy" in the title Privy Councillor.

7. The number thirty-six might also have to do with the 360 degrees of geometric figures. Pushkin seems not to have been interested in geometrical numerology, either Hellenic Pythagorean numerology or the emphasis placed on geometry by such Great Magi as Francesco Giorgi in *De harmonia mundi* (architectural symbolism) and John Dee in *The Perfect arte of Nauigation* (cartography). Mackey associates 36 = 360 degrees with the Triple Trinity (3 + 6 + 0 = 9) (1924, 2:513). Pushkin's awareness of the combination 3 x 3 might have extended this far.

specific mention is made of three of the many letters through which the courtship is conducted, and then the text is given of a fourth letter—the fatal letter in which Lizaveta Ivanovna becomes a "blind accomplice" in the old countess's death by unwittingly betraying access to the old woman's room. In the epigraph to chapter 5, "the late Baroness von V***" is dressed "all in white." In the chapter itself the countess lies in her coffin in "a white satin dress." The apparition later appears in Germann's quarters as "a woman in a white dress," and he thinks of her as "the white woman" before he recognizes the countess. Once again entities and motifs echo among structural parts in triadic arrangements or in combinations of three and one.

Germann has four encounters with the countess. The confrontation in her room is real. The incidents where her corpse in the coffin seems to wink at him, where the ghost visits him and gives him the secret of the three cards, and the climax where Germann imagines that the old woman's surrogate, the queen of spades, winks at him, are fantasy. Germann also encounters Lizaveta Ivanovna four times. Their confrontation in her room after the death of the countess is direct, and they speak to each other. The other three encounters—when she first sees him through the window, when he stands by the carriage and slips her a letter, and when she faints after he falls away from the coffin at the countess's funeral—are indirect, and they do not speak to each other. When Tomsky asks his grandmother for permission to introduce a friend, Lizaveta Ivanovna's heart begins to beat because she thinks he might bring Germann to meet her; while Germann waits for the countess to return from the ball, his heart beats evenly; when he pleads for the secret of the three cards, he asks the old woman whether any human feeling has ever beat in her bosom. And when Germann leaves the mansion via the secret staircase he realizes that the old woman's heart "has this day ceased to beat." The number sixty is repeated three times in relation to the old countess, and used once in relation to Chekalinsky. Reference is made to the old countess "sixty years before," to her life in Paris "sixty years ago," and to the fact that she dresses "exactly as she did sixty years ago." Mention is made of the "sixty-year-old" Chekalinsky. In Vinogradov's view, this link suggests that Chekalinsky is symbolically or actually the old woman's illegitimate son, and therefore the ironic instrument of her vengeance on Germann (1936, 595–96).

Burgin's ingenious study of "The Queen of Spades" demonstrates that this and other allusions establish a secret relationship among the old countess, Count Saint-Germain, Chaplitsky, and their successor Chekalinsky. Where Germann gains the secret by calculation, the first three gained it properly; Chekalinsky is their instrument of justice. Every hint that Germann drops in his attempt to gain the secret of the cards bears terrible irony and brings him inexorably closer to the revenge of a satanic "cabal" whose secret existence he unknowingly threatens (1974). And finally, it should be noted that "The Queen of Spades" is a tale of four, not three cards. The "three trusty cards" trey, seven, and ace are counterposed to the fourth card, the queen of spades that Germann plays instead of the ace. This is a tale of terrible fate (*rok*), as well as common fate (*sud'ba*) and chance (*sluchai*).

The links among words, events, motifs, and allusions are also by simple threes. At the ball Lizaveta Ivanovna dances with Tomsky, and his teasing is interrupted by the approach of three ladies requesting another dance. The old countess's age is given thrice, the time five o'clock in the morning is given thrice. The image of crossed arms appears three times: Lizaveta Ivanovna sits with her bare arms crossed when Germann enters his room, she later notices Germann sitting on the window sill with his arms crossed, and the countess lies in her coffin with her arms crossed on her chest. The conclusion disposes of the fates of three characters. The secret of the three cards is revealed to Germann on three conditions: he must play each card separately on three consecutive nights, he must marry Lizaveta Ivanovna, and he must never play again. In the opening of chapter 6 Germann's obsession with the cards is dramatized by a thrice-chanted "three, seven, ace." (The repetition of the three cards appears four times again—in Germann's favorite saying, in the old countess's revelation of the secret, in the succession of punts, and by Germann in the insane asylum.) And of course, the three cards are played in succession by three characters—Saint-Germain, the countess, and Chaplitsky—and on three separate nights by Germann.

Numbers are often present by implication. The key numbers are often given by using a number that does not "fit," and thereby seems to violate the system 3–7–1. This is one reason why scholars have been confused about the tale, and in fact Pushkin deliberately leads his reader astray by offering a five or the "number of confusion" two, instead of a three, seven, or one. But there are no anomalies in his use of the system—the other numbers are surrogates. When Pushkin repeats the word once in association with the word week and then sets the time sequence as "two days after the evening" on which the tale begins, he signifies that the action of this scene occurs on the third day of the tale. He sets the time sequences as "about two days later" and "two days later" in two other instances, but in these cases, too, the number two implies a sequence on the third day after the event mentioned. Even so trivial a detail as the number of pages read in a book turns out to be numerically significant. When Lizaveta Ivanovna reads the Russian novel to the countess, she manages to read one page before being interrupted and "two more pages" before being stopped altogether. More important in this respect are the times *not* given for the old countess's death and her appearance in Germann's quarters. While Germann waits for the countess's return from the ball, the clocks strike twelve, one, and two (three times; in Russian time-telling they announce the first, second, and third hours of the day). She returns shortly after two. Her toilet and the confrontation would take just about one hour, thus suggesting that she died at three in the morning. Similarly, Germann awakens in his room three nights later "at a quarter to three," just in time for the countess to arrive and reveal the secret of the three cards at three o'clock.

Germann's use of the secret of the three cards—his "duel" with Chekalinsky—is based on the most careful and ironic linking of significant numbers in the tale. Faro, also called Bank and Stoss or Stuss (Russian *shtos*), was played in so many versions that the game played in America (by Mississippi riverboat gamblers, among others) does not even resemble the game played in Europe and Russia (Culbertson 1952, 356–58). Faro is not, like bridge, a game of skill, or a game of luck that requires skill, like poker. In the game played by Germann (and Pushkin), the dealer or banker (or *tailleur*) and the "punters," those who play against him, each play with their own deck of cards. The bank might play against as many as thirty punters. The players "punt" by placing any card face up or face down ("dark card") on the table, together with a stake (called "coup"—to beat, to hit). The banker deals or "tallies" by laying out his cards face up in pairs, one on the right, one on the left. The punter wins if the card matches the banker's card on the left; if the card matches the banker's card on the right, the punter loses.

On the first night Germann punts the trey. When Chekalinsky deals, laying out the cards on the right and left, "the nine fell to the right, the trey to the left." Germann wins. On the second night Germann punts the seven. When Chekalinsky deals, "the jack turned up on the right, the seven on the left." Germann wins again. On the third night Germann thinks he punts the ace, and when Chekalinsky deals, "the queen fell to the right, the ace to the left." Germann thinks he has won, but he discovers to his horror that he has "mispulled" (*obdernut'sia*) the card. That is, he punted the queen of spades instead of the ace from his deck. "Your queen has been beaten [*ubita*, 'killed']," Chekalinsky says gently, but with intense relief. The three is matched to the nine, the seven to the eleventh card in the suit, and the queen is matched to the queen, the twelfth card in the suit, instead of the ace. The queen of spades winks, and Germann goes mad and ends his days in "cell number 17" of the Obukhovsky Hospital. There, as we learn in the epilogue, he mumbles incessantly: "Trey, seven, ace! Trey, seven, queen!" According to one authority, "the practical Cabala is nothing else but magic endeavoring to induce marvelous effects through the power of the spoken word" (Seligmann 1948, 344). In effect, Germann recites a double Christian-Jewish cabalistic incantation based on the numbers of the two systems: Three, seven, one! Three, seven, twelve! (For explications of cabalistic incantations, see Seligmann 1948, 338–47; Cavendish 1967, 63; and Wilson 1971, 202–5.)

Pushkin, Cartomancy, and the Cabala

Numbers do not occur at random in "The Queen of Spades." They are used overtly and covertly in accordance with a well-devised system. We must understand the overt and covert usages at all levels of this tale if we are to appreciate its remarkable consistency and the numerological system on which it is based. There has to be a unity, too, to Pushkin's knowledge of the thaumaturgical skills he uses—they are too specific not to have been acquired from particular sources. Pushkin's knowledge of numerology and cartomancy can be traced by identifying possible sources in the esoteric tradition.

The migration of Christian adaptations of the Jewish Cabala through the esoteric tradition to Freemasonry and Rosicrucianism draws in the cartomantic system known as the Tarot and the card game faro. How familiar Pushkin was with the esoteric tradition in general or the Cabala in particular is not known. The names of the Great Magi of the esoteric tradition do not appear or appear without particular significance in the index volume of his complete collected works and the survey of his personal library (Modzalevskii 1910). He knew that the system 3–7–1 was cabalistic, and hints at this in a witty reference in his tale: "What!" exclaims the incredulous Narumov upon hearing the first part of Tomsky's anecdote, "you have a grandmother who guesses three cards and you still haven't got her cabalistics [*kabalistika*] out of her?" (1937–59, 8:229).

The Cabala (Hebrew *Kabbalah,* "tradition") is based on gematria, a system that specialists in esotericism describe as the making of a cryptograph in the form of a word whose letters have the numerical value of a word taken as hidden meaning. Or the letters of a word are converted into their numerical equivalents, added up, and then replaced by another word whose letters add up to the same total. The Cabala is an ontological system developed in Babylonia and Greece and passed on to the Hebrews. The Cabala, known in its Hebrew forms as Sephir Yetzira, is a search for texts hidden within texts. The Cabala is based on three correspondences: numerical values, letters, and sounds. Ten values (*sephira*) believed to be numerical powers or to represent spheres of natural power are correlated to the twenty-two letters of the Hebrew alphabet (*yetzira*) and to the sounds they represent (*sipura*). The letters are said to function as twenty-two "paths" of meaning among the numerical values or powers, and to represent the twenty-two acts of Genesis; or the *yetzira* and *sephira* are added for a total of thirty-two values.

The letters are grouped into a 3–7–12 system: the three mother letters, the seven double letters, and the twelve single letters (Scholem 1960, 1987, and especially 1971b). The new Christian combination 3–7–1 required considerable reworking of the original Jewish combinations and their symbolism (Cavendish 1967, 99, 117; Seligmann 1948, 343–46, 353–57; Wilson 1971, 200–225). But the order of the numbers (3–7–1) was preserved with great care. The numbers did not remain within the confines of Lullism. The system was developed in the natural sciences, astrology, alchemy, theosophy, and the humanities.

The Cabala is one expression of the larger esoteric practice of bibliomancy, and the numerical-numerological usages of "The Queen of Spades" evoke all kinds of biblical symbolism that go with the system itself. Jewish Cabalists are bibliomancers who interpret the ineffable meanings of the Talmud; Christian Cabalists apply the system to the New Testament, particularly the *Book of Revelation*. The New Testament seven is, among other things, the seven angels to the right and the seven angels to the left of the One on the Throne in *Revelation*. The other prominent biblical number that appears in "The Queen of Spades" is the number forty (in the number 47). The number recurs throughout both Testaments: the forty years the Hebrews wandered through the wilderness, the forty years of Philistine domination of Israel, the forty days of Elijah's solitude, the forty days of Joseph's fast, Goliath's defiance of the Hebrew army for forty days, the forty or twice forty days required for purification of Hebrew women after childbirth, the destruction of Ninevah after a stipulated forty days, Christ's forty days in the wilderness, His appearance to His disciples for forty days, the forty days of Lent, the forty days and forty nights of the Deluge before which Noah prepared seven days and after which he set free the raven on the third day and the dove after three times seven days. Four is apparently associated with seven in the Christian Cabala not only because of the tertiary-quaternary link, but also under the influence of Pythagorean numerology, the key numbers of which are 7, 10, 40, and 100. More generally, as Hopper has noted, "the phases of the moon indicated to early man an important relationship between 4 and 7." Men knew from earliest times that just as the month is naturally composed of four phases of seven days each, so the year is composed of four seasons of three months each. Jewish numerology derived from gematria emphasizes numerous biblical associations of the monad, triad, tetrad, and heptad (Hopper 1938, 14–15, 26–27, 61–62).

When Pushkin adapted the 3–7–1 system to his tale, he acquired with it other traditions of myth and religion. Among his usages that stem from the New Testament and the Christian Cabala is the device of associating the numbers forty and seven, sometimes with a doubling of the number forty. The most prominent of these are the forty days of Lent and the seven days of Holy Week.[8] Pushkin might be hinting at this association where he has Narumov congratulate Germann for breaking his Lenten fast (*post*) by suddenly deciding to play faro. Awareness of the significance of doubling the forty might provide a numerical link with the numbers seventeen and 47,000 in the text and the countess's age eighty-seven (40 + 40 + 7). In this regard two numerical-numerological idiosyncracies of doubling are worth mention. When conjoined with the seventeen, the only number given in figures in the text, the number forty-seven works back to three: 47 = 17 + 30 (=3). The same thing happens when seventeen is conjoined with the countess's age: 87 = 17 + 70 (=7). (For thorough sources on aspects of numbers and numerology, see Jobes 1961–62 and Chambers 1967.)

The system is also basic to the cartomantic system known as the Tarot. The Tarot has seventy-eight cards: fifty-six Minor Arcana (ace through ten and four royal cards in four suits—cups, pentacles, scepters or wands, and swords) and twenty-two Major Arcana. The combinations of the Major Arcana are complicated number sequences from one through ten, ten through 100, and 100 through 900. The Major Arcana originate from the twenty-two paths of the Cabala, and like them symbolize lines among natural forces. As with the Cabala, the lines are organized on the numerological principle 3 + 7 + 12 = 22. The fifty-two cards of the playing deck are comparable to the Minor Arcana in that a suit of playing cards can be augmented by counting the ace as both low and high cards or by using the joker (Hoy 1971, 133–65). The origins of the Tarot are unknown except for the fact that it succeeded and was based on

---

8. The Orthodox calendar adds Lent and Holy Week; other Christian calendars overlap them, with Holy Week beginning on the last day of Lent.

the Cabala.⁹ One advocate of the Tarot describes it as "an ontological system summing up . . . numerology, geometrics, astrology, mythology, and theosophy" (Hoy 1971, 3–4). The Tarot can be "read" by an effectively infinite number of possible numerical-numerological combinations achieved by randomly or logically juxtaposing its graphic figures and a large number of symbolic elements that comprise the figures. The Christian system 3–7–1 is not alien to the Tarot: one of the most powerful divinations is based on twenty-one cards laid out in a three-seven pattern, using a "one" card as a control or "significator" of the "signifiers" (Hoy 1971, 48–49).

There is no evidence that Pushkin knew the Tarot. The text of "The Queen of Spades" yields no apparent indications of Tarot symbolism. The Russian playing-card culture of the eighteenth century and Pushkin's time has been examined in a cultural-semiotic study by Yury Lotman (1975b), but neither this study nor Nathan Rosen's Freudian analysis of the symbolism of Germann's graphic visions of the three cards (1975) indicates that Pushkin used any card system other than the playing deck in his tale. Examination of folders of playing cards in the Petersburg Public Library reveals nothing that was not reported by Lotman and Rosen. Standard histories of card decks yield no significant new evidence (Benham 1931; Hargrave 1930). Pushkin used Russian divination cards, of which several systems were common to the culture of his time. The most common decks were composed of thirty-six cards lettered from AA through IuIU and depicted appropriate figures from Russian folklore (Guberti 1881, 326–27). As has been noted, the number thirty-six might be accounted for in the tale by the count of the word *card* (*karta*). It shows up also in the combined count of all forms of the number three and its higher denominations (33 + 3). The Russian divination system does not seem otherwise to be operative in the tale, and its folk figures do not seem to appear in the tale, not even in the figures Germann hallucinates in the numbers during his obsession with the three cards after the secret is revealed to him. The tale's main epigraph— "The queen of spades signifies secret ill-will"—and its attribution to *The Modern Book of Divination* relate to the standard playing deck, not to the Russian divination deck, which does not feature a queen of spades.

The only possible connection between "The Queen of Spades" and the Tarot is a remote association: the card game faro originates in the Tarot. The

---

9. Claims that the Tarot goes back to the Egyptian pharaohs are disproved by modern esotericists, who have left no doubt that the Tarot is a graphic form of the orthographic system of the Cabala (Seligmann 1948, 423).

word *faro* is believed to be a corruption of the word *pharoah* and an etymological and historical relative of the word *tarot*. The simple turning over and matching of cards to left or right makes faro an extremely boring game. When money is staked on the single turn of a card, however, the game becomes more than slightly absorbing. It is made even more exciting by the system of tally. In Pushkin's time faro offered two methods of tally. To play *mirandole*, as Surin does at the start of the tale, means to gamble a stake on each separate deal of the cards (*coup*). The punter then either wins or loses his or her stake. To play parolet (*paroli*) or *na rute,* the Russian term used by Surin at the start of the tale, means to let the stake and winnings ride on a single card through a series of coups. The numerical combinations for tallying the stakes and winnings when parolet is played, are as follows:

first punt	$1 + 1 = 2$	"un et le va"	
second punt	$3 + 1 = 4$	"trois et le va"	(*parolet*)
third punt	$7 + 1 = 8$	"sept et le va"	(*parolet-paix*)

That is, the stake does not simply double through the run, it increases onefold on the first punt, three fold on the second, sevenfold on the third, and so on (Chkhaidze 1960, 456–58; Chkhaidze 1973, 84–87).[10]

Germann does not play parolet. He is prevented from doing so by the condition that he must punt three different cards. He does, however, aim to achieve the same end by the simple ploy of gambling both his original stake and his winnings on the second and third punts. On the first night Germann stakes 47,000 rubles and wins 47,000 rubles (1 + 1). On the second night Germann bets his original stake and his winnings—94,000 rubles. He wins. Although Pushkin does not specify the amount, Germann now has 188,000, of which one "part" is his original stake, three units his winnings from Chekalinsky (3 + 1). On the third night Germann gambles his original stake and winnings.

---

10. The leading Pushkinist B. V. Tomashevsky has long been credited for first discovering the origin of the three numbers in the tally system. He reported his discovery to the French Pushkinist André Meynieux in 1937. Meynieux did not report the discovery until 1958 when he published the last volume of Pushkin's complete collected works in French (Tomashevskii 1953–58, 500). For some reason, Tomashevsky never developed the discovery. According to a verbal assertion by the Dostoyevsky scholar M. A. Altman it was he who discovered the link in the 1920s and reported it to Tomashevsky (Session of the Comparative Literature Section, Institute of Russian Literature, Leningrad, 26 October 1977). Other scholars discussed the tally system and some of its implications, but only Chkhaidze worked the system out fully and explained many of its implications to the tale (1960, 1973). The correct combinations are not achieved by doubling—two, four, eight—as, for example, Vladimir Nabokov explicated the system (1964, 2:258–61).

Had he won, he would have his original stake and seven units of winnings (7 + 1). Scholars have made much of the fact that Pushkin's calculations of Germann's winnings, based as they are on the number forty-seven, seem to violate the system 3–7–1. To complicate matters, on the back of a letter Pushkin once calculated Germann's winnings for both 47,000 and 67,000 rubles, a comparison that prompted Chkhaidze to speculate that Pushkin intended to up the stakes in a revised version of the tale (1973). In fact, not only is the number forty-seven fully compatible with the system 3–7–1, it is the only number whose sequences provide numerologically elegant results of calculations of Germann's winnings:

47	4 + 7 = 11	1 + 1 = 2
94	9 + 4 = 13	3 + 1 = 4
188	1 + 8 + 8 = 17	7 + 1 = 8

That is, forty-seven is the only number that, when calculated *mirandole,* works out to the system of tally *parolet.* The number sixty-seven does not work out, and neither would any of the numbers Pushkinists have suggested might have been more logical choices—37,000, say, or 33,000.

The system of tally is important not only numerically, but psychologically, for it provides a rational answer to the frequently asked question, "Where did Germann obtain the secret of the three cards?" and thereby nullifies the supernatural answer, "From the ghost of the old countess." Germann is a fanatic and frustrated cardplayer who never permitted himself "to take a card in hand," even while following the turns of play each night "with feverish trembling." When his imagination is aroused by Tomsky's anecdote of his grandmother's possession of a secret method of predicting three winning cards in a row, Germann dreams so intensely of winning parolet that the method even becomes his favorite saying—"these are my three trusty cards," "this is what will triple, multiply seven-fold my capital." And so, when the old countess dies without revealing the secret of the three cards—dies after Germann has worked so hard to deceive Lizaveta Ivanovna and come so close to gaining his fervently coveted "peace and independence"—it is little wonder that he persuades himself (with the help of a little wine) that the ghost of the old countess visits him and gives him the secret. The tally system of the game of faro is itself the source of the three secret numbers, that is, and its participation in the tale explains Germann's motivations with great psychological credibility: he is fixated on the numbers *before* he resolves to obtain the secret.

Here, as in no other work by Pushkin, we have one of the clearest examples of his determination to provide credible psychological explanations for romantic events. The secret of the three cards, which reached Pushkin through centuries of esoteric tradition, comes to Germann not through the kind of supernatural intervention that is the stuff of so many other romantic works, but in the form of the arithmetical logic that is the very basis of thaumaturgical practices. Germann's logic, however, is every bit as acausal as that of any of the pre-Cartesian Great Magi: the cause-and-effect connection between the system of tally and secret of the three cards is as illogical as the alternative supernatural explanation. The romantic irony here is striking: the psychologically "realistic" credibility is as fully romantic as Germann's imagination.

Sooner or later, in one way or another, the text of "The Queen of Spades" yields an answer to the many mystifying questions it raises. The source and probable meaning of the epigraph "Homme sans moeurs et sans religion!" The reason for the order of the three cards—"Trey, seven, ace!" However, three of the most often asked questions—questions raised by the cards themselves—have never been answered. First, given that Germann received the secret not through supernatural intervention but by a trick of the mind, how is it that the cards actually did turn up in the order predicted? Second, how did Germann happen to punt the queen of spades instead of the ace? And third, why did the old countess (or Germann in his delusion) add the stipulation that the cards have to be played on three successive nights? After all, Saint-Germain gave the countess, and the countess gave Chaplitsky, the opportunity to win instantly. The first question might be moot. Certainly an experienced gambler would not ask it. The answer, in both the vast literature of gambling stories and in real life, is that such remarkable strokes of luck happen all the time. This might be the answer to the second question, too. In the excitement of the moment gamblers often play the wrong card. There might also be a Freudian explanation. Like his illustrious successor in Russian literature, Raskolnikov of Dostoyevsky's novel *Crime and Punishment,* Germann desires to be punished. He does, after all, have a burden of conscience to bear. To this it might be added that he is, psychologically, a loser to begin with.

The key to this possible explanation is the Russian word *obdernut'sia* (mispulled). All Germann had to do was "pull" the ace from the top of the deck and "punt" or "hit" (*bit'*) it against the cards Chekalinsky was laying on the table. Instead, he actually reached three cards down and pulled—or rather "mispulled"—the queen of spades. He may have done this unconsciously, but nevertheless he had to have done it deliberately. If this is so, then Pushkin's irony is again striking, because the verb *obdernut'sia* is reflexive (the suffix *-sia*); Germann "turned [the card] around" *against himself.* It also means that he "hit" with the wrong card—a semantic turn that cruelly enhances the irony of Chekalinsky's response: "Your queen has been hit/beaten/killed." No wonder Germann went insane!

As for the third question, there is no apparent answer. The stipulation does not prevent Germann from achieving the same results that would have been his had he played parolet. The prolonging of the play adds suspense, but Pushkin could just as easily have made three punts on a single night as exciting as punts on three different nights. The condition does not suggest any special irony or possible deception. The only apparent answer, therefore, is that despite Pushkin's apparent resolve to provide an explanation for most of the tale's mystifications, he deliberately left some questions open. After all, "The Queen of Spades" has intrigued readers for over a century and a half. She will probably continue to do so for another century and a half.

8

Freemasonry in "The Queen of Spades"

"... in the name of all that is sacred in life ..."
—Aleksandr Pushkin, "The Queen of Spades"

Pushkin's mastery of numerology and cartomancy is exceptional. He was not an adept in the sense that a Master Mason is an adept; nothing in existing evidence suggests that he was an expert in the esoteric tradition. Rather, he knew what he knew, and he mastered the skills he needed to create a major—and highly unusual—literary masterpiece. Where did Pushkin acquire the skills? He did not leave evidence of the source of his knowledge. There is good reason to believe, however, that the general or particular source of his knowledge was the same direct or indirect source of his contemporaries' knowledge—Freemasonry. It is to other aspects of Freemasonry and the relationships between thaumaturgy and literature that we have to turn for further understanding of the development of the esoteric tradition in Russia.

Pushkin and Numerology: Sources

Pushkin's knowledge of numerology could have come from one or many sources available to him as a Freemason, and while it is not possible to point at one particular source, at least two explicate the system 3–7–1 in similar ways. One of these sources is the mystic Louis-Claude de Saint-Martin, the theosophist whom historians of Russian Freemasonry consider the most important influence on the Moscow Mystic Masons (Pypin 1916, 141–42; Vernadskii 1917, 162–63). A posthumous publication of Saint-Martin's teachings on numerology (1807), published in part again in 1843 as *Des nombres,* indicates that his "formules numériques" correspond to the rules applied by Pushkin in "The Queen of Spades." As an example of the first of the three basic operations, addition, he uses the illustration $1 + 2 + 3 + 4 + 5 + 6 = 21$. The example Saint-Martin gives for multiplication—3×7—also yields 21. He understands this numerical formula as either multiplication or "squaring," that is, $3 \times 3 = 9$. For his third numerical formula, addition combined with multiplication, he uses the Triple Trinity as his example: $9 \times 9 = 81$ ($8 + 1 = 9$) (1946, 37–39). Saint-Martin indicates appreciation for the biblical link between seven and forty with the example $5 \times 8 = 40 + 7 = 47$, but he does not seem otherwise to value the system 3–7–1 as such. The numbers two and six are important to him, and he also emphasizes the great power of the number eight by illustrating the power of multiplication with the formulas $2 \times 2 = 4 \times 2 = 8$ and $7 \times 5 = 35$ ($3 + 5 = 8$). Five and seven thus join two, six, and eight in his hierarchy of numerological powers, and he again gives an interesting example: $5 \times 5 = 25$ ($2 + 5 = 7$) (1946, 40–47). Perhaps this association of two, five, and seven derives from the same source as Pushkin's use of the number 275, but Saint-Martin does not show interest in cartomancy or playing cards.

According to Vernadsky, the chief source of Russian knowledge of "the cabalistic-numerical science" was Baron Georg von Welling, whose *Opus Mago-Cabbalisticum et Theosophicum* also influenced Saint-Martin. A copy of the superior edition of 1760 was brought to Moscow among the other "Divine Wisdom [*Bogomudrye*] works" listed by Vernadsky. Welling's work was adapted into Russian by the Masonic leader I. P. Elagin (Vernadskii 1917, 126). According to a copy of Elagin's translation among his papers in the Moscow archives, "Divine . . . writing consists of its secret meaning, understanding of which is incorporated in the cabalistic-numerical science; this must prove to us what the *Kabala* is."[1] Examples of some of the orthographic-numerological

---

1. I am obliged to Stephen Baehr for this lead and its source: TsGADA, fond 8, khranilishche 216, chast' 6, list 53 ob.

operations practiced by Elagin, Lopukhin, and other Moscow Mystic Masons are furnished in their correspondence published by Ya. L. Barskov (1915, 230) and by Pypin (1916, 47, 62–63). However, a reading of Welling does not yield an explication of the system 3–7–1. His work is instead a systematization of a large number of cabalistic symbols, replete with graphic illustrations and theosophical explications. The Masonic authority who explicated Welling's system most lucidly was Baron de Tschoudy.

In Tschoudy's view, "arcane knowledge" was the possession of "great masters." He assesses the contributions of these masters in *Der flammende Stern*, particularly in a series titled "Articles of the Nameless Philosophers," whom he reveals to be, among others, Ficino, Pico, Giorgi, Reuchlin, Andreae, Fludd, Böhme, Swedenborg, and their great teacher Plato (1866, 1:263–64; 2:65–70, 160–61, 168–69). He includes Welling among these masters, and *Der Signatstern* also offers an elaborate "explication of Welling's numerological system" (1866, 2:138–47). The most important revelations of cabalistic writings are not only the names of the great adepts, but the "hieroglyphic signs or allegorical words" that convey their ineffable teachings. "Cabalistics" ("devices" for the manipulation of words with the assistance of numerical formulas) and numerology are equally important to the duty of Freemasons to preserve the memory of a deceased brother without betraying that brother's Masonic identity. The importance of this duty has already been seen with reference to the function of the accomplice of death prescribed to the Moscow Mystic Masons by Baron Schroeder (Barskov 1915, 227).

The numbers and numerical combinations explicated by Tschoudy are based on the numbers three, seven, and one, and they correspond in almost every respect to the system 3–7–1 used by Pushkin. Tschoudy considers these to be the "most powerful . . . cabalistic numbers," and he gives examples extracted from his readings of Welling. Among the most powerful numerological combinations are $3 \times 7 = 21$ and the Triple Trinity. He offers a geometric analysis of the Masonic triangle in which he finds that "all is three." The number one is the Unity, and in his symbolic system the number seven represents the seven days, the seven years, the seven secrets, and the seven liberal arts. These number usages form the basis of his Order of the Flaming Star. The importance he ascribes to the quaternary-tertiary relationship is shown by the very ordering of his system of degrees into the three basic practical or working degrees and seven theoretical degrees ($3 + 4 = 7$).

Baron de Tschoudy joins others in ascribing great power to the Triple Trinity $3 \times 3 = 9$, whose operations he explicates in *Der flammende Stern* (1:263–64). In an exhaustive analysis of numerology in *The Divine Comedy*, Hopper points out that in medieval symbolism the number three is inseparable from "the One God" and is "the sole root of nine." Beatrice is associated with the number nine throughout the work. For Dante, the number nine symbolizes, among other things, "the nine spheres of Heaven" and the "nine circles of Hell." The "one poem" is composed of three canticles, each comprising—symbolically—thirty-three cantos. (The actual realization of this symbolic structure is 34 + 33 + 33 cantos because Dante wished to account in this anomaly for the age of Christ when He was crucified.) In Dante's system the Triple Trinity is systematically associated not only with the monad, but also the diad, triad, tetrad, heptad, and decad. In the poem's order of moral priorities, the heptad symbolizes the seven virtues and seven vices (Hopper 1938, 138–39, 151–53).

Among other possible sources of Pushkin's knowledge, it is worth noting that Pushkinists have wrongly credited a report that Pushkin obtained the anecdote of Saint-Germain's three cards from his friend Prince P. A. Vyazemsky (Iakubovich 1933, 62). There is no indication in biographies of the notorious charlatan that he ever claimed to be able to predict three cards. A facsimile of Saint-Germain's most prominent work, *La Très Sainte Trinosophie* (1949), shows no interest in the system 3–7–1. As Tomsky reports in his anecdote, Saint-Germain did "pass himself off as the Eternal Jew, as the inventor of an elixir of life and the philosophers' stone and so forth."[2] Casanova did report in his memoirs that Saint-Germain was a spy (1833–37, 8:7),[3] and he was right (Seligmann 1948, 474–79).[4] Also wrongly credited are reports that Pushkin developed

---

2. If Pushkin was familiar with Cagliostro's works (which is doubtful), he would undoubtedly have enjoyed the count's prescriptions for the elixir of life or "Panacea" he claimed to have inherited from Saint-Germain. In one (possibly two) works known and described by an anonymous exposer of Cagliostro's hoaxes, "la Régénération physique et morale," Cagliostro (or Saint-Germain) prescribes drops of the Panacea in combinations like 21 + 3 + 3 + 3 + 3 + 3. After a visitation by "the seven primitive spirits" on the thirty-third day and the passage of another seven days (33 + 7 = 40), the "patient" will not only be morally regenerated, but inspired with divine knowledge. Physical regeneration is also achieved by administration of drops in combinations of three, six, and twelve, and of days in threes, with stipulations on the seventeenth, twenty-first, and thirty-third days. After a retreat from the world in early May the patient may return to the world on the fortieth day secure in the knowledge he will live 5557 years—"if he so wishes" ([Barberi] 1792, 258–62, 143–45).

3. Pushkin owned a copy of the 1833 edition of *Mémoires de Jacques Casanova de Seingalt* (Modzalevskii 1910, no. 706). Casanova is also the source of other anecdotes about Saint-Germain and Cagliostro, including one about an encounter with Saint-Germain in which the inventor of the elixir of life attempted to treat Casanova with his "Panacea." Casanova wisely demurred because he knew that Saint-Germain hated him (1833–37, 9:236–39).

4. Just as important to Pushkin, probably, is that Saint-Germain visited Petersburg at the time Catherine II became empress, and there as elsewhere gained a reputation by demonstrating his magical powers. There also he wore out his welcome and was banished from Russia (Seligmann 1948, 474–79; also Chetteoui 1947).

Tomsky's anecdote from rumors about the other great charlatan of the eighteenth century, Joseph Balsamo, "Commonly Called Count Cagliostro."[5] Cagliostro did not claim to predict three lucky cards; others claimed for him that he predicted five winning lottery numbers—8, 20, 25, 55, 57 ([Lucia] 1787, 19, 21).[6]

It has already been noted that Pushkin is not indebted to Swedenborg for his numerological usages; neither is he indebted to the Swedish theosophist for the epigraph to chapter 5.[7] Saint-Germain, Swedenborg, and Casanova are introduced into "The Queen of Spades" more for play than as leads to any momentous meaning. This is especially true of Casanova, whose memoirs yield several finely ironic numerical and gambling connections. Pushkin must have noted, for example, that Casanova played faro in Petersburg and was offended to learn that Russian aristocrats do not pay their gambling debts (1833–37, 9:271–73).[8] Casanova reports that he once lost 100 Spanish quadruples, the equivalent of 700 Venetian sequins, at the bank of the famous gambler Canano. He thereupon placed 100 sequins on a card, punted paroli (*parolet*), punted le sept et le va (*parolet-paix*), and won back his 100 quadruples. He then placed fifty sequins on a card, punted paroli, paix de paroli, and so won his own

---

5. The error seems to have been started in the 1920s and was repeated by leading Pushkinists (Kashin 1927, 32; Grossman 1928, 143–44; Lerner 1929, 141; Tsiavlovskii 1936–38, 4:741).

6. The source of this error can be explained by Petersburg lore. During a sojourn in Petersburg Cagliostro predicted that a skeptical lady at the court of Catherine II would have three accidents. Cagliostro gained great credibility in Petersburg society when his prediction came true. As was his wont, he overexploited the opportunity and soon joined Saint-Germain in banishment (Ribadeau Dumas 1967, 72; also Chetteoui 1947).

7. Nevertheless, searches for Pushkin's interest in Swedenborg have yielded a few rewards. The quotation from "Privy Councillor Swedenborg" reads: "That night there appeared to me the late Baroness von V***. She was all in white and said to me: 'Greetings, Mr. Councillor!'" Pushkinists have searched Swedenborg's thoroughly indexed works without finding this quotation, and one elaborate study of Pushkin's attitude to Swedenborg proved only that a relative attempted without success to interest the poet in Swedenborgism (Sharypkin 1974). More successful was Vinogradov's research. Taking a cue from Pushkin's notes on another story, Vinogradov searched E. T. Van der Velde's "Arwed Gillenstein," a gambling story on the theme of the murder of Charles XII. There he found a hero who, like Germann, is an engineer, and who is guided by "Councillor Swedenborg" to victory in a card game with the future assassin of the Swedish king (1936, 95–96). A point missed by researchers would seem to be that Pushkin invented the quotation in order to parody a prominent aspect of Swedenborg's writings. Swedenborg, like Germann, experienced visitations from beyond the grave, which, he claimed, revealed to him what other mortals knew not. His theosophy is enunciated in the form of encounters with real persons or spirits, all of whom he confounds by posing a paradox. His writings are filled with accounts beginning with a formula such as, "There appeared to me a beautiful girl with a radiant face, passing quickly upwards towards the right . . . not a child nor yet a woman—becomingly clothed with a dress of shining black" (n.d., 3:311). Swedenborg always outwits his interlocutors—even Jesus Christ.

8. Casanova, too, was banished from Russia for scandalous behavior.

money back and then some (1833–37, 8:255–56). Note that in the first run Casanova anted one-seventh of his losses and, in an adroit calculation of quadruples and sequins, recovered his losses exactly (700 sequins equals 100 quadruples).[9]

The Legend of Hyram Abif

One of the most productive interpretations of "The Queen of Spades," by Harry Weber (1968), treats it as a parody of the ancient Masonic legend of Hyram-Abif, the purported hero-martyr and builder of King Solomon's temples who died under torture rather than reveal the secrets of the craft, the Hyram-Abif whose "grave" marks the center of the Masonic lodges during the rite of initiation. The ironies of the tale's Masonic hints and allusions are sharp.

Pushkin recorded the precise date of his initiation into the Kishinev lodge of Ovid, one of the twenty-five lodges obedient to the Grand Lodge of Astraea, as 4 May 1821 (1937–59, 7:303). The Grand Lodge recognized both the Strict Observance Swedish Rites, which it tried to discourage, and the modernized Ancient English system. Ovid was the only lodge authorized to use a "Scottish Rite." This has led scholars to identify it with the system of thirty-three degrees of the American Free and Accepted Rites. But the Grand Lodge of Astraea was authorized to practice only the three craft degrees, and examination of the text of the rite of advancement to the Second Degree of Fellow Craft Mason for the lodge of Ovid does not show any significant differences from the rites of other Russian lodges.[10] Pushkin would have had to memorize and participate in the rite of the death of Hyram-Abif in order to be initiated. He probably gained some knowledge of the required thaumaturgical skills during the Kishinev period, even though he was not greatly attracted to the craft at that time. He could have become more adept, if he had wanted to, at the time he wrote "The Queen of Spades" in the early 1830s. The lodges were closed by that time, but this did not prevent Freemasons from working

---

9. The incident is one part of an account of Casanova's faro exploits that he calls his "war with Canano." On another evening at Canano's Casanova staked the beautiful Irene, who had been told by her father that the secret of winning at faro is never to punt one card at a time. Despite this, she cannot muster the courage to punt beyond *paroli*, and so loses three coups in a row. During this interlude Casanova finds time to seduce the beautiful Zenobie and skillfully contrives for her to achieve her fourteenth orgasm with his third (1833–37, 8:248–49). If Pushkin did not have this numerical accomplishment in mind when he wrote "The Queen of Spades," he should have.

10. Institute of Russian Literature, Razdel II, opis' 2, no. 104.

"in silence." Access to the documents of the Grand Lodge of Astraea was certainly no problem for him: the Grand Master of the Grand Lodge Count V. V. Musin-Pushkin-Bryus was his cousin. If he had obtained his knowledge under his vow of secrecy, he would have observed the vow. This did not prevent him from using his knowledge for the writing of his tale: Goethe used his Rosicrucian knowledge in his poetry, Mozart used Masonic symbolism in *The Magic Flute*.

The lodge of Ovid was closed with the other lodges by Alexander's order of 12 August 1822. Pushkin believed the chief cause was the radical activity of his own lodge of Ovid. In a letter to Vasily Zhukovsky after the failure of the revolt of 14 December 1825, he wrote: "I was a Mason in the Kish[inev] lodge, that is, in the one because of which all the lodges in Russia were destroyed. Lastly, I had connections with the greater part of the present conspirators" (Shaw 1967, 1:302). Pushkinists believe that Pushkin's admissions were addressed not to Zhukovsky, but to Nicholas I, on whose behalf Zhukovsky had requested Pushkin to clarify his involvement in the Decembrist affair. Pushkin probably exaggerated, but the lodge of Ovid was intensely political. Its Master, Colonel P. S. Pushchin, was a political activist, as was another member, Pushchin's mentor and commander General M. F. Orlov. Orlov was a founding member of both the Union of Salvation and the Union of Welfare; one Decembrist plan called for him to take over after power was seized. Pushkin met the Decembrist Pavel Pestel in Kishinev at this time, and Rayevsky was a member of Ovid until his arrest in 1821. Pushkin warned Rayevsky of his impending arrest (Chereiskii 1975, 339–40). In 1821 Pushkin wrote a Masonic poem "To General Pushchin" in which the Masonic hammer, symbol of authority, links Freemasonry with the struggle for freedom (1937–59, 1:204):

> Thou shalt take hammer in hand
> And call the rise: freedom:
> I praise thee, loyal brother!
> O worthy Mason!

Pushkin did not cease to be a Freemason when the lodges were banned. The vow of secrecy and receipt of the secrets of the craft are a lifetime, irrevocable commitment. In a letter of 5 March 1833 to M. P. Pogodin, attempting to persuade the historian to join him in his historical research in state archives, Pushkin promised: "You will produce such marvelous things that we and our posterity will pray [to] God for you" (Shaw 1967, 2:567). Pogodin recognized this as an allusion to the legend of Hyram-Abif, for he replied: "But let them sing my memory, but let them cut out my tongue in as many strips as they wish!" Pushkin's reference to the prayers of posterity has to do with the Masonic initiate's received obligation to revere the great Masonic hero-martyr and to remember all fallen brothers. Pogodin's reply continues the ritualistic recitation: he will preserve the secrets of the archives as faithfully as Hyram-Abif preserved the secrets of the craft. In the legend of Hyram-Abif, which is the basis of Freemasonry, King Solomon's master architect formed a masonic guild and devised the signs, the signals, and the words by which its members could secretly identify their craft, skill level, and rights to wages. When three impostors attempted to force Hyram-Abif to reveal the secrets so that they could falsely claim wages, the hero-martyr allowed his tongue to be sliced into strips rather than betray his oath of secrecy. Every initiated Freemason must swear to uphold the example of Hyram-Abif (Weber 1968, 446–47).

Masonic Symbolism and Ritual

The rite of initiation is the rite of the love of death that proved to be so important to Kondraty Ryleyev. The description of the rite in *Der Signatstern* (1866, 1:63–73) is similar to standard descriptions in English, German, and other encyclopedias (Lenhoff and Posner 1932; Mackey 1924). "Journeys" around the "grave of Hyram-Abif" are made in sequences of three or 3 x 3 from the left and right (east and west), the initiate is "killed" and resurrected, questions are asked and answered, again in sequences of three. The initiate pleads three times for initiation into the secrets of the craft. According to Weber's interpretation of "The Queen of Spades," Germann's stealthy invasion of the old countess's mansion in chapter 3, his suspenseful wait for her return from the ball amidst her once-fashionable, now eccentric eighteenth-century furnishings, and his urgent pleas for the secret of the three cards that can make his fortune—is a carefully arranged parody of the Masonic supplicant's entrance into the Temple of Solomon and his pleas for admittance into the secrets of the craft.

The tale is seen as replete with such Masonic symbolism as Germann's third plea on his knees, the mention of the "appointed hour" and the patterned striking of the clocks, and the left-right sequences of motion and direction. The Masonic and Rosicrucian symbols the rose, Venus, and a virgin appear in the portrait of the young beauty with a rose in her hair and the old countess's cap adorned with roses, in the old woman's reputation in Paris sixty years before as "la Vénus moscovite," and in the jeopardy to Lizaveta Ivanovna's virginity by Germann's clandestine courtship. The mystery of the Masonic temple is evoked by the green lamps, ancient chairs arranged in "sorrowful symmetry" along the walls, portraits painted in Paris by Madame Lebrun, a star, table clocks by Leroy. The mystique of Freemasonry is invoked by allusions to Count Saint-Germain, Swedenborg, and Casanova. Weber finds a hint of Masonic symbolism in the choice of doors to the left and right of the stairs when Germann enters the mansion. He draws a parallel between the old countess lying with her arms crossed in the coffin and the practice of some rites of placing the initiate in a coffin with his arms crossed (1968, 435–37, 438–41).

Weber's work is convincing because of his documentation from research in Russian Freemasonry, particularly the work of Pypin (1916) and T. O. Sokolovskaya (1915a, 1915b). Although the rites vary from lodge to lodge and orient to orient, the essential elements are common to all. The initiate is led by his sponsor, often up a flight of stairs, to the door of the temple where the Doorkeeper obtains permission to introduce the initiate by a designated number of knocks and questions. The time is asked. The initiate is brought blindfolded into the temple and made to face different directions and answer a memorized ritualistic series of questions pertaining to each direction. Questions are asked by the Warden or Wardens; most are asked by the Master of the Lodge. Times and directions are stipulated, often to the striking of clocks. The initiate is led around the temple in one or both directions, clockwise and counterclockwise, right and left, west and east, sometimes thrice. Other questions are asked in stipulated numbers and orders, usually by threes. The initiate rolls up one leg of his trousers to the knee and a sword is pointed at his bare chest. In some rites he swears by the honor of his mother, symbolized by a red rose if she is alive, by a white rose if she is dead. Symbols are spoken and explicated. The legend of Hyram-Abif is explained. The initiate is led to the Master, who warns him three times of the seriousness of the vows he is about to take and the secrets that are about to be revealed to him. He indicates his understanding and pleads for the secrets, the third time on bended knee. His third plea is accepted and the oath is administered, after which the blindfold is removed to reveal the identities of his new brothers. The symbolism of the craft—the work of the mason, builder, architect—is then revealed to him, and he is instructed to work diligently to build a perfect mind, body, and soul (see Pypin 1916, 42–80).

Weber points out that asking the time, as someone asks the absent-minded

Germann in chapter 6, is essential to the rite of initiation, and that the tale's left-right sequences (including the deals of the cards in the game faro) correspond to the fundamental left-right, east-west (Orient-Occident) motions, signals, directions, and locations of the Masonic temple. The symmetry of the old countess's furniture along the walls corresponds to the symmetrical orientation of the officers and members of the lodge along the walls of the temple. The receipt of a key, as when Lizaveta Ivanovna gives Germann the key so that he can leave by the staircase, corresponds to the Masonic key given to the initiate as a symbol of receipt of the secrets of the craft.[11] The "galvanic" motions of the old woman's head bobbing to the left and right are similar to "galvanic" devices used to govern the movements of a skeleton in the decor of at least one Russian lodge. The doors to the left and right of the stairs are similarly reminiscent of the locations of doors to the Masonic temple at the left and right. There is an ironic parallel between the Masonic ritual phrase, "That which my soul yearns for, but does not attain," and Lizaveta Ivanovna's realization about Germann, "Money, that is what his soul yearns for!" The tale contains such possible hints of Freemasonry as the guests at the ball who pay their respects to the countess "in accordance with an established ritual" (1968, 436–42).[12]

Other possible connections are the countess's losses to the Duc d'Orleans and the fact that the latter was the Grand Master of the Grand Orient of France (Mackey 1924, 1:528). Or Germann's decision to exploit Lizaveta Ivanovna in order to obtain the secret of the three cards—"That moment decided his fate!"—and the moment when the Master of the Lodge accepts the initiate's aspirations to the secrets of the craft—"Your fate has been decided!" (Sokolovskaia 1915b, 93). Or Germann's failed quest for the secret and the most typical plot of Masonic literary works, which deals with the fall of a character "whose knowledge is insufficient to distinguish between appearance and reality and who thus falls prey to beckoning temptation and deceptive disguises" (Baehr 1976, 124).

---

11. Note the irony: Germann is given the key to leave, not to enter, and he descends, not ascends, the stairs of the mansion he has invaded.

12. Weber also points out the similarities between the names of the characters Chaplitsky and Chekalinsky and the prominent Russian Freemasons Chaplits and Chekalevsky, and a possible connection between the Obukhov Hospital where Germann ends his days and the fact that the director of the hospital was Dr. Georg Heinrich Ellison, principal founder of the Grand Lodge of Astraea.

Freemasonry in "The Queen of Spades"

Weber's interpretation is reinforced by parallels between Pushkin's tale and details provided by Sokolovskaya. Among these is her description of St. John's Rituals, which define the craft degrees. Among the features she mentions that have correspondences with "The Queen of Spades" are a three-cornered lampholder, the placement of three symbolic lamps, sometimes in groups of three, dim lights and shadows, striking clocks, three knocks on the door of the temple, and "a staircase which leads to heaven." Staircases are important to Masonic symbolism in that the rite of initiation is called "the first step of the Masonic staircase" to moral and spiritual perfection. The staircase (also, symbolically, the ladder) has seven steps, each symbolizing a Masonic virtue (1915b, 85–98). Sokolovskaya pays special attention to a Masonic sign ("the signs, the signals, and the words") that seems to have a place in Pushkin's tale, the depiction of the three main characters at significant moments with their arms crossed over the breast. According to Sokolovskaya, the crossing of the arms in this way followed the Christian tradition and was a sign of identification and a signal of distress (1908, 82).[13]

Correspondences are also to be found in the Masonic holdings of the Institute of Russian Literature in Saint Petersburg. Among the allegorical images illustrated in one document, for example, are seven candles in three holders, crossed ladders with seven rungs each, and the signs for the seven "positive qualities" (virtues) of a Freemason. A text of the rituals for opening and closing the lodge and for the rite of initiation shows many of the elements mentioned by Weber, Pypin, and Sokolovskaya: three knocks on a door (or table), questions and answers in sets of three, a request for the time, three symbolic journeys around the temple, the arrangement of the officers of the lodge along the four walls, elucidations of the three signs and the seven virtues, repeated in the Master's injunctions to the initiate.[14]

The irony of Pushkin's parody of the Masonic rite of initiation is strong. Germann in effect violates the sanctity of the Masonic temple by invading the

---

13. Sokolovskaya relates a story of the Decembrist G. S. Batenkov who was saved from death in 1812 when French officers, who turned out to be Freemasons, found him unconscious on the battlefield with his arms inadvertently crossed in the Masonic plea for help. (For Baten'kov's own account, see Pypin 1916, 467–68.) In a study of Russian Rosicrucianism Sokolovskaya describes a ceremony in which such gestures as crossing the arms and kneeling in supplication are symbolic (1906, 89–93). Batenkov was the Masonic brother to whom Rayevsky addressed his epistles.

14. Institute of Russian Literature, Razdel II, opis' 2, nos. 51, 105.

countess's mansion. Indicative of this is that the numerically arranged sequences in which he pleads for the secret of the cards conform to the patterns of the Masonic rite of initiation. He appeals to the countess's "feelings of a spouse, a lover, a mother," he promises that "not only I, but my children, grandchildren, and great-grandchildren will bless your memory," and he even makes this urgent plea with Masonic correctness on bended knee. Similarly, the supplicant in the rite of initiation begs "three times three" for admittance into the order in the name of that which is sacred: parent(s), wife, and children, or three universal values (family, fatherland, God), or three personal values (honor, life, soul). Just as the Master of the Lodge warns the supplicant in three ways that betrayal of his oath of secrecy will jeopardize his soul, Germann reminds the countess that her use of the secret of the three cards might be accompanied "by a terrible sin, by the loss of eternal bliss, by a satanic pact," and expresses his willingness to take her sin on his soul. In Masonic terms, this corruption of a serious warning into a satanic bargain constitutes blasphemy. And when Germann follows this plea with the threat of a pistol, he compounds his sin with the sin of profanity. Germann's pleas are not the supplication of an altruistic initiate who seeks moral perfection. His is the sacrilege of a calculating man whose greedy quest for money and social acceptance results in the death of an old woman.

The old countess's responses are also ironic. Where the Master of the Lodge does most of the speaking, in the form of questions that prompt the initiate's answers, the countess either does not respond or she responds with a denial or protest. Her response to Germann's angry threat is to die. In the rite of initiation the Grand Master asks the supplicant "three times three" whether he is truly prepared to accept the secrets of the craft (whether he is prepared in his soul, whether he understands the seriousness of his plea, whether he swears to preserve the secrets he is about to be told). When he is satisfied with the supplicant's answers, the Grand Master thrice pronounces acceptance of the initiate—in the name of the Grand Architect of the Universe, in accordance with the authority invested in him, and with the consent of all brothers present and absent (see Sokolovskaia 1915b, 90–98).

Other ironies are revealed by correspondences between the seven Masonic virtues and the qualities ascribed to Germann in "The Queen of Spades." As has been noted, the Masonic virtues varied even within the Orient of Petersburg, Grand Lodge of Astraea, but the Grand Lodge's documents generally agree despite different terms and different languages. In one variant or another these virtues figure into Pushkin's tale. Some are claimed for Germann by himself, in his favorite saying: "No! calculation, moderation, and industriousness, these are my three trusty cards: this is what will . . . bring me peace and independence." Calculation is not exactly what Freemasons mean when they call for discretion, prudence, disinterestedness, or altruism, but it makes for a finely ironic substitute. Independence is hardly obedience, but industriousness is certainly a kind of perseverance and Germann's moderation certainly goes well with the virtues patience and temperance. Ironic, too, are the two virtues Pushkin specifies in the epigraph to chapter 5: "Homme sans moeurs et sans religion!" Germann is certainly a man without morals and without religion. He is just as certainly prudent when he attends the old countess's funeral services, just in case and because, as Pushkin notes, he is superstitious. Germann is also without love of humanity, and he is certainly not generous. Given that he never touches either cards or the interest on his capital until he has a sure thing, he is not courageous, although of course he is not only perseverant but patient, moderate, discreet, and prudent.

Germann possesses the proper virtues—until he abandons them because his romantic imagination is carried away by his greed for money. This irony, and especially the irony of Germann's stealthy invasion of the countess's mansion, have another parallel in a warning issued by the Second (Junior) Warden when he reveals the seven virtues to the initiate: "Nous avons été calme, car nous avons travaillé, nous avons été secret, car aucun profane n'a pu s'approcher des nous, nous avons été prudens, car nous avons garde l'entrée de notre temple."[15] "The Queen of Spades" is not only ironic, it is profane.

Gematria in "The Queen of Spades"

Readers of "The Queen of Spades" have been especially drawn to Pushkin's detailed description of the interior of the old countess's mansion in chapter 3. The description contains many of the tale's most intriguing symbols, and the accoutrements are a key to the cultural environment of the tale or "spirit of the time" (Alekseev 1972, 79–84). The description dramatizes Germann's invasion of the mansion and creates the ominous mood for his plea for the secret of the three cards. Weber finds many of the tale's Masonic symbols in this scene. Especially prominent is the description of the old countess's boudoir,

---

15. Ibid., no. 105.

with its ancient icons, golden lampstand, divans with feather pillows, Chinese wallpaper, its "two portraits painted in Paris by *Me Lebrun*" and its "porcelain shepherdesses, table clocks in the work of the glorious Leroy, little boxes, hairpins, fans, and various ladies gewgaws invented at the end of the last century together with the Montgolfièr balloon and Mesmér's magnetism" (Pushkin 1937–59, 8:239–40).[16] This part of the description is significant because it seems to contain a series of anagrams hidden in the text. The character of these anagrams suggests knowledge of the practice of gematria, the basic numerological-orthographic system of the Cabala.

Through a process of transposition or reversal of syllables, elimination or addition of letters, and metathesis, it is possible to form words pertinent to the tale's card terminology. From the Russian adjective *farforovye* (porcelain), for example, it is easy to form the word faro: *far(fo)ro*. The Russian word for the number three, *tri*, can be found thrice in the passage: *sT(a)RInnym, simeTRIi,* and *porTREta* (e > i). The number seven, *sem'*, is also present thrice—in the words *vSEM, vMESte,* and *MESmerovym*. The third card, the ace (*tuz*), seems possibly to be accounted for in the words *pasTUSHki* (sh > z) and *magneTIZmom* (i > u). The numerical value of the ace seems to be present thrice in the form of the word *raz* (as in the cadence *raz, dva, tri*, "one, two, three"): *obRAZami, ROZoiu* (o > a), *RAZnye*. The anagram also accounts for *az*, another word for the ace. The word *pasTUSHki* also contains the reverse word *shut* (joker or jester). A metathetic (r > l) or syllabic recombination of the two consecutive words *ruLETki, VeerA* suggests the word *valet* (jack). The consecutive words *KORObochki, RULetki* run in the anagram or logograph *korol'* (king), and the king is also present in the prominently marked French name *Leroy:* the phrase *slavnogo Leroy* provides the syllables needed to form the French anagram "le nouveau roi slave." The word *dama* (queen) is present in

---

16. There is no evidence that Pushkin knew anything more than cultural hearsay about Christian Rosenkreutz, but it might be mentioned that his description of the interior of the old countess's mansion suggests not only the accoutrements of a Masonic lodge, but the documents on which some Rosicrucian and Masonic interiors are based, Johannes Andreae's *The Hermetick Romance, or The Chymical Wedding* and *The Fame and Confession of the Fraternity of the Rosie Cross (Famas Fraternitas)*. The work is replete with seven days, seven rites, forty maidens, seven flames, three-stanza and seven-stanza verses, and spiral staircases (Allen 1968, 68). The third of the seven rites that comprise the Chemical Wedding, known commonly as the Royal Wedding, takes place in a Palace that is described as a place "where one can wander for years without exploring all its marvelous rooms, staircases, clocks, astronomical instruments, doors, paintings, lights and torches" (Seligmann 1948, 444). If Pushkin did happen to have Masonic adaptations of the Royal Wedding in mind when he wrote his description of the countess's mansion, this adds irony to his irreverent choice of scripture for the young orator's unwittingly appropriate paraphrase of the Parable of the Ten Virgins at the old countess's funeral: "The angel of death found her engaged in pious meditation and waiting for the midnight bridegroom."

the adjective *DAMskie*. The commonly used French slang term for the queen of spades, "la dame brune," is present in a recombination of the second name marked out in French, *Me Lebrun:* Madame Lebrun > "la (le) dame brun(e)."[17]

Any tightly organized literary text can be made to yield anagrams, but cabalists (and cryptographers) recognize that anagrams that yield meaning in their context and are governed by logical morphological and numerical or numerological principles are not a product of chance. The general term for this practice is logomachy, a skill or game of making words. Logomachic practice involves anagrams—words or phrases made by transposing, recombining, or reversing syllables, metathesizing vowels and consonants (letters or sounds), eliminating or interposing letters, placing words containing needed syllables in proximity to each other, and other morphological processes. Logomachy can be as simple or as complex as the writing of crossword puzzles or crostics, but these quite different systems cannot be used in texts unless, as in poetry or medieval illuminated manuscripts, the exact arrangement of words can be guaranteed in subsequent texts. Another general term for the practice of logomachy, when it is combined with numbers, is cryptography: writing in ciphers or secret arrangements of letters, words, phrases, or entire texts controlled by numerical formulas. The basic process of cryptography is substitution. Cryptography involves the making of cryptograms (Greek *kryptos, gramma*) or cryptographs (Greek *kryptos, grafeia*).

Pushkin's practice seems to be a variant of gematria as it was incorporated into the Christian Cabala. The word gematria is believed to have been formed from a metathesis of the Greek word *grammateia*, and has been less convincingly traced to the Greek word *geometria*, as in the Pythagorean numerological system based on geometry. The practice of gematria is also associated with *Gemara,* the latter of the two portions of the Talmud, consisting of a commentary on the older part (*Mishnah*). Gematria is not one but many sets of hermeneutic rules. Gerschom Scholem defines seven basic types of gematria and mentions that as many as seventy-five different forms have been identified (1971a, 373–74). Gematria was originally a method for interpreting the secret meaning of existing texts and later became the practice of actually lodging hidden or

---

17. Although Davydov endorses my analyses of this and other passages containing hidden or disguised numerical and morphological phenomena, and most of his analyses coincide with my own, he opposes his "cryptographic readings" to what he calls my "numerological or . . . gematic readings" (1989b, 120–21). However, as I point out here and in the articles Davydov cites, my approach includes cryptography. Moreover, where he cites his own findings in another passage of a two, eight, king, and queen as contradictions to my findings, my analyses account for the king and queen, and, as I have demonstrated, the two—the "number of confusion"—is a surrogate for the number three.

encoded matter in texts for religious, theosophical, or thaumaturgical purposes. Scholem distinguishes between the Speculative and Practical Cabala (1971b, 632–34).

Whereas Scholem is careful to define the *sephira* as numerical values rather than numbers (1971a, 369) and gives preference to the notion that they are spheres of natural power (1971b, 507–8), other scholars assume that the *yetzira* are letters and the *sephira* numbers. Scholem defines gematria as a set of "hermeneutic rules for interpreting the Torah. . . . It consists of explaining a word or group of words according to the numerical values of the letters, or of substituting other letters of the alphabet for them in accordance with a set system" (1971a, 369). With this definition he disperses the widespread confusion arising from the differences between the Jewish and Christian Cabala. Whereas the letters of the Hebrew alphabet *are* the numbers (letters, numbers, and sounds are simultaneous), numbers had to be assigned to letters in literary cultures where orthographic and numerical signs do not coincide. Not all forms of the Christian Cabala retained the Hebrew system of adding or substituting values. Systems of both strictly orthographic-morphological and cryptographic logomachy were also developed.

A possible use of some form of these latter adaptations of gematria seems to be operative in the text of chapter 3 of "The Queen of Spades." In at least one instance the usage combines morphological process with the system 3–7–1. It can be graphically represented with reasonable clarity for those who do not know Russian. The scene where Germann waits outside the mansion until the countess departs for the ball begins with these words:

> Germann trepetal kak tigr, ozhidaia naznachennogo vremeni. V desiat' chasov vechera on uzhe stoial pered domom grafini. Pogoda byla uzhasna: veter vyl, mokryi sneg padal khlop'iami; fonari svetilis'. . . . (1937–59, 8:239)

> Germann quivered like a tiger, awaiting the designated time. At ten o'clock in the evening he was already standing in front of the countess's home. The weather was terrible: the wind howled, a wet snow was falling in clots; the streetlamps shone. . . .

The first sentence of this passage in Russian contains seven words. The second, which begins with the time "At ten o'clock," contains ten words, for a total of seventeen. The next sentence begins with three words separated syntactically from the remaining words by a full colon, for a total of twenty. The next seven words, beginning with the twenty-first (3 x 7), read as follows:

veter vyl, mokryi sneg padal khlop'iami; fonari

The first three and the seventh words of this strand yield eight syllables (7 + 1):

ve ter vyl mo kry fo na ri

By removing the last syllable, seven syllables remain:

ve ter vyl mo kry fo nar

When these syllables are transposed and recombined, the anagram achieved is:

ko nra ti f ry le ev   Kon(d)raty F. Ryleev

All seven syllables have been used.[18]

No other segment of this passage yields the name of Kondraty Ryleyev with such a precise use of the system 3–7–1. The syllables for Kondraty Ryleyev or Kondraty F. Ryleyev do, however, seem to pervade the same passage and the immediately following description of the interior of the countess's mansion. These syllables formed from rearrangements of letters by purely morphological logomachic practice (or of sounds), are as follows (1937–59, 8:239–40):

> vanka na toshchei kliache svoei vysmatrivaia
> nakonets grafininu karetu podali germann videl kak
> rykhlomu snegu shveitsar zaper dveri okna pomerkli
> on podoshel k fonariu . . . na chasy bylo dvadtsat'
> on ostalsia pod fonarem ustremiv glaza na . . . strelku i vyzhidaia
> germann stupil na grafinino kryl'tso . . . iarko . . . shveitsara ne bylo
> raboty slavnogo leroy korobochki ruletki veera
> raznye damskie igrushki izobretennye v kontse . . . stoletiia

---

18. The process can be seen more closely by noting that *fonar* achieves *konraty* by removing the *f*, substituting the adjacent *k*, and adding the syllable *te* from *ter* (pronounced "ti" in Russian). Ryleyev is achieved after using the *k* from *kry*, running the resultant syllable *ry* together with *(v)yl* after dropping the intervening *v*. The remaining syllables for the surname Ryleyev are provided by adding *e[y]ev* from *ve(t)e(r)*. The *f* remains for the initial.

The syllables seem to appear again in one of the tale's key phrases, "The anecdote of the three cards acted powerfully on his imagination" (1937–59, 8:235): "*Anekdot o trekh kartakh sil'no podeistvoval na ego voobrazhenie.*" They also appear at the start of chapter 5, in the funeral scene (1937–59, 8:246): "Germann otpravilsia v *** monastyr'. . . byli . . . grafini raskaianii on ne mog odnako sovershenno . . . sovesti tverdivshei imeia malo istinnoi very on imel . . . predrassudkov on veril. . . ."

Key segments and syllables are achieved from repetition of such words as *fonar'* and *grafinia,* and by use of such ideal words as *nakonets, kontse, odnako.* The key syllable *ryl* appears throughout in such words as *kryl'tso, strelku,* and *ruletki.* The principle of redundancy seems to be operative—ample lexical elements are available in close contact with one another. Redundancy is contrary to standard cryptographic practice, where the sample must be small to avoid detection and exact so that the decoder will not be led astray by superfluous elements. But the use of redundancy to pervade the passage is ideal for a literary work: the sounds intrude without the reader's conscious awareness. Sound is just as important as orthography in the Cabala, and would be important to a poet such as Pushkin too. It is not possible to prove a negative, but the text of "The Queen of Spades" does not seem to yield other cryptonyms for Kondraty Ryleyev. Neither does the text seem to yield more than a few random syllables resembling other Decembrists' names (*est' uzhe* [Bestuzhev], *rumian* [Ryumin]). A search for anagrams resembling the names of the other four hanged Decembrists yields no results.

The presence of so many apt logomachic elements is intriguing. The anagrams designating words for numbers and cards are in keeping with Pushkin's love of word games. Davydov has shown that Pushkin practiced logomachy in "The Shot" and *The Captain's Daughter* (1983, 1989a).[19] But if the name of Kondraty Ryleyev is the result of a conscious knowledge and use of some form of gematria, we cannot speak of games. The execution of Ryleyev was a traumatic event for Pushkin's generation; Pushkin spent many years searching for the graves of the five hanged Decembrists. Pushkin brooded as deeply about the Decembrist conspiracy during the writing of "The Queen of Spades" as he did at any other time after receiving the news of 13 July 1826. If he brooded about *le pendu* while writing these passages, it would be natural

---

19. Davydov uses the general term *paronomasia* to describe his analyses of what he calls onomancy (divination by letters of a name), logogriphs (word puzzles), and anagrammatism and anaphony (words made by transposing letters or sounds of other words). He cites as an example of logomachy in Pushkin's poetry a study of the lyric poem "Anchar" by Blagoy who notes that the poem's words and sound patterns are generated from the syllables of the title (1973).

for him to subconsciously write sentences filled with the syllables of Ryleyev's names. It is not likely, however, that subconscious creativity works to the extent that is represented by the numerically derived cryptonym at the opening of the passage.

Pushkin's use of gematria is commensurate with the other morphological, stylistic, structural, and semantic practices in the tale. The name Ryleyev is a natural concomitant of the links between "The Queen of Spades" and "The Frigate Hope," and with all the painful matters raised by Bestuzhev in his Decembrist confession and message to Pushkin. Another possibly nonrandom anagram in the passage suggests a connection with Freemasonry. As Germann waits, quivering like a tiger outside the countess's mansion, "the old woman wrapped in a sable cape" is carried out and placed in a waiting carriage (1937–59, 8:239). In Russian the phrase "old woman wrapped" is *starukhu ukutannuiu*. The first syllables of the phrase *starukhu uku* form a phonetic or orthographic anagram: *sta(v') ruku ukhu*, "place (thy) hand to (thine) ear." The remainder of the segment, *tannuiu*, suggests the key word *taina* (secret) in its adjectival form *tainuiu* (feminine singular accusative). The anagram is an eerie evocation of the Master of the Lodge placing his hand to his ear in the symbolic query, "Who asks entry here?"

Cabalism, Troubled Conscience, Psychological Exorcism

The possibility of the use of gematria in "The Queen of Spades" renews the question of the Rosicrucian instruction brought to Moscow by Baron Schroeder. "When a brother of the order dies," every brother must strive to ensure the immortality of the deceased, and "make every possible arrangement to ensure that not so much as a single piece of paper containing the secret writing" will fall into alien hands, a contingency that "can bring harm to the peace of a soul even if it has already departed in a state of purity" (Barskov 1915, 227). The key word is "geheimliche Schriften," translated into Russian in another version as *tainopis'* (secret script) (Pekarskii 1909, 87). Relevant here is the Practical Cabala, the creation of cabalistic documents, as opposed to the analysis of existing holy writ. Practical cabalistic documents are meant to be read aloud. The reader unknowingly gives voice to signs, signals, words; the listener hears without conscious awareness. The sacred is conveyed, the secrecy is preserved. Such cabalistic practices are used for many purposes, one being to express reverence for the memory of a deceased friend or relative. Gematria is a thaumaturgical skill. The lodging of secret meaning or messages in texts was a means of covert incantation or divination. A text created in this way was believed to bring good luck; ward off evil; exorcise demons; and divine past, present, and future. Scholem calls this aspect of the Practical Cabala vulgar. The Practical Cabala is not a forbidden practice, but according to Jewish ethics "only the most perfectly virtuous individuals are permitted to perform [such operations]," and "whoever else seeks to perform such acts does so at his own grave physical and spiritual peril" (Scholem 1971b, 632). Scholem does not liken gematria itself to its gross, superstitious variants. Quite the contrary. The Practical Cabala serves deeply religious and psychological needs. It lends meaning to events. It offers comfort to the bereaved, and it helps perpetuate memories of the deceased. According to Seligmann, "The Cabala is a metaphysical system by which the elect shall know God and the Universe. It will raise him above common knowledge and make him understand the profound meaning and the plan of creation. These secrets are immanent in Holy Writ, yet not to be grasped by him who understands the texts literally" (1948, 343). Gematria is the basis of an ontological system and a hermeneutic method. It is also a way to express thoughts and feelings too painful to be expressed in overt written communication. It provides a covert textual level for associations too complex, and perhaps even too abhorrent or dangerous, to be expressed by overt means.

In this, "The Queen of Spades" and "The Frigate Hope" are cabalistic documents. Like Bestuzhev, Pushkin needed to give expression to thoughts he wished to express, but could not bring himself to communicate overtly to others, or did not dare to say openly for political reasons, or wished to express only to a select few friends who could decode the text—to his own and Ryleyev's Masonic brothers. He turned the uninitiated away with irony in the same way that Bestuzhev covered the serious meaning of "The Frigate Hope" with a barrage of witticisms. For Pushkin, gematria could have served as a form of psychological exorcism, a way to relieve his mind of painful memories and troubling matters of conscience. Above all, the practice enabled Pushkin to revere the memory of the Decembrist and to commemorate a friend and poet whose fate might have been his own.

9

Literature and Thaumaturgy: Sources and Tradition

What is it, our work? We study.
        —I. V. Lopukhin

This study of the relationships between literature and thaumaturgy in Russian romantic literature has traced a path through many seemingly disparate subjects that despite their often bewildering complexities, are ultimately connected. This is the character of the esoteric tradition: the modus operandi is to mislead, but the message, however obscured, is there and it yields to empirical research, formal analysis, and heuristic interpretation. A hidden culture existed and helped shape Russian romantic literature. The path from the Star of Hope to the system 3–7–1 is marked by many misleading links and associations, but they can be clarified and the path discovered. Knowledge of the existence of this hidden culture significantly changes our perception of the Russian romantics and their work. This new perception cannot be achieved without, first, understanding what the esoteric tradition is and, second, developing a method that eschews the discredited practice of autonomous speculation.

    A word commonly used at present to describe the practices analyzed in this study is the occult. Occultism is a bona fide phenomenon that needs to be studied, but the occult is only one of many phenomena that make up the esoteric tradition as a whole. Esotericism is a kind of logic that prevailed in European thought in the Medieval and Renaissance periods. Esoteric logic is pre-Cartesian: connections are made between phenomena without the mental discipline made obligatory by the principle of cause and effect. Esoteric logic carried European culture a long way, not least by laying the gnoseological basis for the development of science and theology. Esoteric logic was discredited by Cartesian philosophy, but continued in the work of eighteenth-century mystics and charlatans, and continues to this day. This is why a methodology that excludes autonomous speculation is necessary: precisely because acausal logic is nebulous—disconnected, illogical, "most seemingly strange"—we need to carefully analyze, logically verify, and sensibly interpret. A model for this kind of study is available in the field of modern esoteric studies whose most authoritative scholars combine empirical measure with heuristic interpretation.

The paths along which the esoteric tradition entered Russia in the eighteenth century and made its way to the nineteenth-century romantics can be traced further; other paths need to be traced through the romantic movement and beyond. Evidence is needed—not only contextual but textual. Text-object analysis is needed to discover and verify the presence of thaumaturgical practices in literary works and clarify their function. Textual evidence is, as stated at the start of this study, empirical: the implications of using thaumaturgical skills to create literary texts are not easily judged, but the text itself can be analyzed.

Analysis, however productive, does not necessarily achieve understanding of more than the text itself; that is, of that quality which is intuitively created and intuitively received, that which the romantics called the consequence of imagination. Said otherwise (and again), the presence of thaumaturgical phenomena in a text yields its own verification, but the interpretation of their meaning is not possible without appreciation. Neither is interpretation possible without knowledge of context. Thaumaturgical texts are strongly marked by intertextuality. With regard to the relationships between literature and thaumaturgy, skills are acquired, transmitted, and transmuted from one need to another, in various forms of writing, as a dynamic process of disguised but nonetheless effective communication of meaning. Text-context and text-subtext analyses are essential to the appreciation of thaumaturgical discourse because a code must be broken. Upon first consideration, it might seem that a code is intended to hinder communication. In fact, its intent is to facilitate communication. Meaning is disguised, but it is arcane only in that it is hidden from the uninitiated. For the adept, however, the meaning is accessible—communication is facilitated by possession of the key to the code. The task of the literary scholar who deals with these kinds of texts is therefore to break the code by finding the key. The key might be in the text itself. This is the case with Pushkin's "Queen of Spades" with its many applications of the system 3–7–1: the text itself yields the information needed to break the code and test it by trial and error. The key or keys might be lodged in another text, or another text might yield the information needed to discover the key—such is the case with Bestuzhev's "Frigate Hope" or Zhukovsky's transformation of the Masonic symbolism of the flaming star into the Star of Hope. In both instances biographical information—the author's intent—is indispensable. Whatever the case, interpretation, empirical or heuristic, must be verified. The presence of a code often raises as many questions as it answers, and autonomous speculation must be avoided by clearly distinguishing between verifiable *links* and suggestive *associations*.

Concerning the whole context—the influence of the esoteric tradition on Russian culture—one must ask, What was a given writer's attitude toward the tradition? As has been noted with reference to Freemasonry, not all Freemasons are serious. The sentimentalist writer and national historian N. M. Karamzin was in his early years as devoted to Freemasonry as any of the Moscow Mystic Masons, but he was not drawn to esotericism and eventually became a skeptic. This attitude is probably why Karamzin's successor Vasily Zhukovsky adapted Masonic symbolism to his poetry without endorsing Freemasonry per se. Zhukovsky admired I. P. Turgenev and I. V. Lopukhin not for their adeptness in the craft but for their high moral characters. He appreciated the example they set by their devotion to the ideal of the free personality, and their profoundly Orthodox beliefs accorded with his own Christian aesthetics.

Skepticism about Freemasonry was probably shared by most of Zhukovsky's contemporaries of the early romantic sentimental-elegiac trend: in the Arzamas Brotherhood they parodied the pseudo-Masonic rituals of Admiral A. S. Shishkov's Society of Lovers of the Russian Word. Skepticism is certainly the attitude of Karamzin's legal ward Prince P. A. Vyazemsky, whose strict Voltairean principles made him a skeptic and atheist at once.[1] Nor is it easy to conceive that the romantic poets of the Pushkin Pleiad, worldly aristocrats that they were, could have committed themselves with any degree of seriousness to Masonic beliefs. Pushkin and his Lyceum friend Baron Anton Delvig were initi-

---

1. Regardless of his attitude toward Freemasonry, Prince Vyazemsky and his family's remarkable Ostafevsky Archives provide significant knowledge about Freemasonry in the widest context of Russian culture of the first half of the nineteenth century. Another invaluable source is the Turgenev family archives preserved by the equally indefatigable diarist Aleksandr Turgenev, son of I. P. Turgenev and close friend of Zhukovsky.

ated into the craft, but nothing in their lives or poetry suggests serious interest. As for Aleksandr Bestuzhev and such other leading figures of the romantic period as the dramatist A. S. Griboyedov, their personalities suggest that they found in the lodges not meaning, but opportunity for social prestige and political influence. Younger poets like N. M. Yazykov and A. I. Polezhayev seem to have been neither adept nor informed. If Freemasonry came to Yazykov at all, it was in the form of the great influence exerted on his later beliefs by Slavophile ideology.

V. F. Rayevsky and Kondraty Ryleyev, on the other hand, were serious Freemasons, who even after they lost faith in Freemasonry as a vehicle of political change continued to espouse both the symbolism and the skills of the craft. Among those who can be considered serious Freemasons, however, we have to ask another question, namely, what was the character of a given writer's commitment to the craft? Rayevsky was drawn to rational Freemasonry and to the craft as a revolutionary phenomenon. Ryleyev, however, was a man whose commitments had to be all or nothing. He was drawn to esotericism and he took the symbolism of the virtue of the love of death so seriously that he was willing to carry it into reality. Less is known about the attraction to the craft of Pushkin's other Lyceum comrade V. K. Küchelbecker, but he, too, was a serious Decembrist whose political commitments and attraction to Freemasonry were strong. Among other cultural figures who were serious Freemasons and whose works can provide needed knowledge are the ultraconservative linguist Shishkov, the historian M. P. Pogodin, the journalist N. I. Grech, and the memoirist F. F. Vigel. The early romantic poet V. L. Pushkin, uncle of the poet, worked actively in his Masonic lodge. Two of the most serious Russian Freemasons were the poet and memoirist F. N. Glinka, author of Masonic songs, and the writer and journalist A. E. Izmaylov. The former was Master of the lodge of Michel l'élu, a leader of the Union of Welfare, and leader of the left wing of the two literary societies almost taken over by Ryleyev and Bestuzhev. (Izmaylov headed the right wing of both societies.) For that matter, those scholars who are presently studying the history of Russian culture as it was developed in the early nineteenth century in literary-political-cultural societies have to note that the membership of these two and other societies is often identical to the membership of the elite Masonic lodges.

As one example, the Masonic origins of the romantic grouping of the 1820s known as the Lovers of Wisdom are apparent. These young philosopher poets, especially the poet D. V. Venetinov and the writer V. F. Odoyevsky, were obviously taken with the emphasis placed on enlightenment as the true way to self-perfection, self-knowledge, and self-sacrifice by the Moscow Mystical Masons. Their greatest commitment was to Friedrich Schelling's romantic idealist aesthetics—their faith that poetry is philosophy. Schelling was a serious Freemason—he played an important role in the modernization of the craft—and his influence on these "young Russian Schellingians" was strong. The connections between Freemasonry and romantic idealist philosophy constitute a formidable research task, but the young professors of philosophy at Moscow Imperial University who introduced Kant, Schelling, and the Schlegel brothers into Russia in the 1810s were drawn to Freemasonry. Their immediate influence was on their students who became the Lovers of Wisdom, and this in turn opens the way to the role of Freemasonry in the Slavophile movement of the 1830s–1850s and the organic aesthetics of the Russian romantic idealist philosopher Apollon Grigorev.

Russian Freemasonry per se was not operative after the closing of the lodges in 1822, but interest in Masonic symbolism remained viable. If the realist writer A. F. Pisemsky's novel *The Masons* is credited, the possibility that Freemasons continued their work "in silence" cannot be discounted. Those writers whose attachment to German philosophy was strong, particularly those who were educated in Germany, had access to Masonic knowledge. A recent study of V. F. Odoyevsky shows that in his later career this polymath became adept in the esoteric teachings of Saint-Martin, Jacob Böhme, Robert Fludd, and other theosophers of the esoteric tradition. Odoyevsky even practiced alchemy, numerology, and cabalistics (Cornwell 1986, 97–106). The poet Fyodor Tyutchev spent most of his adult life as a diplomat in Germany. A recent study by Sarah Pratt of this metaphysical romantic poet and the metaphysical poet Evgeny Baratynsky does not mention Freemasonry, but many of her analyses of the romantic idealist poetry of these two men suggest elements reminiscent of Masonic symbolism (Pratt 1985).

The sources of the thaumaturgical knowledge of Russian writers and poets are also an important question. One problem here has been noted: the suppression of the lodges by Catherine II and, especially, her order to burn the library of N. I. Novikov. Essential here is the bibliographer Evgeny Beshenkovsky's discovery of the inventory of Novikov's library, described in part by Ivan Martynov (1976) and by Kenneth Craven (1988). Unfortunately, although Craven has reported the impending publication of the inventory by the Harriman Institute at Columbia University (1988, 401), this important research tool has not been forthcoming. The problem here is not that the sources of the esoteric knowledge of the Moscow Mystic Masons have not been identified. The researches of Pypin, Vernadsky, Sokolovskaya, and other early twentieth-century historians of Russian Freemasonry are excellent in this respect. Craven has added significantly to the list of the European esoterics who influenced eighteenth-century Russian thought. Introductions to and commentaries on the works of Russian authors frequently point to Masonic influences. But as of this time, the works of the European esoterics have not been read for the particulars of their influence. This applies not only to the more remote sources—Ficino, Lull, Dee, Giorgi—but even to those frequently mentioned as specific influences, such as Fludd, Böhme, Swedenborg, or Saint-Martin. We do not yet know who and when, and we do not know how thaumaturgical devices and esoteric symbolism shaped Russian culture of the romantic period, or before, or after. Simply stated, Novikov, Lopukhin, Turgenev, and other Moscow Mystic Masons were far more erudite than is appreciated, and they passed on more of their knowledge of esoterica than is realized. It might very well be that they knew not only Tschoudy but also many other theosophers not yet even mentioned in studies of late eighteenth- and early nineteenth-century Russian culture.

A serious problem here is not only that the paths were cut off by Catherine's suppression of Freemasonry in the 1790s, but that the excellent research in Russian Freemasonry begun in the early twentieth century was halted in the Soviet period when Freemasonry was considered a state crime. In the 1970s and 1980s Party scholars launched a full-scale debate over the alleged role of Freemasons in the revolution of February 1917 (Avrekh 1990 and sources cited there). There is an irony here, of course: the most serious modern advocates of international conspiracy are themselves fearful of some "Secret Brotherhood." Nevertheless, despite these detractions, study of the role of Freemasonry in Russian culture has begun. Several Russian scholars have explored the Masonic beliefs of the Novikov group; Stephen Baehr has provided excellent studies of esotericism and Freemasonry in eighteenth-century Russian literature (1976, 1987, 1991). Interest in Freemasonry and other aspects of the esoteric tradition is also now substantial in Russia and the other Commonwealth countries, and a number of professional research groups have been formed in Kiev, Moscow, and Petersburg.[2] Freemasonry in Russian literature is still a subject less rather

---

2. In addition, Freemasonry itself is being revived with the opening of lodges in Russia and Ukraine, and the rich Masonic culture of the postrevolutionary émigrés is being revived or supplanted by a new generation of émigrés in the United States and Paris. (For a contrary view of Freemasonry among the earlier émigrés in Paris, see Berberova 1986.)

than better known for a more than slight presence in literary history, but strong interest is indicated by recent reprints of *The Memoirs of Senator Lopukhin* (1859) and the collection of articles published by S. P. Melgunov and N. P. Sidorov, *Masonry in Its Past and Present* (1915).

One difficulty of dealing with the esoteric tradition has to do with the impossibility, at least at this stage of the investigation, of separating the history of the esoteric tradition from questions of literature proper. Textual analyses alone cannot sustain the burden of evidence: the sources of knowledge in essentially philosophical (theosophical) treatises and the social, political, and cultural context in which a text was created have to be identified and explicated. This has proved true of the path through the Decembrist conspiracy traced in this study. It will also prove true of attempts to trace the influence of the esoteric tradition through the cultural-organizational activities of the many friendship, literary, and other societies of the late eighteenth–early nineteenth centuries. However, not every path need lead inevitably through such a broad context. Davydov's purely formal analyses of anagrammatism in Pushkin's prose have been remarkably successful. Russian romantic poetry will surely yield a wealth of further knowledge about the use of thaumaturgical devices to shape form and style and about the role of esoteric, particularly Masonic, symbolism in the development of romantic aesthetics. This applies not only to Zhukovsky and the other romantics discussed in this study, but to such poets as, to cite only a few, V. K. Küchelbecker, Evgeny Baratynsky, Fyodor Tyutchev, and the "latent romantic poets" of the 1850s–1860s Maykov, Fet, and Mey. As for work in other disciplines, surely there is more to be discovered about the role of Freemasonry in the Decembrist conspiracy, and surely there is much to be learned about the influence of the esoteric tradition on the Schellingian poets of the Society of Lovers of Wisdom, the Slavophiles, and the intriguing metaphysical prose writer V. F. Odoyevsky. What, for example, was the role of such esotericists as Fludd, Böhme, Saint-Martin, Andreae, and Swedenborg in the development of Russian philosophy? What, for that matter, was the full role of the unexpectedly influential Baron de Tschoudy?

When I began this study, I hoped that the complex Russian literature of the eighteenth century could be avoided, or at least left to the remarkable group of Russian specialists organized around the collections *XVIII vek* and its Western counterpart *The International Eighteenth-Century Russia Studies Group*. This proved impossible: the key to understanding the esoteric tradition in Russian culture is the Moscow Mystic Masons. The path of research I chose for this study originates in the thought of two especially adept eighteenth-century

Freemasons, I. V. Lopukhin and I. P. Turgenev, but there are other paths and other early Freemasons. The admiration for these pioneer theosophists expressed by N. M. Karamzin in *Letters of a Russian Traveler* ought to prompt serious reexamination of their influence on Russian thought. The materials assembled by the late nineteenth–early twentieth-century scholars of Freemasonry provide extensive information about the character of their work and, just as important, their study of the European esoteric tradition.

The time has also come to begin examining in close detail the kinds of thaumaturgical practices that attracted Russian writers and that they used in their works. Happily, this work has already begun and was given a great boost by the conference "The Occult in Modern Russian and Soviet Culture" held at Fordham University in June 1991 and by the conference "Five Hundred Years of Gnosticism in Europe" held in Moscow in March 1993. Among the subjects treated at the former conference were magic and divination, the Cabala, mystical sects, shamanism, satanism and black magic, spiritualism, theosophy and hermeticism, numerology, sacerdotal properties of poetic language and form, Rosicrucianism, cosmism, and Freemasonry. Among the Russian cultural figures discovered to have been attracted to esotericism are Dostoyevsky, Khlebnikov, Bulgakov, Olesha, and Platonov. Several Slavic scholars who know Hebrew have begun exploring the influence of the Cabala in Russian history. The latter conference brought European and Russian specialists of the esoteric tradition together for the first time. Not the least important paper read at this conference was M. Ya. Bilinkis's review of the legendary "Hermetic Library" of the Novikov group. Invaluable as a research model here are the efforts of Gerschom Scholem and Frances Yates.

The role of the esoteric tradition in Russian culture is a problem of both intellectual and literary history. It is also the province of philosophy, theology, and science and of politics, social history, and culturology as well. So far as literary study is concerned, thaumaturgical literature poses questions of both the text as such and reader-reception. This book is neither a reader-reception study nor an application of semiotic or Bakhtinian discourse theory. Questions of audience and sign-systems have been raised throughout, however, and it has been assumed that thaumaturgical literature is a dialogic process—an atypical dialogic process not accounted for in the work of Mikhail Bakhtin, but a nonetheless valid process of broad cultural communication and rich intertextuality. Here it is important for literary study that thaumaturgy is more than a simple use of skills by an adept few to communicate matters of interest only to those minor few. The esoteric tradition in Russia, still not fully understood, and thaumaturgical texts, many still not decoded, constitute a culture that, although hidden, is a part of Russian culture as a whole. Closer and broader knowledge of this culture can open ways to a new understanding of Russian literature. When asked, what is it, this work you do? I. V. Lopukhin replied, "We study." Study of thaumaturgy in literature is as elusive as Zhukovsky's Star of Hope and often as deceptive as Pushkin's secret of the three cards. But the phenomenon is there to be discovered and appreciated. Knowledge of it can be as promising as Zhukovsky's poetry and even as arithmetically certain as Pushkin's 3–7–1.

Reference Materials

Russian sources are quoted in text in English translation and their titles are cited in text in English translation wherever needed for information of those who do not read Russian. Original titles, names, and other bibliographic information are given in transliterated Russian in Reference Materials. Russian terms and words are transliterated in parentheses wherever needed to ensure accuracy. Texts that cannot be explicated without reference to the original are given in transliteration with accompanying line-by-line English translations.

Materials in French, German, and Latin are quoted in English translation except where the original is needed to ensure accuracy; titles are given in the language of the original in text and in Reference Materials. Technical terms, particularly Masonic and other esoteric terms, have been checked to ensure that equivalents are identical in all languages. The modified Library of Congress system for transliteration of Russian is used for citations in text and Reference Materials and for words as words in text. This orthographic system facilitates location of Russian sources in most library catalogues and information-retrieval systems, and is sufficiently phonetic to provide a reliable transcription of sounds and shapes of words as words. A yet simpler transliteration system is used for proper names in the text and in discursive notes. This system is oriented toward pronunciation for English speakers. Mentally "translating" from one system to another (from, for example, "Alekseyev" to "Alekseev," or from "Ya. L. Barskov" to "Ia. L. Barskov") should pose no difficulty.

Afanas'ev, Viktor. 1982. *Ryleev. Zhizneopisanie.* Moscow: Molodaia gvardiia.
Agrippa, Henry Cornelius. 1531. *De occulta philosophia.* Antwerp.
———. 1533. *De vanitate scientarium.* Antwerp. Also *Of the vanitie and uncertaintie of artes and sciences.* Edited by Catherine M. Dunn. Northridge: California State University Press, 1974.
Akhmatova, Anna. 1977. *O Pushkine. Stat'i i zametki.* Leningrad: Sovetskii pisatel'. 3d ed. Moscow: Kniga, 1989.
Alekseev, M. P. 1930. "Pushkin i Bestuzhev. Po povodu odnoi kartiny." In *Pushkin i ego sovremenniki,* 38–39:241–51. Leningrad: AN SSSR.
———. 1972. "Pushkin i nauka ego vremeni." In *Pushkin,* 5–159. Leningrad: Nauka. Also in *Pushkin. Issledovaniia i materialy,* 1:9–125. Moscow and Leningrad: AN SSSR, 1956.
———, and B. S. Meilakh, eds. 1951. *Dekabristy i ikh vremia.* Moscow: AN SSSR.
Allen, Paul M., ed. 1968. *A Christian Rosenkreutz Anthology.* Blauvelt, N.Y.: Rudolf Steiner Publications.

Allgemeines Handbuch der Freimauerei. 1867. 2 vols. Leipzig: Verein deutscher Freimaurer.
Altshuller, Mark. 1982. "Masonskie motivy 'Vtorogo toma.'" *Revue des études slaves* 54:591–607.
Arkhipova, A. V., and V. G. Bazanov. 1967. "V. F. Raevskii i dekabristskaia literatura." In V. F. Raevskii, *Polnoe sobranie stikhotvorenii,* 2d ed., 5–50. Biblioteka poeta, bol'shaia seriia. Leningrad: Sovetskii pisatel'.
Avrekh, A. Ia. 1990. *Masony i revoliutsiia.* Moscow: Politizdat.
Azadovskii, Mark, ed. 1951. *Vospominaniia Bestuzhevykh.* Moscow and Leningrad: AN SSSR.
Babinski, Hubert F. 1974. *The Mazepa Legend in European Romanticism.* New York and London: Columbia University Press.
Baehr, Stephen L. 1976. "The Masonic Component in Eighteenth-Century Russian Literature." In *Russian Literature in the Age of Catherine the Great,* 121–39. Oxford: Willem A. Meeuws.
———. 1987. "Freemasonry in Russian Literature: Eighteenth Century." In *Modern Encyclopedia of Russian and Soviet Literature,* 8:30–36. Gulf Breeze, Fla.: Academic International Press.
———. 1991. *The Paradise Myth in Eighteenth-Century Russia: Utopian Patterns in Early Secular Russian Literature and Culture.* Stanford: Stanford University Press.
Bakounine, Tatiana. 1967. *Répertoire biographique des Francs-Maçons russes.* Paris: L'Institut d'études slaves.
Barberi [pseud.]. 1792. *The Life of Joseph Balsamo, Commonly Called Count Cagliostro.* Dublin.
Barskov, Ia. L., ed. 1915. *Perepiska moskovskikh masonov XVIII-go veka.* Petrograd.
Bazanov, V. G. 1953. *Ocherki dekabristskoi literatury. Publitsistika, proza, kritika.* Moscow: Khudlit.
———. 1961. *Ocherki dekabristskoi literatury. Poeziia.* Moscow: Khudlit.
———. 1964. *Uchenaia respublika.* Moscow and Leningrad: Nauka.
Bel'chikov, N. F. 1957. "A. I. Polezhaev." In A. I. Polezhaev, *Stikhotvoreniia i poemy,* 2d ed., 5–35. Biblioteka poeta, bol'shaia seriia. Moscow and Leningrad: Sovetskii pisatel'.
Belousov, R. 1965. "Zagadki Grafini ★★★." *Smena,* no. 22:30.
Bem, A. 1934–35. "'Faust' v tvorchestve Pushkina." *Slavia* 13:378–99.
Benham, William Gurney. 1931. *Playing Cards: History of the Pack.* London and Melbourne: Ward, Lock.
Berberova, Nina. 1986. *Liudi i lozhi: Russkie masony XX stoletiia.* New York: Russica.
[Berdnikov, I. D.], comp. 1900. *Katalog masonskikh rukopisei moskovskago i rumiantsovskogo muzeev.* Moscow.
Berlin, Isaiah. 1957. *The Hedgehog and the Fox.* New York: New American Library.
Bertenev, P. I. 1925. *Rasskazy o Pushkine, zapisannye so slov ego druzei.* Moscow: S. Sabashnikov.
Bestuzhev-Marlinskii, A. A. 1958. *Sochineniia.* 2 vols. Moscow and Leningrad: Khudlit.
Bitsilli, P. V. 1932. "Zametki o Pushkine." *Slavia* 11:556–60.
Blagoi, D. D. 1967. *Tvorcheskii put' Pushkina (1826–1830).* Moscow: Sovetskii pisatel'.
———. 1973. "Mysl' i zvuk v poezii." In *Slavianskie literatury,* 99–139. VII International Congress of Slavists. Moscow: AN SSSR.
Blau, Joseph L. 1944. *The Christian Interpretation of the Cabala in the Renaissance.* New York: Columbia University Press. Reprint. Port Washington, N.Y.: Kennikat Press, 1965.
Böhme, Jacob. 1623. *Mysterium magnum, oder Erklärung über das erste Buch Mosis.* Amsterdam.
Bogdanovich, M. I. 1869–71. *Istoriia tsarstvovaniia Imperatora Aleksandra I i Rossii v ego vremia.* 6 vols. Moscow.

Bourychkine, Paul [P. A. Buryshkin]. 1967. *Bibliographie sur la Franc-Maçonnerie en Russie.* Paris and The Hague: Mouton.
Burgin, Diana Lewis. 1974. "The Mystery of 'Pikovaja dama': A New Interpretation." In *Mnezomina*, 46–56. Munich: Fink.
Butler, Christopher. 1970. *Number Symbolism.* New York: Barnes & Noble.
Casanova, Jacques. 1833–37. *Mémoires de Jacques Casanova de Seingalt.* 10 vols. Paris: Paulin.
Cavendish, Richard. 1967. *The Black Arts.* New York: G. P. Putnam's Sons.
Chambers, R. 1967. *The Book of Days.* Detroit: Gale Research.
Chereiskii, L. A. 1975. *Pushkin i ego okruzhenie.* Leningrad: Nauka.
Chetteoui, Wilfrid-René. 1947. *Cagliostro et Catherine II.* Paris: Champs-Elysées.
Chkhaidze, L. V. 1960. "O real'nom znachenii motiva trekh kart v 'Pikovoj dame.'" In *Pushkin. Issledovaniia i materialy,* 3:455–60. Moscow and Leningrad: AN SSSR.
———. 1973. "Pometki Pushkina na pis'me k nemu A. P. Pleshcheeva." In *Vremennik pushkinskoi komissii 1971,* 82–88. Leningrad: Nauka.
Chukovskaia, Lidiia. 1976. *Zapiski ob Anne Akhmatovoi.* Vol. 1. Paris: YMCA Press.
Clayton, John Douglas. 1971. *Parody and Burlesque in the Work of A. S. Pushkin: A Critical Study.* Ph.D. diss., University of Illinois.
———. 1974. "'Spadar Dame,' 'Pique-Dame,' and 'Pikovaja dama': A German Source for Pushkin?" *Germano-Slavica,* no. 4:5–10.
Cornwell, Neil. 1986. *The Life, Times and Milieu of V. F. Odoyevsky.* Athens: University of Ohio Press.
Craven, Kenneth. 1988. "The First Chamber of Novikov's Masonic Library." In *Russia and the World of the Eighteenth Century,* 401–10. Columbus, Ohio: Slavica.
Culbertson, Ely. 1952. *Culbertson's Card Games, Complete with Official Rules.* New York: Greystone Press.
Davydov, Sergei. 1983. "The Sound and Theme in the Prose of A. S. Pushkin: A Logo-Semantic Study of Paronomasia." *Slavic and East European Journal* 27, no. 1:1–18.
———. 1987. "Real'noe i fantasticheskoe v 'Pikovoi dame.'" *Revue des études slaves* 59, no. 1–2:263–67.
———. 1989a. "'The Shot' by Aleksandr Pushkin and Its Trajectories." In *Issues in Russian Literature Before 1917,* ed. J. Douglas Clayton, 62–74. Columbus, Ohio: Slavica.
———. 1989b. "The Ace in Pushkin's 'The Queen of Spades.'" In *Alexander Pushkin: Symposium III,* ed. A. A. Kodjak and S. Rudy, 118–33. New York: New York University Press.
Debreczeny, Paul. 1983. *The Other Pushkin.* Stanford: Stanford University Press.
Dee, John. 1564. *Monas hieroglyphica.* Antwerp. Translated by J. W. Hamilton-Jones, under the title *The Hieroglyphic Monad.* London: John M. Watkins, 1947.
———. 1577. *General and rare memorials pertayning to the Perfect arte of Nauigation.* London.
Donesenie Sledstvennoi komissii. 1826a. Saint Petersburg. [95 pp. pripleteno k Verkhovnoi ugolovnoi sud nad zloumyshlennikami.]
Donesenie Sledstvennoi komissii, pechatano po vysochaishemu poveleniiu. 1826b. Saint Petersburg. [50 pp.]
Druzhnikov, Yuri. 1991. *Prisoner of Russia: Understanding the Other Pushkin.* Orange, Conn.: Antiquary.
Efros, Abram. 1934. "Dekabristy v risunkakh Pushkina." In *Literaturnoe nasledstvo* 16–18. Leningrad: Zhurnal'no-gazetnoe ob''edinenie.
Eydelman, N. Ia. 1979. *Pushkin i dekabristy.* Moscow: Khudlit.
Eikhenbaum, B. M. 1969. *O poezii.* Leningrad: Sovetskii pisatel'.
Erlich, Victor. 1964. *The Double Image.* Baltimore: Johns Hopkins University Press.

Erman, Georg Adolph. 1850. *Travels in Siberia.* 2 vols. Philadelphia. [This is a translation of part of *Reise um die Erde.* Berlin, 1838–45.]

Faivre, Antoine. 1969. "En Russie." In *Eckartshausen et la théosophie chrétienne,* 620–38. Paris: Klincksieck.

———. 1973. *L'Ésotérisme au XVIIIe siècle en France et en Allemagne.* Paris: Seghers.

———. 1986. "Pensées de Dieu, images de l'homme (figures, miroirs et engendrements selon J. Boehme, Fr. C. Oetinger et Franz von Baader)." In *Cahiers de l'Université Saint-Jean de Jérusalem,* 12:110–19. Paris: Berg International.

———. 1987. "Esotericism." In *The Encyclopedia of Religion,* ed. Mircea Elliade, 5:155–63. New York: Macmillan.

———. 1992. *Que sais-je? L'ésotérisme.* Paris: Presses Universitaires de France.

Ferd, Josef Schneider. 1909. "Die romantische Schicksalidee." In *Die Freimaurer und ihr Einfluss auf die geistige Kultur in Deutschland am Ende des XVIII Jahrhunderts,* 184–229. Prague: Taussig & Taussig.

Florinsky, Michael T. 1955. *Russia: A History and an Interpretation.* 2 vols. New York: Columbia University Press.

Fludd, Robert. 1617–21. *Utriusque cosmi, majoris et minoris.* 3 vols. Frankfurt? [Volume 3 was not published.]

Fowler, Alastair, ed. 1970a. *Silent Poetry: Essays in Numerological Analysis.* New York: Routledge & Kegan Paul.

———. 1970b. *Triumphal Forms: Structural Patterns in Elizabethan Poetry.* Cambridge: Cambridge University Press.

French, Peter J. 1972. *John Dee: The World of an Elizabethan Magus.* London: Routledge & Kegan Paul.

Fridlender, G. M. 1987. "Spornye i ocherednye voprosy izucheniia Zhukovskogo." In *Zhukovskii i russkaia kul'tura,* 5–31. Leningrad: AN SSSR.

Gillel'son, M. I. 1974. *Molodoi Pushkin i arzamasskoe bratstvo.* Leningrad: Nauka.

Giorgi, Francesco. 1525. *De harmonia mundi.* Venice.

Gorbachevskii, I. I. 1963. *Zapiski. Pis'ma.* Moscow: AN SSSR.

Gorodetskii, B. P. 1964. "Pushkin posle vosstaniia dekabristov (zagadochnaia zapis' Pushkina 1826 g.)." In *Problemy sravnitel'noi filologii,* 378–86. Leningrad: AN SSSR.

———. 1970. *Lirika Pushkina.* Leningrad: Prosveshchenie.

Grech, N. I. 1886. *Zapiski o moei zhizni.* Saint Petersburg.

Gregg, Richard A. 1966. "Balzac and the Women in 'The Queen of Spades.'" *Slavic and East European Journal* 10, no. 3:279–82.

Grossman, L. P. 1928. "Iskusstvo anekdota u Pushkina." In *Etiudy o Pushkine,* 45–79. Moscow and Petrograd: L. D. Frenkel'. Also published under the title "The Art of the Anecdote in Pushkin." *Russian Literature Triquarterly,* no. 10 (1974):129–48.

Guberti, N. 1881. "Lubochnye gadatel'nye kartochki." *Rossiiskaia bibliografiia* 3, no. 91:326–27.

Gukovskii, G. A. 1957. *Pushkin i problemy realisticheskogo stilia.* Moscow: Khudlit.

———. 1965. *Pushkin i russkie romantiki.* Moscow: Khudlit.

Hargrave, Catherine Perry. 1930. *A History of Playing Cards and a Bibliography of Cards and Gaming.* Boston and Cincinnati: Houghton Mifflin.

Haugwitz, Christian August Heinrich Kurt von. 1785. *Hirten-brief.* Leipzig.

Hermes Trismegistus. 1964. *Thrice-Greatest Hermes.* Translated by G.R.S. Mead. 3 vols. London: John M. Watkins.

Hillgarth, J. N. 1971. *Ramon Lull and Lullism in Fourteenth-Century France.* Oxford: Clarendon Press.

Hopper, Vincent Foster. 1938. *Medieval Number Symbolism*. New York: Columbia University Press.
Hoy, David. 1971. *The Meaning of Tarot*. Nashville and London: Aurora.
Iakubovich, D. P. 1933. "O 'Pikovoi dame.'" In *Pushkin. 1833 g.*, 7–68. Leningrad: Pushkinskoe obshchestvo.
Iazykov, N. M. 1964. *Polnoe sobranie sochinenii*. 2d ed. Biblioteka poeta, bol'shaia seriia. Moscow and Leningrad: Sovetskii pisatel'.
Iezuitova, R. V. 1989. *Zhukovskii i ego vremia*. Leningrad: Nauka.
Izmailov, N. V. 1926. "A. A. Bestuzhev-Marlinskii do 14 dekabria 1825 g." In *Pamiati dekabristov*, 3 vols. 1:1–99. Leningrad: AN SSSR.
———. 1936. "Retsenziia na knigu 'Rukoiu Pushkina.'" In *Vremennik pushkinskoi komissii*, 2:426. Moscow and Leningrad: AN SSSR.
———. 1937. "Fantasticheskaia povest'." In *Russkaia povest' XIX veka*, 134–69. Leningrad: Nauka.
Jobes, Gertrude. 1961–62. *Dictionary of Mythology, Folklore and Symbols*. 3 vols. New York: Scarecrow Press.
Kanunova, F. Z. 1973. *Estetika russkoi romanticheskoi povesti*. Tomsk: Tomsk University Press.
———. 1987. "O filosofsko-istoricheskikh vozzreniiakh Zhukovskogo." In *Zhukovskii i russkaia kul'tura*, 289–305. Leningrad: AN SSSR.
Kanunova, F. Z., and A. S. Ianushkevich. 1985. "Svoeobrazie romanticheskoi estetiki i kritiki V. A. Zhukovskogo." In V. A. Zhukovskii, *Estetika i kritika*, 7–47. Moscow: Iskusstvo.
Karamzin, N. M. 1988. *Pis'ma russkogo puteshestvennika*. Moscow: Pravda.
Karatygin, P. A. 1929–30. *Zapiski*. 2 vols. Leningrad: Academia.
Kashin, N. P. 1927. "Po povodu 'Pikovoi damy.'" In *Pushkin i ego sovremenniki*, 31–32:25–34. Leningrad: AN SSSR.
Kaspryk, Andrew. 1990. "V. A. Zhukovsky's 'Ja muzu junuju, byvalo . . .': An Interpretation." *Graduate Essays on Slavic Languages and literatures* 3:48–58.
Khodorov, A. E. 1975. "Ukrainskie siuzhety poezii K. F. Ryleeva." In *Literaturnoe nasledie dekabristov*, 121–41. Leningrad: Nauka.
Kirchweger, Anton Joseph. 1723. *Aurea Catena Homeri, oder Eine Beschreibung von dem Ursprung der Natur und natürlichen Dingen*. Frankfurt and Leipzig.
Kotliarevskii, Nestor. 1908. *Ryleev*. Saint Petersburg.
Krestova, L. V. 1963. "Pushkin i dekabristy." In *Vremennik pushkinskoi komissii*, 41–48. Moscow and Leningrad: AN SSSR.
Le Forestier, René. N.d. *La Franc-maçonnerie occultiste au XVIIIe siècle et l'ordre des Élus Coens*. Paris: Darbon-Ainé.
Lebedev, N. M. 1954. "Otrasl' Ryleeva v Severnom obshchestve." In *Ocherki iz istorii dvizheniia dekabristov*, 320–403. Moscow: Gospolit.
Lednicki, Waclaw. 1955. *Pushkin's Bronze Horseman: The Story of a Masterpiece*. Berkeley and Los Angeles: University of California Press. Reprint. Westport, Conn.: Greenwood Press, 1978.
Leighton, Lauren G. 1975. *Alexander Bestuzhev-Marlinsky*. Boston: Twayne.
———. 1982. "Freemasonry in Russia: The Grand Lodge of Astraea, 1815–1822." *Slavonic and East European Review* 60, no. 2:244–61.
Lennhoff, Eugen, and Oskar Posner, eds. 1932. *Internationaler Freimaurer Lexicon*. Zurich, Leipzig, Vienna: Amalthea.
Lerner, N. O. 1929. "Istoriia 'Pikovoi damy.'" In *Rasskazy o Pushkine*, 132–63. Leningrad: Priboi.

Lezhnev, A. Z. 1966. *Proza Pushkina.* 2d ed. Moscow: Khudlit. Translated by Roberta Reeder, under the title *Pushkin's Prose.* Ann Arbor, Mich.: Ardis, 1983.

Lincoln, W. Bruce. 1978. "Decembrists." In *Modern Encyclopedia of Russian and Soviet History,* 8:229–37. Gulf Breeze, Fla.: Academic International Press.

Longinov, M. N. 1857. *Novikov i Shvarts.* Moscow.

———. 1867. *Novikov i moskovskie martinisty.* Moscow.

Lopukhin, I. V. 1790. *Nravouchitel'nyi katikhizis istinnykh frank masonov.* Moscow. [Subsequent editions appeared in 1791, 1798, and 1859.]

———. 1791. *Dukhovnyi rytsar' ili ishchushchii premudrosti.* Moscow. 2d ed. Moscow, 1810.

———. 1798. *Nekotorye Cherty o Vnutrennei Tserkvi, o Edinom Puti Istiny i o Razlichnykh Putiakh Zabluzhdeniia i Gibeli.* Moscow. 2d ed. Moscow, 1801. See also D.H.S. Nicholson's translation from the French, published under the title *Some Characteristics of the Interior Church.* London: Theosophical Publishing Society, 1912.

———. 1859. *Zapiski senatora I. V. Lopukhina.* London: Trubner. Reprint. Moscow: Nauka, 1990; Newtonville, Mass.: Oriental Research Partners, 1976.

———. 1913. *Masonskie trudy. Materialy po istorii russkogo masonstva XVIII veka.* Moscow.

———. 1924. *The Spiritual Knight/Duchovnyi rycar.* Translated by Boris Telepneff. London: n.p.

Lotman, Iu. M. 1973. "Ideinaia struktura poemy Pushkina 'Andzhelo.'" In *Uchenye zapiski. Pushkinskii sbornik,* 3–23. Pskov: University of Pskov.

———. 1975a. "Dekabrist v povsednevnoi zhizni." In *Literaturnoe nasledie dekabristov,* 25–74. Moscow: Nauka.

———. 1975b. "Tema kart i kartochnoi igry v russkoi literature nachala XIX veka." *Uchenye zapiski Tartuskogo universiteta, Trudy po znakovym sistemam* 7:120–42.

Lotman, Lidiia. 1981. "I ia by kak shut < . . . >." In *Vremennik pushkinskoi komissii 1978,* 46–59. Leningrad: AN SSSR.

Lucia [pseud.]. 1787. *The Life of Count Cagliostro.* 2d ed. London.

Mackey, Albert G. 1924. *An Encyclopedia of Freemasonry.* New and rev. ed. 2 vols. Chicago, New York, London: Masonic History.

Maikov, L. N. 1899. *Pushkin. Ocherki.* Saint Petersburg.

Mann, Iu. V. 1976. *Poetika russkogo romantizma.* Moscow: Nauka.

Marlinskii, A. A. *See* Bestuzhev-Marlinskii, A. A.

Mart'ianov, P. K. 1885. "Tri vstrechi." *Istoricheskii vestnik* 25, no. 11:413–21. See also volume 1 of *Dela i liudi veka.* 3 vols. Saint Petersburg, 1893–96.

Martynov, Ivan. 1976. *V mire knig.* No. 3.

Mason, John. 1745. *Self-Knowledge: A Treatise showing the Nature and Benefit of this Important Science and the Way to Attain It.* London. 2d ed. London, 1784. Translated into Russian by I. P. Turgenev, under the title *O poznanii samogo sebia.* Moscow, 1783. 2d [Russian] ed. 1786.

Mazour, A. G. 1937. *The First Russian Revolution. 1825.* Berkeley: University of California Press. Reprint. Stanford: Stanford University Press, 1961.

Meilakh, B. S. 1958a. "Pushkin v khode sledstviia i suda nad dekabristami." In *Pushkin i ego epokha,* 345–62. Moscow: Khudlit.

———. 1958b. "Vmeste s dekabristami." In *Pushkin i ego epokha,* 282–341. Moscow: Khudlit.

Mel'gunov, S. P., and N. P. Sidorov, eds. 1915. *Masonstvo v ego proshlom i nastoiashchem.* 2 vols. Moscow. Reprint. Moscow: SP "IKPA," 1991.

Mikhailova, N. I. 1974. "Povestvovatel'naia struktura 'Pikovoi damy.'" *Vestnik moskovskogo universiteta,* seriia 10, no. 3:10–19.

Mikkelson, Gerald E. 1980. "Pushkin's 'Arion': A Lone Survivor's Cry." *Slavic and East European Journal* 25, no. 1:1–13.
Modzalevskii, B. L. 1910. *Biblioteka A. S. Pushkina*. Saint Petersburg. Reprinted with a supplementary volume. Moscow: Kniga, 1988.
Mordovchenko, N. I. 1959. *Russkaia kritika pervoi chetverti XIX veka*. Moscow and Leningrad: AN SSSR.
Morozov, O. M. 1910. "Shifrovannoe stikhotvorenie Pushkina." In *Pushkin i ego sovremenniki*, 13:1–12. Saint Petersburg.
Nabokov, V. N., editor, translator, and commentator. 1964. *Eugene Onegin*. By Alexander Pushkin. 4 vols. New York: Pantheon.
Nauert, Charles G. 1965. *Agrippa and the Crisis of Renaissance Thought*. Urbana: University of Illinois Press.
Nechkina, M. V. 1937. "Dekabristy i Pushkin." In *Pushkin. Sbornik kriticheskikh statei*, 292–99. Moscow: Uchpedgiz.
———. 1947. *A. S. Griboedov i dekabristy*. Moscow: Khudlit.
———. 1951. *Vosstanie 14-go dekabria 1825 goda*. Moscow: AN SSSR.
———. 1955. *Dvizhenie dekabristov*. 2 vols. Moscow: AN SSSR.
———. 1978. "Decembrists' Uprising of 1825." In *Modern Encyclopedia of Russian and Soviet History*, 8:237–47. Gulf Breeze, Fla.: Academic International Press.
Nezelenov, A. I. 1889. *Literaturnye napravleniia v Ekaterinskuiu epokhu*. Saint Petersburg.
Oksman, Iu. G. 1926. *Dekabristy. Otryvki iz istochnikov*. Moscow and Leningrad: Gosizdat.
O'Meara, Patrick. 1984. *K. F. Ryleev: A Political Biography of the Decembrist Poet*. Princeton: Princeton University Press.
Ovsiannikova, S. A. 1954. "A. A. Bestuzhev i ego rol' v dvizhenii dekabristov." In *Ocherki iz istorii dvizheniia dekabristov*, 404–50. Moscow: Gospolit.
Papius (Papus), Doktor [Gerald Encausse]. 1911. *Tenezis i razvitie Masonskikh Simvolov*. Translated from French. Saint Petersburg.
de Pasqually, Martines [Martinez Pasqualis]. 1899. *Traité de la réintégration des êtres* (1754). Paris.
Pauls, John. 1963. "Two Treatments of Mazeppa: Ryleyev's and Pushkin's." *Slavic and East European Studies* 8, no. 1–2:97–109.
Pekarskii, P. P. 1909. "Dopolneniia k istorii masonstva v Rossii XVIII stoletiia." *Sbornik statei, chitannykh v otdelenii russkogo iazyka i slovesnosti Imp. akademiia. nauk* 7, no. 4:1–224.
Petrovskii, S. A. 1889. "Ocherki iz istorii russkogo masonstva v XVIII veke." *Khristianskoe chtenie* 7–8:123–63; 9–10:353–89; 11–12:571–602.
Piksanov, N. K. 1915. "I. V. Lopukhin." In *Masonstvo v ego proshlom i nastoiashchem*, 2 vols., 1:227–55. Moscow.
———. 1947. "Masonskaia literatura." In *Istoriia russkoi literatury*, 41–84. Moscow and Leningrad: AN SSSR.
Pokrovskii, A. A., et al., eds. 1925–86. *Vosstanie dekabristov*. 14 vols. Moscow and Leningrad: Tsentrarkhiv.
Polevoi, K. A. 1861. "Pis'ma A. A. Bestuzheva (Marlinskogo) k N. A. i K. A. Polevym." *Russkii vestnik* 32, no. 3:285–335; no. 4:425–87.
Polezhaev, A. I. 1957. *Stikhotvoreniia i poemy*. Biblioteka poeta, bol'shaia seriia. Leningrad: Sovetskii pisatel'.
Pordage, John [Johann Pordadsche]. 1715. *Göttliche und wahre Metaphysica oder Wunderbare*. 3 vols. Frankfurt and Leipzig.
Porokh, I. V. 1954. "Vosstanie chernigovskogo polka." In *Ocherki iz istorii dvizheniia dekabristov*, 121–85. Moscow: Gospolit.

Pratt, Sarah. 1984. *Russian Metaphysical Romanticism: The Poetry of Tiutchev and Boratynskii.* Stanford: Stanford University Press.
Prokhorov, V. G., ed. 1926. "A. A. Bestuzhev v Iakutske." In *Pamiati dekabristov,* 3 vols., 2:189–226. Leningrad: AN SSSR.
Prokopovich-Antonskii, A. A. 1785–89. *Detskoe chtenie dlia serdtsa i razuma.* Moscow.
Pushchin, I. I. 1979. *Zapiski o Pushkine.* Moscow: Sovetskaia Rossiia.
Pushkin, A. S. 1937–59. *Polnoe sobranie sochinenii.* 16 vols. and suppl. vol. Moscow and Leningrad: AN SSSR.
Pypin, A. N. 1916. *Russkoe masonstvo. XVIII i pervaia chetvert' XIX v.* Petrograd.
Raeff, Marc, ed. and trans. 1966. *The Decembrist Movement.* Englewood Cliffs, N.J.: Prentice-Hall.
Raevskii, N. A. 1976a. *Drug Pushkina Pavel Voinovich Nashchokin.* Leningrad: Nauka.
———. 1976b. *Portrety zagovorili.* 2d ed. enl. Alma-Ata: Khazushy.
Raevskii, V. F. 1967. *Polnoe sobranie sochinenii.* 2d ed. Biblioteka poeta, bol'shaia seriia. Moscow and Leningrad: Sovetskii pisatel'.
Reuchlin, Johann. 1494. *De verbo mirifico.* Basel.
———. 1517. *De arte cabalistica.* Hagenau. Also *De arte cabalistica* [facs.]. Stuttgart-Bad Cannstadt, 1964. Translated by Martin Goodman and Sarah Goodman, under the title *On the Art of the Kabbalah.* New York: Abaris Books, 1983.
Ribadeau Dumas, François. 1967. *Cagliostro.* London: George Allen & Unwin.
Riha, Thomas, ed. 1964. *Readings in Russian Civilization.* 3 vols. Chicago: University of Chicago Press.
Roberts, J. M. 1972. *The Mythology of the Secret Societies.* London: Secker & Warburg.
Rosen, Nathan. 1975. "The Magic Cards in 'The Queen of Spades.'" *Slavic and East European Journal* 19, no. 3:255–75.
Rovinskii, D. A., comp. 1881–93. *Russkie narodnye kartinki.* 5 vols. Saint Petersburg.
Rozhdestvenskii, V. A. 1966. *Chitaia Pushkina.* 2d ed. Leningrad: Detlit.
Ryleev, K. F. 1934. *Sochineniia.* Moscow: Academia.
———. 1971. *Polnoe sobranie stikhotvorenii.* 2d ed. Biblioteka poeta, bol'shaia seriia. Leningrad: Sovetskii pisatel'.
Sablin, B. M. 1906. *Dekabristy i tainye obshchestva v Rossii.* Moscow.
Saint-Germain, Count. 1949. *The Most Holy Trinosophia.* 3d ed. Los Angeles: Philosophers Press.
Saint-Martin, Louis Claude de. 1775. *Des erreurs et de la vérité.* Edinburgh.
———. 1790. *L'Homme de désir.* Lyon.
———. 1797? *De l'esprit des choses.* N.p.: Laran an 8.
———. 1807. *Oeuvres posthumes.* Tours.
———. 1946. *Des nombres.* Paris, 1843. 2d ed. Edited by Robert Dumas. Paris: L. Schauer.
Sakharov, V. I. 1988. "U istokov. Druzheskoe literaturnoe obshchestvo 1801 goda." In *Stranitsy russkogo romantizma,* 31–47. Moscow: Sovetskaia Rossiia.
Sakulin, P. N. 1928–29. "Masonizm." In *Russkaia literatura,* 2 vols., 2:337–46. Moscow: Gos. akademiia. khud. nauk.
Schilder, N. K. 1904–5. *Imperator Aleksandr Pervyi, ego zhizn' i tsarstvovanie.* 2d ed. 4 vols. Saint Petersburg.
Schneider, Heinrich. 1947. *Quest for Mysteries: The Masonic Background for Literature in Eighteenth-Century Germany.* Ithaca: Cornell University Press.
Scholem, Gershom. 1960. *Jewish Gnosticism, Merkabah Mysticism, and Talmudic Tradition.* New York: Jewish Theological Seminary of America.
———. 1961. *Major Trends in Jewish Mysticism.* New York: Schocken Books.
———. 1965. *On the Kabbalah and Its Symbolism.* New York: Schocken Books.

———. 1971a. "Gematria." In *Encyclopedia Judaica,* 10:369–74. Jerusalem: Keter Publishing House.
———. 1971b. "Kabbalah." In *Encyclopedia Judaica,* 10:489–653. Jerusalem: Keter Publishing House.
———. 1978. *The Kabbalah.* New York: New American Library.
———. 1987. *The Origins of the Kabbalah.* Philadelphia: Jewish Publications Society; Princeton: Princeton University Press.
Seligmann, Curt. 1948. *The History of Magic.* New York: Pantheon Books.
Semenko, I. M. 1980. "V. A. Zhukovskii." In V. A. Zhukovskii, *Sochineniia,* 1:5–39. 3 vols. Moscow: Khudlit.
Semevskii, M. I. 1870a. "Aleksandr Bestuzhev na Kavkaze." *Russkii vestnik,* no. 6:485–524; no. 7:72–85.
———. 1870b. "Bestuzhev v Iakutske." *Russkii vestnik,* no. 5:213–64.
———. 1908. "Dekabristy-Masony." *Minuvshie gody,* no. 2:1–50; no. 3:127–70; no. 5–6:379–433.
Sharypkin, D. M. 1974. "Vokrug 'Pikovoi damy.'" In *Vremennik pushkinskoi komissii 1972,* 128–38. Leningrad: AN SSSR.
Shaw, J. Thomas. 1962. "The Conclusion of Pushkin's 'Queen of Spades.'" In *Studies in Russian and Polish Literature in Honor of Waclaw Lednicki,* 114–26. The Hague: Mouton.
———. 1963. "Pushkin's 'The Shot.'" *Indiana Slavic Studies* 3:113–29.
———, ed. and trans. 1967. *The Letters of Alexander Pushkin.* 3 vols. in 1. Madison: University of Wisconsin Press.
———. 1981. "The Problem of Unity of Authorial-Narrator's Stance in Pushkin's Evgenii Onegin." *Russian Language Journal* 35, no. 120:25–42.
Der Signatstern, oder die enthüllten sämmtliche sieben Grade und Geheimnisse der mystischen Freimaurerei, nebst dem Orden der Magus oder Ritter des Lichts. 1866. 2 vols. Stuttgart.
Slonimskii, A. L. 1959. *Masterstvo Pushkina.* Moscow: Goslit.
Sokolov, D. N. 1910. "Po povodu shifrovannogo stikhotvoreniia Pushkina." In *Pushkin i ego sovremenniki,* 4:1–11. Saint Petersburg.
Sokolovskaia, T. O. 1906. "Brat'ia zlatorozovogo kresta." *Russkii arkhiv* 9:89–93.
———. 1908. *Russkoe masonstvo i ego znachenie v istorii obshchestvennogo dvizheniia.* Saint Petersburg.
———. 1915a. "Masonskie sistemy." In *Masonstvo v ego proshlom i nastoiashchem,* 2 vols., 2:52–59. Moscow.
———. 1915b. "Obriadnost' vol'nykh kamenshchikov." In *Masonstvo v ego proshlom i nastoiashchem,* 2 vols., 2:80–117. Moscow.
Stenbock-Fermor, Elizabeth. 1964. "Some Neglected Features of the Epigraphs in *The Captain's Daughter* and Other Stories of Pushkin." *International Journal of Slavic Linguistics and Poetics* 8:110–23.
Stepanov, N. L. 1962. *Proza Pushkina.* Moscow: AN SSSR.
Swedenborg, Emanuel. 1918. *Heaven and Its Wonders and Hell.* New York: Houghton Mifflin.
———. N. d. *The Works of Emanuel Swedenborg.* 32 vols. Boston and New York: American Swedenborg Society.
Syroechkovskii, B., ed. 1924. "Zapiski [Nikolaia I] o 14 dekabria 1825 g." *Krasnyi arkhiv* 6:222–34.
Tamarchenko, N. D. 1971. "O poetike 'Pikovoi damy' A. S. Pushkina." In *Voprosy teorii i istorii literatury,* 45–62. Kazan: Kazanskii gosudarstvennyi pedagogicheskii institut.

Tarasov, E. I. 1915. "Moskovskoe Obshchestvo rozenkreitserov." In *Masonstvo v ego proshlom i nastoiashchem*, 2 vols., 2:1–26. Moscow: Zadruga i K. F. Nekrasov.
Tefft, Stanton K., ed. 1980. *Secrecy: A Cross-Cultural Perspective*. New York and London: Human Sciences Press.
Tiutchev, F. I. 1987. *Polnoe sobranie stikhotvorenii*. 3d ed. Biblioteka poeta, bol'shaia seriia. Leningrad: Sovetskii pisatel'.
Tomashevskii, Boris. 1927. *Pis'ma Pushkina k E. M. Khitrovo*. Leningrad: AN SSSR.
———. 1934. "Desiataia glava 'Evgeniia Onegina' (istoriia razgadki)." In *Literaturnoe nasledstvo*, 16–18:379–420. Moscow: Zhurnal'no-gazetnoe ob"edinenie. Also in *Pushkin. Vtoraia kniga*, 200–244. Moscow and Leningrad: AN SSSR, 1961.
———. 1953–58. "[Letter to André Meynieux]." In A. S. Pouchkine, *Oeuvres complètes*, 3 vols., 3:500. Paris: A. Bonne.
———. 1956. "Voprosy iazyka v tvorchestve Pushkina." In *Pushkin. Issledovaniia i materialy*, 1:126–84. Leningrad: AN SSSR.
Tschoudy (Tschudy), Théodore Henri, baron de [pseud., De Lussy]. 1766. *L'Étoile flamboyante des Franc-Maçons, considerée sous tous les aspects*. 2 vols. Frankfurt and Paris.
———. 1866. *Der flammende Stern und die königliche geheime Kunst, oder die Gesellschaft der Freymaurer, von allen Seiten beträchtet. Zugleich Fortsetzung des "Freimaurerischen Signatstern."* 2 vols. Stuttgart. See also *Der Flammende Stern*. 2 vols. Berlin, 1779.
Tsiavlovskaia, T. G. 1975. "Otkliki na sud'by dekabristov v tvorchestve Pushkina." In *Literaturnoe nasledie dekabristov*, 195–218. Leningrad: Nauka.
———. 1983. *Risunki Pushkina*. Moscow: Iskusstvo.
Tsiavlovskii, M. A. 1936–38. "Kommentarii." In A. S. Pushkin, *Polnoe sobranie sochinenii*, 6 vols., 4:738–43. Moscow and Leningrad: Academia.
Tukalevskii, V. L. 1911. *Iskaniia russkikh masonov*. Saint Petersburg.
Vatsuro, V. E., and B. S. Meilakh. 1966. "Pushkin i deiatel'nost' tainykh obshchestv." In *Pushkin. Itogi i problemy izucheniia*, 168–97. Moscow and Leningrad: Nauka.
Vernadskii, G. V. 1917. *Russkoe masonstvo v tsarstvovanie Ekateriny II*. Petrograd.
Veselovskii, A. N. 1918. *V. A. Zhukovskii. Poeziia chuvstva i "serdechnogo voobrazheniia."* Petrograd.
Vickery, Walter. 1976. "'Arion': An Example of Post-Decembrist Semantics." In *Alexander Pushkin: A Symposium*. New York: New York University Press.
Vinogradov, V. V. 1936. "Stil' 'Pikovoi damy.'" In *Vremennik pushkinskoi komissii*, 1:74–147. Moscow and Leningrad: AN SSSR.
———, comp. 1956. *Slovar' iazyka Pushkina*. 4 vols. Moscow and Leningrad: AN SSSR.
Vladimirova, I. [pseud.], et al. 1981. "A. A. Blok i russkaia kul'tura XVIII veka. 1." In *Blokovskii sbornik IV (Nasledie A. Bloka i aktual'nye problemy poetiki)*. Tartu, Estonia: University of Tartu.
Voltaire. 1820–26. *Oeuvres complètes*. 70 vols. Paris: A. E. Lequien.
Waite, A. E. 1924. *The Brotherhood of the Rosy Cross*. London: W. Rider & Son.
———. 1970. *New Encyclopedia of Freemasonry*. 2 vols. in 1. New York: Weathervane Books.
Walker, Franklin. 1969. "K. F. Ryleev: A Self-Sacrifice for Freedom." *Slavonic and East European Review* 47, no. 4:436–46.
Weber, Harry B. 1968. "'Pikovaia dama': A Case for Freemasonry in Russian Literature." *Slavic and East European Journal* 12, no. 4:435–47.
Webster, Charles. 1982. *From Parcelsus to Newton: Magic and the Making of Modern Science*. Cambridge: Cambridge University Press.
Welling, Georg von [Georgius Anglus Sallwigt]. 1735. *Opus Mago-Cabbalisticum et Theosophicum*. Homburg von der Hohe. 2d [authoritative] ed. Frankfurt, 1760.

Williams, Gareth. 1981. "Pushkin and Jules Janin: A Contribution to the Literary Background of 'The Queen of Spades.'" *Quinquereme* 4:206–24.
Wilson, Colin. 1971. *The Occult*. New York: Random House.
Yates, Frances A. 1964. *Giordano Bruno and the Hermetic Tradition*. Chicago: University of Chicago Press.
———. 1972. *The Rosicrucian Enlightenment*. London: Routledge & Kegan Paul.
———. 1975. *Astraea: The Imperial Theme in the Sixteenth Century*. London: Routledge & Kegan Paul.
———. 1979. *The Occult Philosophy in the Elizabethan Age*. London and Boston: Routledge & Kegan Paul.
Zakharov, N. S. 1954. "Peterburgskoe soveshchanie dekabristov v 1824 g." In *Ocherki iz istorii dvizheniia dekabristov*, 84–120. Moscow: Gospolit.
Zhukovskii, V. A. 1980. *Sochineniia*. 3 vols. Moscow: Khudlit.

Index

Aesopic language, 3, 85
Afanas'ev, Viktor, 74
"Agitational Songs," 19–20, 113
Agrippa, Henry Cornelius, 23, 28
   De occulta philosophica, 23
   De vanite scientarium, 23
Akhmatova, Anna, 123, 153, 154
alchemy, 2, 24, 25, 31, 33, 137, 167, 169
Aleksandra Fedorovna, Grand Duchess, 48
Alekseyev, M. P., 85, 112, 133, 157, 187
Alexander I, 11, 12–14, 15, 16, 20, 26, 30, 31, 54, 62, 71–72, 97, 104, 107, 109, 123, 125, 126, 127
Alexander II, 38
Allen, Paul M., 24, 188
Altman, M. A., 170
Altshuller, Mark, 89
Andreae, Johannes. *See* Rosenkreutz, Christian
Aristotle, Aristotelian, 22
Arkhipova, A. V., 59
Arnim, Achim von, 128
Arsen'ev, V. S., 26
Arzamas Brotherhood, 36–37, 41–42, 197
astrology, 2, 24, 133, 137, 167
Avrekh, A. Ia., 200
Azadovskii, M. A., 76, 97, 104, 105

Babinski, Hubert F., 77
Bacon, Roger, 28
Baehr, Stephen, 26, 176, 184, 200
Bakhtin, M. M., 202
Bakounine, Tatiana, 25–26, 28, 92
Balsamo, Joseph. *See* Cagliostro, Count

Balzac, Honoré, 155, 156
   "L'Auberge rouge," 156
   "La Peau de chagrin," 156
Baratynsky, E. A., 199, 201
Barskov, Ya. L., 25, 27, 89–90, 177, 193
Batenkov, G. S., 61, 62, 185
Bazanov, V. G., 14, 17, 21, 59, 101–3, 104
Beaumarchais, 156
Bel'chikov, N. F., 63
Belousov, R., 156
Bely, Andrey, 142
Bem, A., 133, 155
Benckendorf, A. Kh., 31
Benham, William Gurney, 169
Berberova, Nina, 200
Berdnikov, I. D., 26
Berlin, Isaiah, 134
Bertenev, P. I., 156
Beshenkovsky, Evgeny, 28, 199
Bestuzhev, A. A. (Marlinsky), 2, 3, 8–9, 13, 14, 15, 16, 18, 19–20, 70–71, 72, 73, 74, 82–84, 85–87, 89, 90, 91–110, 111–30, 131, 149–52, 161, 162, 192, 193, 194, 197, 198
   "Agitational Songs," 19–20, 113
   "Ammalat-Bey," 19
   "Castle Eisen," 19
   "Castle Neihausen," 19
   "Castle Wenden," 19
   "Dream," 20, 70–71, 83–84, 113, 115–17, 118, 122
   "Frigate Hope," 8–9, 19, 93–110, 111, 113, 114, 117–22, 129, 130, 131, 149–52, 162, 194, 197
   "Gedeon," 19

"Glances," 111
"Letter to Doctor Erman," 85
"Raiders," 19
"Roman and Olga," 19
"Test," 111–12, 113
"Tournament at Reval," 19, 129
"Traitor," 19
Bestuzhev, A. F., 15, 85
Bestuzhev, M. A., 15, 16, 72, 82, 96, 97, 98, 99, 104–5, 106–7
Bestuzhev, N. A., 15, 16, 72, 76, 82, 96, 97–98, 99, 105, 106–7
"Memoir on Ryleyev," 76
Bestuzhev, P. A., 93
Bible, 22, 27, 137, 167, 168
Bilinkis, M. Ya., 202
Birkina, Sonyushka, 157
Bitsilli, P. V., 156, 162
Blagoy, D. D., 114, 192
Blau, Joseph L., 22
Blavatsky, Madame, 2
Blok, A. A., 89
Bogdanovich, M. I., 125
Böhme, Jakob, 24, 27, 28, 55, 177, 199, 200, 201
Mysterium magnum, 24
Bonnet, Charles, 25
Bourychkine, Paul, 25–26
Boyan, 18
Bruno, Giordano, 22
Brutus, 15, 20, 71, 72, 75, 79–80, 107, 109
Buffon, 156
Bulgakov, Mikhail, 202
Bulgarin, F. V., 17, 74, 92, 102
Burgin, Diana Lewis, 155, 163–64
Burns, Robert, 1
Butler, Christopher, 133
Byron, Lord, 4, 18, 38, 40, 71, 73, 77, 83, 92, 111, 127
Mazeppa, 83
Prisoner of Chillon, 38

Cabala, Cabalism, 2, 4, 5, 9, 21, 22–23, 24, 31, 32, 33, 37, 55, 90, 94, 122, 131–32, 133, 134, 135, 137, 152, 159, 161, 163–64, 166–69, 176–77, 187–94, 199, 202
Cagliostro, Count (Joseph Balsamo), 24, 155, 178–79
Roman Rites of the Egyptian Order of Masons, 24

calendarology, 2, 4, 9, 37, 94, 101–5, 106–9, 122–28, 133, 134, 137, 159
Cartesianism, 2, 5, 23, 172, 196
cartomancy, 2, 9, 37, 122, 123, 133, 134, 135, 137, 156, 159–60, 162, 164–66, 168–73, 175, 176, 178–80
Casanova, Jacques, 1, 155, 178, 179–80, 183
Catherine II, 26, 28, 39, 54, 123, 178, 179, 199, 200
Cato, 75
Cavendish, Richard, 135, 161, 166, 167
Cervantes, 2, 134
Chambers, R., 101, 168
Charles XII, 77, 179
Chénier, André, 71
Chereiskii, L. A., 31, 181
Chernov, K. P., 74–75
Chernova, Mariya, 74–75
Chetteoui, Wilfrid-René, 24, 178, 179
Chkhaidze, L. V., 134, 170–71
Chukovskaia, Lidiia, 153
civicism, 8, 16, 17, 70
Clayton, J. Douglas, 154, 156, 157
Constantine, Grand Duke, 11, 13, 107
Corday, Charlotte, 20
Cornwell, Neil, 199
Craven, Kenneth, 25, 28, 199, 200
Culbertson, Ely, 165

Dante, 2, 21, 99, 134, 136, 160, 177–78
Divine Comedy, 99, 177–78
Dantes (D'Anthes), 39
Davydov, Denis, 20
"Hungry Cur," 20
Davydov, Sergei, 134, 145, 146, 156, 157, 189, 201
Davydovs, 15
Debreczeny, Paul, 156
Decembrism, 2–4, 6, 7, 8–9, 11–21, 31, 32, 35, 37, 38, 41, 59–65, 66, 67–90, 91–110, 111–29, 131, 181, 185, 190–93, 198, 201
Dee, John, 23, 28, 162, 200
General and rare memorials pertayning to the Perfect arte of Nauigation, 23, 162
Monas hieroglyphica, 23
Delvig, Baron A. A., 57, 75, 197
Descartes, René. *See* Cartesianism
Dolgorukaya, Natalya, 18
Donskoy, Dimitry, 18

Dostoyevsky, F. M., 134, 170, 172, 202
  Crime and Punishment, 172
Druzhnikov, Yuri, 133
Duc d'Orleans, 156, 160
duma, 18, 71, 75–76
Dumas, Alexandre, 93, 130

Eckartshausen, Carl von, 25
Eckleff, Count von, 30, 67
Efros, Abram, 128
Eikhenbaum, B. M., 37
Elagin, I. P., 26, 176, 177
Elizabeth I, 23
Ellison, Georg Heinrich, 184
Erman, Georg Adolph, 85–87, 89, 90, 95, 107
  Travels in Siberia, 85–87
esoterica, esotericism, 1–2, 4–7, 8, 9, 21–25, 26, 27–28, 31–32, 33, 35–37, 54–55, 65–66, 87, 99–100, 117, 131–32, 155, 175, 176–80, 188, 195–203
Eydelman, N. Ya., 21, 119, 124

Faivre, Antoine, 7, 21, 25
Ferd, Josef Schneider, 127–28
Fessler, Ignatius, 30
Fet, A. A., 201
Fichte, J. G., 30
Ficino, Marsilio, 55, 177, 200
Fielding, Henry, 136
  Tom Jones, 136
Florinsky, Michael T., 157
Fludd, Robert, 24, 27, 177, 199, 200, 201
  Utriusque cosmi historia, 24, 27
Fowler, Alastair, 5, 23, 133
Freemasonry, 1, 2, 4, 7, 8, 9, 21, 22, 24, 25–33, 35, 36–37, 39, 41, 53, 54–57, 59, 62, 65–66, 67–68, 74, 87–90, 92, 99–100, 127–28, 131, 133–34, 135, 136, 175, 176, 180–94, 197–203
French, Peter J., 22
Fridlender, G. M., 41
friendship, cult of, 39, 41–42, 82–84

Gamaleya, S. I., 27
gematria, 9, 149–51, 166–67, 168, 187–93
Gillelson, M. I., 42
Giorgi, Francesco, 22, 28, 55, 162, 177, 200
  De harmonia mundi, 22, 162
Glinka, F. N., 198

Goethe, 1, 21, 25, 122, 126, 127, 128, 133, 138, 155, 157, 160
  Faust I, 122, 126, 127, 133, 138, 155, 157, 160
  Wilhelm Meister, 128
Gogol, N. V., 38, 142
Golytsina, Countess N. P., 155–56
Gorbachevsky, I. I., 72, 119
Gorodetskii, B. P., 114, 128
Gray, Thomas, 38
  "Elegy Written in a Country Churchyard," 38
Grech, N. I., 16, 74, 82–83, 92, 198
  Notes on My Life, 82–83
Gregg, Richard, 156
Griboyedov, A. S., 16, 21, 198
  Woe from Wit, 21
Grigorev, A. A., 199
Grossman, L. P., 179
Guberti, N., 162, 169
Gukovskii, G. A., 37, 155
Guyon, Jeanne Maria, 25

Hargrave, Catherine Perry, 169
Haugwitz, Christian von, 24, 27, 32
  Hirten-brief, 24, 32
Hebel, Johann, 40, 46
  "Der Morgenstern," 46
Helmont, Jean Baptist van, 25
Herman, Armand, 157
Hermes Trismegistus, hermeticism, 22, 23, 27, 32, 54, 202
  Corpus Hermeticum, 22
Herzen, A. I., 54
Heun, Karl, 156
  "Der holländische Jude," 156
Hillgarth, J. N., 22
Hoffmann, E. T. A., 156
Hopper, Vincent, 5, 99, 168, 177–78
Hoy, David, 168–69
Hugo, Victor, 130, 150, 156
Huizenga, Johan, 134
humanism, 22, 23
Hund, Johann Gottlieb von, 30, 67
Hyram-Abif, legend of, 9, 88–90, 180–82

Iakubovich, D. P., 178
Iezuitova, R. V., 37, 61
Illuminati, Illuminism, 2, 25, 29

International Eighteenth-Century Russian Studies Group, 201
Ivan the Terrible, 18
Izmailov, N. V., 133, 140, 144
Izmaylov, A. E., 198

Jobes, Gertrude, 168
Jung-Stilling, Heinrich, 25
Juvenal, 100

Kakhovskoy, P. G., 16, 72, 97, 98
Kant, Immanuel, 199
Kanunova, F. Z., 104, 122
Karamzin, N. M., 18, 25, 36, 37, 38, 41, 67, 197, 202
  History of the Russian State, 18
  Letters of a Russian Traveler, 25, 202
Karatygin, P. A., 157
Kashin, N. P., 144, 179
Katenin, P. A., 20
Khlebnikov, Velemir, 202
Khodorov, A. E., 77
Kipling, Rudyard, 1
Kirchweger, A. I., 24, 27, 32
  Aurea Catena Homeri, 24, 32
Kleist, Ludwig von, 25
Klopstock, Friedrich Gottlieb, 25
Knights of Malta, 29
Kotliarevskii, N. A., 124
Krestova, L. V., 128
Küchelbecker, V. K., 16, 19, 20, 57, 71, 198, 201
Kurbsky, Prince, 18
Kutuzov, A. M., 27

Labzin, A. F., 27
Lamartine, Alphonse de, 71
La Motte-Fouque, 156
Lavater, Johannes Caspar, 25
Lax Observance, 29–30, 67
Lebedev, N. M., 13, 72, 97
Lebrun, Madame, 183, 188, 189
Le Carré, John, 1
Lednicki, Waclaw, 21
Le Forestier, René, 30, 146
Leighton, Lauren G., 28, 31
Lerner, N. O., 156, 179
Leroy, 183, 188
Leskov, N. S., 142

Lessing, Gotthold Ephraim, 1, 25, 30
Lezhnev, A. Z., 140, 143
Lincoln, W. Bruce, 15
Livijn, Clas Johan, 156
Longinov, M. N., 25, 26, 27
Lopukhin, I. V., 26, 27, 32, 36, 39, 54–57, 65, 87, 88, 89, 117, 177, 197, 200, 201, 202, 203
  Memoirs of Senator Lopukhin, 54, 201
  "A Morally Edifying Catechism of the True Free Masons," 27, 54, 55
  "On the Church Within Thee," 27, 32, 54, 87
  "The Spiritual Knight, or The Seeker of Supreme Wisdom," 27, 54, 55–56, 89
Lotman, Lidya, 128–29
Lotman, Yu. M., 75, 119, 123–24, 169
Lovers of Wisdom, 18, 198–99, 201
Lull, Ramon, Lullism, 22, 23, 167, 200
Lurie, Isaac, 22

Machiavelli, Niccolò, 14
Mackey, Albert G., 88, 136, 162, 184
Magi, Great, 1, 5, 21, 22, 23, 28, 32, 162, 166, 172
Maikov, L. N., 112
Mann, Iu. V., 43
Marlinsky. *See* Bestuzhev, A. A.
Mart'ianov, P. K., 112
Martines de Pasqually (Martines Pasqualis), 24, 26
  Traité de la réintégration des êtres, 24
Martynov, Ivan, 28, 199
Mason, John, 39
  Self-Knowledge, 39
Matthisson, F. von, 46
  "Elysium," 46
Maykov, A. N., 201
Mazepa, 69, 77–81, 82, 85, 86
Mazour, A. G., 12
Medici circle, 22
Meilakh, B. S., 21, 114, 124
Melgunov, S. P., 26, 201
Merkabah mysticisim, 5, 21
Mesmér, 160, 188
Mey, L. A., 201
Meynieux, André, 170
Mikhaylova, N. I., 143
Mikkelson, Gerald, 21, 114–15

Miller, Georg Friedrich, 78, 85, 86
Millevoye, Charles Hubert, 40, 68
  "La Fleur," 40, 68
Milton, John, 21, 134, 136
Modzalevskii, B. L., 133, 166, 178
Montgolfièr, 160, 188
Mordvinov, N. S., 74
Morozov, O. M., 21
Moscow Mystic Masons (Novikov group), 8, 24–25, 27, 28, 32, 35, 39, 53, 67, 89, 131, 176, 177, 197, 199, 200, 201, 202
Moses, 22
Mozart, 127, 181
  Magic Flute, 181
Musin-Pushkin-Bryus, Count V. V., 157, 181

Nabokov, Vladimir, 21, 123, 125–27, 134, 156, 170
Napoleon, 12, 15, 72, 113, 120–22, 126, 127, 130, 138, 149, 155
Nashchokin, P. V., 156
Nauert, Charles G., 23
Nechkina, M. V., 12, 31, 101, 105, 107, 109, 124
Nezelenov, A. I., 25
Nicholas I, 11–12, 13, 14, 15, 26, 31, 38, 39, 48, 63, 71, 73, 85, 96, 97, 98–99, 100, 101–2, 103, 104–6, 107, 119, 120, 122, 123, 124, 127, 129, 181
Noailles, envoy, 156–57
Northern Bee, 102, 103–4, 106, 108
Northern Flowers, 74
Novikov, N. I., 26–27, 36, 54, 89, 199, 200
Novikov group. *See* Moscow Mystic Masons
Novosiltsev family, 74
numerology, 2, 4, 5, 9, 23, 24, 31, 33, 37, 54, 55, 89, 93, 94, 99, 122, 123, 125, 131–52, 153, 155, 157–73, 175, 176–80, 183, 185–87, 188, 189, 199, 202

Obolensky, E. P., 73
occult, occultism, 2, 195–96, 202
Odoyevsky, A. I., 16, 19, 20
Odoyevsky, V. F., 198–99, 201
Odyssey, The, 38
Oksman, Iu. G., 124
Olesha, Yuri, 202
O'Meara, Patrick, 68, 74, 75

Orlov, M. F., 31, 59, 61–62, 181
Ovsiannikova, S. A., 95, 96, 97

Papius, Doctor, 55, 99
Pascal, 23
Paul I, 26, 39, 54, 123
Paul, Jean, 128
Pauls, John, 78
Pekarskii, P. P., 90, 193
Pestel, Pavel, 12, 13, 14, 15, 31, 59, 72, 73, 95, 181
Peter I, 26, 77, 78, 79, 80–81, 85
Peter III, 123
Petrovskii, S. A., 25
Pico della Mirandola, 22
Piksanov, N. K., 25, 54
Pisemsky, A. F., 199
  Masons, 199
Plato, 22
Platonov, Yury, 202
Plotinus, 22
Pogodin, M. P., 181–82, 198
Pokrovskii A. A., 6, 73, 82, 95, 96–97, 98, 105
Polar Star, 18, 70, 74, 78, 83, 87, 92, 111
Polevoy, K. A., 120
Polezhayev, A. I., 62–65, 114, 198
  "Condemned Man," 64–65
  "Embittered Poet," 64
  "Song of a Drowning Sailor," 63–64, 114
  "To My Genius," 64
Pordage, John (Johann Pordasche), 24, 27, 32
  Göttliche und wahre Metaphysica, 24, 32
Porokh, I. V., 125
Pratt, Sarah, 199
Prokopovich-Antonsky, A. A., 38, 39
  Childrens Readings for the Heart and Mind, 39
Protasova, Maria, 38, 53
Pushchin, I. I., 57, 124
Pushchin, P. S., 181
Pushkin, A. S., 1, 2–3, 7, 8–9, 16, 20, 21, 31, 33, 38, 39, 51, 57–58, 59, 62, 63, 67, 71, 74, 75, 78, 83, 92, 93, 111–30, 131–52, 153–73, 175–94, 197, 203
  "Anchar," 192
  Angelo, 123, 134
  "Arion," 20, 21, 113–15, 117–18, 122, 130
  Bronze Horseman, 21, 113, 134, 154
  Captain's Daughter, 113, 133, 192

Captive of the Caucaus, 38, 120
Count Nulin, 134
"Dagger," 20, 71
Eugene Onegin, 21, 111–12, 113, 120, 121, 125, 133, 134, 149, 154
"Exegi monumentum," 113, 123
"Faust," 133
Fountain at Bakhchisaray, 121
"Gambler's Song," 113
"Journey to Arzerum," 112
"Liberty," 20, 71
Little House in Kolomna, 133, 134
"Message to Siberia," 20
"Noël, Hurrah," 20
Poltava, 78, 134
"Queen of Spades," 7, 9, 21, 113, 122–23, 126, 127, 129, 130, 132–52, 153–73, 175–94, 197
"Shot," 112, 192
Table-Talk, 133
Tales of Belkin, 134
"To Anna Kern," 51, 57–58
"To the Sea," 121–22
Pushkin, V. L., 198
Pypin, A. N., 25, 26–27, 31, 54, 87, 176, 177, 183, 185, 200

Rabelais, 2, 21, 136
Raeff, Marc, 12
Raevskii, N. A., 156
Rayevsky, V. F., 16, 31, 59–62, 65, 67, 69, 76, 114, 181, 185
"Autumn," 60, 114
"Epistle to G. S. Batenkov," 61
"My Farewell to My Friends," 59
"To G. S. Batenkov," 61
"To My Friends in Kishinev," 59–60, 61–62
"To My Rural Retreat," 61
Reuchlin, Johann, 23, 28, 55, 177
De arte cabalistica, 23
De verbo mirifico, 23
Revelation, Book of, 22, 167
Ribadeau-Dumas, François, 179
Richelieu, 160
Riha, Thomas, 96
Roberts, J. M., 32–33
Robespierre, 72, 157
Rosen, Nathan, 134, 144, 169
Rosenkreutz (Rosencreutz), Christian (Johannes Andreae), 24, 27, 28, 55, 177, 188, 201
The Fame and Confession of the Fraternity of the Rosie Cross (Fama fraternitas), 24, 188
The Hermetick Romance, or The Chymical Wedding, 24, 188
Rosicrucians, Rosicrucianism, 2, 24, 27, 29, 30, 31, 32, 182
Rousseau, J. J., 61
Rovinskii, D. A., 101, 133
Rozhdestvenskii, V. A., 114
Ruisbreck, Jan van, 25
Russian Word, Society of Lovers of, 37, 41–42, 197
Ryleyev, K. F., 2, 3, 8, 12, 13–20, 31, 66, 67–90, 91, 92, 95, 96–97, 98, 99–100, 106, 107–9, 110, 111–19, 124, 125–26, 127, 128, 131, 154, 161, 182, 190–93, 198
"Agitational Songs," 19–20, 113
"Dmitry the Pretender," 71
"Ivan Susanin," 75–76
Nalivayko, 19, 76–77, 78
"On the Death of Byron," 73
"Signal-Star," 68–69, 100, 114
"Some Thoughts on Poetry," 111
"To A. A. Bestuzhev," 69–70, 83
"To the Favorite," 75
"Volynsky," 76
Voynarovsky, 8, 19, 69–70, 77–81, 82, 83, 84, 85, 86–87, 90, 91, 95, 98, 106, 115, 116, 117

Sablin, B. M., 109, 125
Saint-Germain, Count, 2, 24, 138, 143, 155, 156, 157, 160, 163, 164, 172, 178, 179, 183
La Très Sainte Trinosophie, 24, 178
Saint-Martin, Louis-Claude de, 24, 26, 27, 28, 39, 54, 176, 199, 200, 201
Des erreurs et de la verité, 24, 27
L'esprit des choses, 24
L'homme de désir, 24
Des nombres, 176
Sakharov, V. I., 36
Sakulin, P. N., 25
Sand, Karl, 20
Schelling, Friedrich, 18, 199, 201
Schilder, N. K., 109

Schiller, Friedrich, 25, 40, 41, 43, 44, 48, 68, 71, 128
  Die Braut von Messina, 128
  "Die Ideale," 41, 44, 48, 68
  "Lied," 43
  "Der Pilgrim," 44
  "Song of the Mountains," 44
Schlegel, August, 199
Schlegel, Friedrich, 199
Schneider, Heinrich, 22
Scholem, Gershom, 5, 136, 167, 189–90, 194, 202
Schroeder, Friedrich, 30
Schroeder, Baron G. J., 26–27, 89–90, 177, 193–94
Schwartz, I. G., 26–27
Scott, Sir Walter, 19, 128–29, 150
  Ivanhoe, 128–29
Seligmann, Curt, 5, 135, 152, 166, 167, 169, 178, 188, 194
Semenko, I. M., 37, 43
Semenova, Nimforoda, 157
Semevsky, M. I., 68, 82, 97–98, 105, 106–7, 108
Shakespeare, 107, 134
Sharypkin, D. M., 179
Shaw, J. Thomas, 21, 51, 62, 119, 123, 125, 139, 157, 181
Shelley, Percy Bysshe, 127
Shishkov, A. S., 197
Sidorov, M. P., 26, 201
Signatstern, Der (Wöllner, Johann Christoph [Chrysophiron]), 25, 36, 55, 177
Slavophiles, 199, 201
Slonimskii, A. L., 144
Sokolovskaya, T. O., 25, 183, 184, 185, 186, 200
Spenser, Edmund, 2, 21
Speransky, M. S., 62
Star of Hope, 8–9, 36–37, 40–66, 68–71, 83–84, 87–90, 91, 95, 99–100, 105–6, 115, 117, 131, 195, 197, 203
Stenbock-Fermor, Elizabeth, 156, 162
Stendhal, 155
Stepanov, N. L., 140
Sterne, Laurence, 2, 21, 155
  Tristram Shandy, 155
Strict Observance, rite of, 29–30, 31, 67, 180
Swedenborg, Emanuel, 2, 24, 27, 28, 55, 137, 155, 160, 177, 179, 183, 200, 201
  Apocalypsis revelata, 24
  Coelestia Arcana, 24, 137
  De Coelo et Inferno, 24
Swedish system, 30, 67, 180
Syroechkovskii, B., 97

Tacitus, 129
Talmud, 167
Tamarchenko, N. D., 140–42
Tarasov, E. I., 39
Tarot, 168–70
Tatishchev, P. A., 27
Tefft, Stanton K., 14
Templarism, 25, 27, 28, 29, 30, 55
thaumaturgy, 2–3, 4, 5–9, 21, 27–28, 31–32, 33, 35, 37, 39, 91, 94, 99–110, 125, 130, 131–32, 133, 134, 152, 172, 175, 180, 193–94, 195–203
Tieck, Johann Ludwig von, 128
Tolstoy, Fedor, 125, 127
Tolstoy, L. N., 26
  War and Peace, 26
Tomashevskii, B. V., 21, 156, 170
Torah, 190
Torson, Konstantin, 72, 98, 104–5
Trubetskoy, N. N., 27
Tschoudy, Théodore Henri, baron de, 25, 28, 36–37, 39, 54–55, 65, 87, 88–89, 90, 117, 177, 200, 201
  Der flammende Stern (L'Étoile flamboyante), 25, 36–37, 55, 87, 88–89, 90, 117, 177
Tsiavlovskaia, T. G., 125, 126, 128
Tsiavlovskii, M. A., 156, 179
Tukalevsky, V. L., 25
Turgenev, Aleksandr, 36, 38, 40–41, 197
Turgenev, Andrey, 36, 38, 39, 40–41
Turgenev, I. P., 27, 36, 38, 39, 40–41, 53, 54, 56, 65, 197, 200, 201, 202
Tyutchev, F. I., 199, 201

Uhland, Johann Ludwig, 25

Van der Velde, E. T., 179
  "Arwed Gillenstein," 179
Vatsuro, V. E., 21, 124
Venevitinov, D. V., 20, 198
  "Homeland," 20
Vernadsky, G. V., 25, 26–27, 176, 200
Veselovsky, A. N., 37, 44, 52–53, 56
Vickery, Walter, 21, 114–15

Vigel, F. F., 198
Vinogradov, V. V., 134, 140, 143, 144, 156, 157, 162, 163
Vladimirova et al., 89
Volkonskys, 15
Voltaire, 77, 126–27, 134, 156, 197
  "Dialogue d'un Parisien et un Russe," 126–27
Vyazemsky, Prince V. A., 16, 75, 123–24, 178, 197

Waite, A. E., 99
Walker, Franklin, 72, 73
Weber, Carl, 149
  Freischutz, 149
Weber, Harry B., 134, 180–84, 185
Webster, Charles, 23
Welling, Baron Georg von, 24, 27, 28, 55, 176–77
  Opus Mago-Cabbalisticum et Theosphicum, 24, 27, 55, 176–77
Wetzel, J. G., 40
  "Nach Osten," 46
Wieland, Christoph Martin, 25
Williams, Gareth, 126–27
Wilson, Colin, 135, 166, 167

Yakubovich, A. I., 16, 71–72, 97, 98, 107
Yates, Frances A., 4–5, 22, 23, 24, 136, 202
Yazykov, N. M., 16, 20, 58–59, 198

"To A. N. Vulf," 58–59
Ypsilanti, Alexander, 31

Zakharov, N. S., 13, 73, 97
Zhukovsky, V. A., 2, 8, 27, 36–65, 68, 76, 83, 114, 117, 131, 181, 197, 201, 203
  "Appearance of Poetry in the Guise of Lalla Rookh," 47–48, 49, 50
  "Blossom," 40
  "Elysium," 46–47
  "Inexpressible," 43
  "Lalla Rookh," 48–49, 50, 57–58
  "Lines on the Death of Her Majesty the Queen of Wurtemberg," 42–43, 47
  "Mountain Road," 44
  "Mysterious Visitor," 48, 50
  "My youthful muse, as was wont to be," 50–51
  "Remember, remember, my beloved friend," 42
  "Remembrance," 42
  "Reveries," 41, 43–44, 48
  "Sailor," 45–46, 68, 114
  "Song," 42, 43
  "To the East," 47
  "To a Fleeting yet Familiar Genius," 43
  "To Turgenev, in Reply to his Letter," 40–41, 53
  "Traveler," 44, 114
Zinnendorf (Ellenberg), J. W., 30

www.ingramcontent.com/pod-product-compliance
Lightning Source LLC
Chambersburg PA
CBHW031549300426
44111CB00006BA/241